COMMUNITY ENGAGEMENT IN HIGHER EDUCATION

Edited by Dan W. Butin

This series examines the limits and possibilities of the theory and practice of community engagement in higher education. It is grounded in the desire to critically, thoughtfully, and thoroughly examine how to support efforts in higher education such that community engagement–a wide yet interrelated set of practices and philosophies such as service-learning, civic engagement, experiential education, public scholarship, participatory action research, and community-based research–is meaningful, sustainable, and impactful to its multiple constituencies. The series is by its nature cross-disciplinary and sees its readership across the breadth of higher education, both within student and academic affairs.

Dan W. Butin is an associate professor and founding dean of the School of Education at Merrimack College and the executive director of the Center for Engaged Democracy. He is the author and editor of more than seventy academic publications, including the books *Service-Learning in Theory and Practice: The Future of Community Engagement in Higher Education* (2010), which won the 2010 Critics Choice Book Award of the American Educational Studies Association; *Service-Learning and Social Justice Education* (2008); *Teaching Social Foundations of Education* (2005); and, most recently with Scott Seider, *The Engaged Campus: Majors and Minors as the New Community Engagement* (2012). Dr. Butin's research focuses on issues of educator preparation and policy, and community engagement. Prior to working in higher education, Dr. Butin was a middle school math and science teacher and the chief financial officer of Teach For America. More about Dr. Butin's work can be found at http://danbutin.org/.

The Engaged Campus: Certificates, Minors, and Majors as the New Community Engagement
edited by Dan W. Butin and Scott Seider

Engaged Learning in the Academy: Challenges and Possibilities
by David Thornton Moore

PREVIOUS PUBLICATIONS

Working Knowledge: Work-based Learning and Education Reform (2004)
With Thomas R. Bailey and Katherine L. Hughes

Engaged Learning in the Academy

Challenges and Possibilities

David Thornton Moore

First published in 2013 by
PALGRAVE MACMILLAN®
in the United States—a division of St. Martin's Press LLC,
175 Fifth Avenue, New York, NY 10010.

Where this book is distributed in the UK, Europe and the rest of the world,
this is by Palgrave Macmillan, a division of Macmillan Publishers Limited,
registered in England, company number 785998, of Houndmills,
Basingstoke, Hampshire RG21 6XS.

Palgrave Macmillan is the global academic imprint of the above companies
and has companies and representatives throughout the world.

Palgrave® and Macmillan® are registered trademarks in the United States,
the United Kingdom, Europe and other countries.

ISBN: 978–1–137–02518–0

Library of Congress Cataloging-in-Publication Data

Moore, David Thornton.
    Engaged learning in the academy : challenges and possibilities /
David Thornton Moore.
        p. cm.
    Includes bibliographical references.
    ISBN 978–1–137–02518–0 (alk. paper)
        1. Learning by discovery. 2. Experiential learning. 3. Education,
    Higher. I. Title.

LB1067.M66 2013
370.15'23—dc23   2012038635

A catalogue record of the book is available from the British Library.

Design by Newgen Imaging Systems (P) Ltd., Chennai, India.

First edition: March 2013

10 9 8 7 6 5 4 3 2 1

To Sandy and Katie
with love and thanks

Contents

Series Editor's Preface

Higher education is splintering before our very eyes: The prominence of for-profit institutions has forced us to redefine the notion of "education for the public good"; online education has upended the very idea of place-based learning; competency-based learning and prior learning assessments have begun to explode the monopoly of the credit hour as the basis of the credentialing function of the academy. This disruptive moment suggests, at least for me, a unique opportunity to set forth a clearer articulation of the "value proposition" of higher education. Namely, what is it that differentiates my practices as a scholar in the college classroom? What is it that I offer to my students that cannot be outsourced or automated? What is my job?

My answer is that education, ideally, is transformational. Above and beyond the content knowledge learned, the skills gained, and the habits of mind formed, education is about opening our minds and our hearts to new ways of examining, exploring, and embracing the world around us. It is about forming, and reforming, our assumptions and models of how to engage with and think about our local and global communities. It is about disrupting our taken-for-granted notions of the world and helping us to build them back up again through careful consideration of facts, values, contexts, and contents.

Such transformation, I want to be clear, is never an obvious or natural occurrence in the higher education classroom. It happens all too infrequently, is all too often fleeting and ephemeral in its results, and, when it does occur, is stratified to the student populations already with privileged status in privileged institutions. And yet, such potential for transformation is what drives our belief in and enactment of the liberating power of the classroom. Such transformation can, and should, be for everyone.

It is thus with gratitude that I read David Moore's book. David has offered us a powerful and nuanced examination of the challenges and possibilities of engaged learning in higher education. For engaged learning can, if anything can, substantiate and ground our discussions and debates about the value of the academy. Engaged learning offers a bridge between the theory of the classroom and the lived reality outside those walls. It, as David offers in his conclusion, "manages to induce the learner to look carefully at her experience, to question her own assumptions, to place the experience in relation to larger institutional and societal processes and discourses, to hear others' voices, to grapple with the question of why things happen the way they do...to engage, in other words, in *serious* critical thinking."

David puts forward his argument in a deliberate and thoughtful manner. David employs multiple conceptual frameworks, offers distinctive strategies and criteria, and provides sustained case studies and examples to make his case. He is always wary of the over-generalizations and the overarching rhetorical claims of the success of experiential learning. His consistent point that "it depends" is a necessary deflationary moment that allows us to glimpse the true potential of engaged learning when it is done well.

David is not afraid to tackle the hard issues, whether it is to challenge the "rhetoric of application" as articulated by proponents of experiential education or my own arguments for the "disciplining" of service-learning. David is able to do so exactly because of his deep knowledge of the field, of the literature, and of his vast experiences. He draws on all of this to offer concrete principles at a vivid level of granularity as well as high-level theorizing to contextualize and clarify how to think about the variety of practices and issues within the field. To give but one example, David's sustained deliberation on the pragmatist idea that knowledge is "something that we *do*" offers the reader an entrance into a way to make sense of the messy and chaotic practice of engaged learning. This is invaluable.

For me, it reaffirms that our experiences outside of textbook covers, classroom walls, and college boundaries can never be neutral, obvious, or transparent practices. Community engagement, and engaged learning more broadly, is (as I have written about before) a culturally saturated, socially consequential, politically volatile, and existentially defining experience. Put simply, it requires the sustained work of reflection, discussion and debate to begin to tease out its myriad complexities and threads and implications.

And if we indeed treat it as the complex phenomenon that it is—exactly as David has encouraged us to do throughout his book—it allows us the beginnings of a foothold for how to hold onto some key principles and practices in higher education. As David himself notes, "experiential learning might be used as a tool of profound transformations in the functions and operations of the academy...[but] these changes will not happen if experiential pedagogies are half-baked or half-hearted."

Note here the deep respect for the situational context. This is what makes David's book worth reading. It is neither an ideological rant nor a quicksand of ambiguity. Rather, it is a focused argument that takes account of the multiplicities and complexities of experiential education at the exact same time that it demands that we attend to its power to transform. We all need to be reminded that our work, while difficult and never done, is at the heart of higher education. I welcome David's contribution and the discussions, debates, and, yes, engagements it will foster.

DAN W. BUTIN

Acknowledgments

As befits a book on the use of experience as a source of learning, this one represents my grappling with a huge array of experiences of my own, some of them centered on my own schooling and professional work, but most of them embodied in relationships with students, colleagues, and friends. As a graduate student in social work in the late 1960s and early 1970s, I did internships three days a week, and struggled back at school to make sense of them in terms of the theories and concepts we were encountering in our academic classes. As a fledgling teacher at an alternative high school in Philadelphia, I sometimes took my students into the field, talking with community activists and city planners, watching neighborhood meetings and public hearings, working in food coops and attending block parties. Once again, while the direct experiences excited us and taught us a lot, it was not easy to think about them in relation to the social studies classes I was teaching, or to the academic ideas I was charged with passing on. When I went back to graduate school, I learned theories and methods for describing other people's firsthand experience and analyzing the learning they teased from it. I have been pursuing that issue ever since: as an educator working with student-interns in a myriad work and service settings; as a researcher observing dozens and dozens of students' internship experiences; and as a participant in the experiential education community, that set of professionals committed to bringing engaged learning into the academy.

My first concerted effort on the research side was a three-year study of the pseudonymous School for External Learning (SEL), a public high school whose students earned most of their credits through internships. Successive teams of research assistants at Teachers College, Columbia University, carried out most of the field work with great diligence, sharp eyes, and an enormous tolerance for ambiguity. In the first (unfunded) year, the researchers received only credit for their contributions: David Cornelio, Shelley Goldman, Thomas Shaw, and Margaret Tipper. In the second and third years, seven different people worked on the project: Berna Green, Suma Kurien, Geraldine McNelly, Tom Shaw, Meg Tipper, Robert Vivolo, and James Walkup. All nine of them did far more than collect data, though they did that with intelligence and efficiency: They interpreted, analyzed, and helped me make sense out of it (in the days before Atlas.ti or NVivo!). Meg Tipper was especially crucial to the project, serving as the site coordinator when I moved to Washington University in St. Louis. I am profoundly grateful to all of them for their hard work, their great insights, and their friendship. The three consultants for the project provided crucial observations, warnings, and suggestions at several junctures. Professor Frederick Erickson, who was my mentor at the Harvard Graduate School of Education, shaped my approach to the problem of understanding experiential learning, although he may not recognize the results. Professors Charles Harrington and R. P. McDermott, then of Teachers College, offered pointed and demanding guidance. Dr. Stephen Wilson used his experience as a researcher at the Center for New Schools (the organization housing the project) to provide much-needed practical and conceptual help. The research was supported in its second and third years by a generous grant from the National Institute of Education, where Dr. Thomas Carroll, the project officer responsible for overseeing our work, was considerably more helpful than his role called for him to be: He contributed logistical supports, detailed conceptual feedback, and no bureaucratic obstacles. The true heroes of the project, of course, were the students and staff at the School for External Learning. Unfortunately, in order to preserve their anonymity and to protect them from my representations of their work, I cannot name them. But through three years of relentless ethnographic scrutiny, endless and inane questions, and little substantive return, they maintained their patience, their good will, their humor, and their commitment to excellent education. They have my heartfelt gratitude.

At Washington University, several colleagues and students provided helpful suggestions and feedback about the SEL study, and pushed me to think harder about my arguments: Lou Smith, Art Wirth, David Dwyer, and John Prunty. When I moved to New York University (NYU) to become the director of the Cooperative Education Program at what is now the Gallatin School of Individualized Study, I received support and encouragement from Herb London, the founding dean, and from Faith Stangler, then as now the director of the school's internship program. In the early days at NYU, I managed to find colleagues from other schools in the metropolitan area to bounce ideas around with: Madeline Holzer, Ken Reardon, Sam Beck, Cathy Farrell, Peter Kleinbard, and others too numerous to mention.

The most fruitful of my professional relationships came through the National Society for Experiential Education (NSEE), where I became active in the early 1980s. My friends and colleagues there impressed me over and over again with their deep commitment to students, to learning, and to social justice; they pushed me to think more rigorously about experiential learning, challenged me to elaborate and extend my ideas, and buoyed me with their spirit. I am especially indebted to Jane Kendall, Garry Hesser, Tim Stanton, Jane Permaul, Dwight Giles, Janet Eyler, Rob Shumer, Steve Schultz, Mary King, Keith Morton, Bob Sigmon, Sally Migliore, Sharon Rubin, Tricia Thorme, Steve Hamilton, and Anne Kaplan, the last of whom slyly roped me into editing the NSEE quarterly for three years. The NSEE community has truly been a professional and spiritual home for 30 years.

During the late 1990s, I was fortunate to be asked to take part in a project at the Institute on Education and the Economy (IEE) at Teachers College, Columbia University, studying the ways in which work-based learning contributes to educational reform. The program was supported by grants from the Pew Charitable Trusts, the DeWitt Wallace–Reader's Digest Fund, and the National Center for Research in Vocational Education. Tom Bailey, the director of IEE, and Kathy Hughes became great colleagues, expanding and refining my understanding of experiential learning every day. Our collaboration resulted in a book—*Working Knowledge* (RoutledgeFalmer, 2004)—and in my deep gratitude to them. A faculty seminar related to the project also pushed my thinking; I am particularly grateful to Henry Levin, Victoria Marsick, Terry Orr, and Clifford Hill.

In 2004, I received a Research Challenge Grant from NYU to conduct a study of college-level experience-based courses; we interviewed students and instructors, and observed a number of concurrent seminars. I appreciate the support of the university, and especially the help of my research assistants, Sasha Ginnetti and Kavita Karni.

In 2007 and 2008, I was invited to be the keynote speaker at Northeastern University's Summer Institute on Experiential Education, where I had the privilege of sitting in on workshops with faculty and administrators from a number of colleges around the country and from as far away as South Africa. The institutes were organized by Tim Donovan, Rick Porter, and Jim Stellar; other presenters included Donna Qualters (who edited a Jossey-Bass collection of articles based on the sessions), Kristen Simonelli, and Joe Raelin, who also organized important conferences at Northeastern on Practice-Oriented Education (POE). All of these people shaped my thinking about learning from experience.

I am grateful to the Gallatin School, my home for over 30 years, for affording me the opportunity to do this work. My successive deans, including Herb London, Dick Koppenaal, Fran White, Ali Mirsepassi, and now Susanne Wofford, have granted me travel time, logistical resources, and access to research assistants, and for that I thank them. While, to be honest, not many of my colleagues in this highly interdisciplinary college find my studies all that interesting—they are scholars in fields from comparative literature to environmental studies, from Latin American history to political theory—they have been uniformly encouraging. Several have in fact worked with me on developing the Community Learning Initiative in Gallatin, our stab at engaging people, organizations, and issues outside the classroom; I want to thank Steve Duncombe, Rene Poitevin, June Foley, and Mark Read. Other NYU colleagues who have shown an interest include Bridget O'Connor and Michael Bronner of the business and workplace education program, Betts Brown of the Metropolitan Studies program, and Laurel George of the College of Arts and Science.

Recently, I attended three summer conferences on the future of community engagement in higher education organized by Dan Butin and Scott Seider, the first two at Boston University and the third at Merrimack College, Dan's home base. Not only did these meetings connect me with even more people involved in this important practice, but they made it possible for me to publish this book as part of their series. For that, and for the support of my editor Burke Gerstenschlager and his assistants Kaylan Connally and Lani Oshima, as well as Sarah Nathan, who shepherded the manuscript through the last stages, I am deeply grateful.

Finally, like most academic authors, I have to thank my family. Over the years, my wife Sandy has put up with endless hours, days, and weeks of my preoccupation with this work, my professional travel, and my reluctance to go out and play. Her patience, support, and affection have carried me through this long, long process. The same goes for my daughter Katie, though she hasn't been around as much since she grew up. She did, however, wield her skills as a professional editor both to clean up the final draft of the book and to reassure me that I wouldn't be embarrassed by the result. I cannot say how grateful I am to them both.

It is the custom in these acknowledgments to thank contributors and then to dissociate them from any responsibility for the final product. In fact, that is the case here as well. All of them have added something to my understanding of the problematics of experiential learning, but none of them has come out exactly where I have. In many cases, they may actually disagree with my analyses and conclusions. Although I owe a great debt to these folks in the evolution of this book, they must not be blamed for its final form.

CHAPTER 1

The Paradox of Experiential Learning in Higher Education

According to the conventional wisdom in higher education today, doing an internship in college boosts a student's chances for landing a good job after graduation. At my own university, well over half the undergraduates do at least one and many do several. Another common belief is that students with serious social and political commitments do some sort of service-learning or civic engagement in college: volunteering in a battered women's shelter, going on an Alternative Spring Break, canvassing for a favored cause. More and more students enroll in study-abroad programs, experiencing other cultures intensively and firsthand. Many conduct original research, sometimes in laboratories or libraries, sometimes in local or distant communities, sometimes in collaboration with a faculty member, sometimes on their own. Observers use a variety of terms to describe these kinds of educational activities: experiential, community-based, engaged. Whatever the label, experience-based, nonclassroom learning in its many forms has become more and more widespread in American colleges and universities, more and more a conventional, almost taken-for-granted element of students' educations (cf. Qualters, 2010; Perlin, 2011).

But a nagging paradox plagues the use of experience as a source of learning in higher education: Although students clamor for it, most institutions offer it, and a vibrant professional community has grown up around it, experiential learning occupies a marginal and rather second-class status in mainstream schools. There are those in the academy who believe deeply in experiential education as a pedagogical practice, who claim great benefits from its use for students, faculty, colleges, and their broader communities alike (cf. Eyler, 2009). A batch of professional associations advocate the practice. But—here is the paradox that makes this phenomenon interesting and important—institutions tend to relegate those experiential programs to the margins of their academic operations, as if the learning were somehow suspect, as if "real" academics don't do that sort of thing. Moreover, despite their apparent popularity, participation in forms like civic engagement appears not to be rising (Butin, 2012).

This paradox is interesting and important because it reveals a fundamental tension in the dominant conception of what a university is and does, raising challenges to the basic premises of higher education: about what qualifies as legitimate and creditable sources of knowledge and modes of learning, about the respective roles of teachers and students in the educational process, about the relationship between the academy and the rest of the world. This book addresses those tensions by describing, analyzing, and assessing the role that experience plays in the academy, and by identifying both the challenges and the opportunities in that role.

Many readers will be familiar with, and indeed advocates of, the practices of experiential education. But in order to establish the grounds for the key insight of this introduction, I will first describe some of the ways in which colleges and universities promote experience-based programs and practices—the basic formats include internships, service-learning, cooperative education, study-abroad, and student research (Qualters, 2010)—in their public pronouncements, their mission statements, and their advertising. I will provide evidence of the popularity of experience-based learning among students, both inside and outside the credit system. And I will outline some of the professional efforts—among scholars, student affairs officials, and administrators alike—to expand and improve experiential education as one element of teaching and learning in their institutions.

But I will also argue that these efforts do not represent the basic position and status of experiential learning in colleges, especially liberal arts schools. I will deconstruct some of the rhetoric pointing toward experience-based opportunities, showing that it often either rests on inflated claims and unexamined assumptions or damns with faint praise. I will explore the location of experiential programs in the structures of universities, and will maintain that they often sit outside the units that carry out the core missions of the schools and enjoy the greatest prestige inside and outside the institutions. Based on these observations, I will raise perplexing questions about the role of experiential learning in the academy. Finally, toward the end of the chapter, I will comment on the structure and content of the book: what sorts of research and theory inform it, and what issues will be addressed in the respective chapters. The point of the introduction, in other words, is not to demonstrate that a myriad of experiential programs exist or that they produce benefits—surely most readers will acknowledge those facts—but to highlight the paradox of the status of experience in the academy. I will begin with the positive side of the story, and move on to the more troubling issues.

Even the most elite colleges and universities offer students some form of experience-based learning. At Harvard, for instance, the Derek Bok Center for Teaching and Learning sponsors the development of credit-bearing Activity-Based Learning (ABL) courses in which

> students do public service, fieldwork, community-based research and internships in conjunction with in-class work. ABL aims to enrich students' academic experience and learning outcomes by connecting theory with practice, and concepts with methods, using data and insight they gain through engagement with the larger world. (Bok Center, 2011)

According to the website, over 1600 students have enrolled in one or more of the 80 iterations of the more than 30 courses offered in this program since 2005. Some courses in Romance languages, for instance, have connected undergraduates with English as a Second language (ESL) children in local schools. In 2010–2011, the Division of Social Science piloted activity-based courses in anthropology, government, history of science, and sociology, giving students "credit for extra reading and for writing a paper that would require intellectual engagement with topics pertinent to an independent activity, while connecting the activity to relevant course work" (Bok Center, 2011).

Amherst College offers a mission statement typical of leading colleges when it says that its students learn to

> seek, value and advance knowledge, *engage the world around them*, and lead principled lives of consequence...[U]ndergraduates assume substantial responsibility for undertaking inquiry and for shaping their education within and *beyond the curriculum*...Amherst College is committed to learning through close colloquy and to expanding the realm of knowledge through scholarly research and artistic creation at the highest level. Its graduates *link learning with leadership—in service to the College, to their communities, and to the world beyond.* (Amherst College, 2011a; emphasis added)

The implication of this statement is that learning is not simply an intellectual matter located inside the head, but that it changes the way one relates to the actual world. This concept finds expression in the college's Center for Community Engagement (CCE), which

> brings together Amherst students, faculty, alumni and community partners to engage the world around them. The Center designs opportunities that are linked to Amherst courses and co-curricular opportunities where students learn the skills and knowledge to be effective public problem-solvers. (Amherst College, 2011b)

The CCE offers consultations to faculty members who want to incorporate service-learning or other off-campus experience into their syllabi, as well as noncredit activities and placements for students at a variety of community-based organizations. In the Spring 2011 semester, the college offered five classes with community-based components. The activities included tutoring high school students in Holyoke, interacting with local musicians, and conducting research based on geographical information systems (GIS); one class met in an area prison, and included inmates as learners (Amherst College, 2011c).

On the public side, many universities offer opportunities for students to engage in experience-based learning. UCLA, like Amherst, has a special office dedicated to this mission: the Center for Community Learning (CCL). Housed in the Division of Undergraduate Education, the CCL promotes civic engagement by undergraduates and faculty through courses, research, and service alongside community partners. The service-learning courses sponsored by the CCL sometimes entail service, and sometimes community-based research. These classes are distinct from the "academic internships" ("195" courses, like History 195) offered through the various departments—not classes, but individual placements with school-based supervision, required journals, and research papers. These are aimed at connecting students with "experiences that manifest the content of the discipline"—not necessarily service-learning, but discipline-specific internships. Moreover, the center sponsors a Civic Engagement minor, which students complete by taking several lower- and upper-division courses, doing at least one internship, and writing a capstone research paper on a policy issue (UCLA, 2011).

In general, then, offering experiential learning opportunities appears to have become a standard practice among American colleges and universities. The National Association of Colleges and Employers (NACE) reported in 2010 that over 86 percent of its responding schools had formal internship and/or cooperative education programs (NACE, 2010). Sometimes these programs are located in the student affairs area; often they are run by career services offices, which place students in paid and unpaid internships, usually not for credit. Sometimes the programs are administered centrally by the office of the provost or some other academic official, and sometimes they are operated by the individual schools and academic departments. These programs and activities can be found on the websites of most colleges and universities. In any case, most institutions appear to have accepted the premise that experiential learning is a legitimate, valued element of their educational programs.

For their part, students have voted with their feet on the importance of experiential education. In many schools, it is the rare student who does not complete at least one internship or service-learning placement (Perlin, 2011). This is especially true of undergraduates in preprofessional programs like business and journalism, but it obtains even in liberal arts colleges, where the connection between a discipline-based major and a career is somewhat more tenuous. One survey by Aramark College Relations claims that "75% of all college seniors have had at least one internship before graduation" (Aramark, 2011). The highly respected National Survey of Student Engagement (NSSE) includes service-learning, internships, and practica as "high-impact practices" that "demand considerable time and effort, provide learning opportunities outside of the classroom, require meaningful interactions with faculty and students, encourage interaction with diverse others, and provide frequent and meaningful feedback"—that is, the survey's sponsors clearly regard experiential learning as a beneficial practice. According to their 2010 results, between 37 percent and 49 percent of college seniors participated in at least one service-learning activity during the previous year, and between 47 percent and 59 percent did an internship or practicum (NSSE, 2010, 23).

To be sure, many students regard internships primarily as a smart career move, a networking tool, a foot in the door of a possible job after graduation. They are probably right: NACE conducted a student survey in 2010 that indicated that "new graduates who took part in an internship program are more likely to have received a job offer than their peers who decided to forgo the experience," and that those graduates received higher salaries than noninterns (NACE, 2010). Showing undergraduates how to leverage internships into career success has spawned a cottage industry for consulting organizations and authors. Intern Bridge, a for-profit company, sponsors research on internships and employment, offers professional development opportunities for career services and human resources practitioners, and coaches students and graduates on job-hunting (Intern Bridge, 2012). Books such as *The Intern Files: How to Get, Keep, and Make the Most of Your Internship* (Fedorko, 2006) and *Hello, Real World!: A Student's*

Approach to Great Internships, Co-Ops and Entry-Level Positions (Liang, 2005) advise students on the transition from school to work—the list could go on. Clearly, internships are on the radar of American college students, particularly in a difficult economic time, when work experience becomes a competitive advantage for prospective employees as a distinctive item on the curriculum vitae.

A lively if curiously fragmented professional community has grown up around the various forms of experiential education. The National Society for Experiential Education (NSEE) pursues an inclusive strategy, trying to meet the needs of a broad array of practitioners: teachers, professors, principals, deans, directors of service-learning programs, professionals in career development and youth employment, counselors, directors of internships and cooperative education programs, school-to-work coordinators, superintendents, college presidents, researchers, and policymakers (NSEE, 2011).

Other organizations in the field are more specialized. The Cooperative Education and Internship Association (CEIA) bills itself as "the leader in work-integrated learning," focusing on experiences that enhance workforce preparation and continuous learning. (Not long ago, by the way, CEIA did not include the word "internship" in its title; curiously, about 20 years ago NSEE removed the same word from its previous title: NSIEE. Organizational strategies too complex to review here lie behind those terminological choices.) Campus Compact, founded 20 years ago by a small group of college presidents, now includes over 1,100 member colleges and universities. Its mission is to "educate college students to become active citizens who are well-equipped to develop creative solutions to society's most pressing issues" (Campus Compact, 2011). It sponsors research on service-learning, advocates the practice among educators and policymakers, and produces professional development materials for practitioners. The Association for Experiential Education (AEE), though it espouses a commitment to "experiential education" in broad terms, primarily attracts practitioners and scholars interested in outdoor and adventure programming—Outward Bound and Project Adventure are key examples.

What seems curious about this very partial list is that this very specialized educational practice has fragmented into so many professional organizations, each attracted to a very particular version of the pedagogy. During the 1980s, leaders of some of those groups tried to create an umbrella association called the Forum of Experiential Education Organizations (FEEO). It briefly included something like 22 member groups, but expired fairly quickly. Apparently, the practices of experiential learning are imagined in so many different ways by educators—the term *experience*, after all, does cover a lot of territory—that they see utility in finding others who specialize in very particular models. In any case, the point here is that there are in fact substantial numbers of professionals in higher education who advocate and practice one or another version of experiential learning, and legions of students eager to participate.

Despite this popularity among faculty, administrators, students, community leaders, and employers, I will argue that experiential education lies at the margins of the academy, that support for it is thin and spotty despite the passion its advocates display, and that many mainstream educators are either ignorant of or resistant to this form of learning. To be sure, the practice has grown substantially over the past few generations. Certainly when I went to college in the 1960s, almost nobody thought of internships as a valid form of education—indeed, the very term *internship* then applied primarily to recent medical school graduates. Instead, we thought of college-level learning as a matter of lectures, seminars, laboratories, and blue-book exams, of abstract theories and abstruse texts, of masterful scholars passing their wisdom on to thickheaded neophytes. Today, at least, schools pay lip service to experiential learning, and not-insubstantial resources are poured into civic engagement projects, community learning centers, alternative spring breaks, student research programs, work-related internships, and the like. Clearly, there is some momentum toward the use of experience as an educational resource—though that may be tailing off (Butin, 2012; National Task Force, 2012). But it could go in a number of directions, not all of them to my mind salutary; or it could wither under the pressures of the accountability and measurement movements, a sort of back-to-basics for higher education, or of a revanchist assertion by the advocates of classic texts and the traditional liberal arts. So I believe it is worth examining the extent, source, and quality of the current support.

Consider the commitments of colleges and universities as they are expressed in mission statements; to be sure, these are not declarations that most faculty and students fully grasp or even know about, but they give some indication of the priorities of the institutions. Harvard College, though it offers a range of experience-based learning opportunities, barely hinted at that form of education in its original mission statement; rather, it focused on "the advancement and education of youth in all manner of good literatures, arts and sciences; [the college's goal is to] create knowledge, to open the minds of students to that knowledge, and to enable students to take best advantage of their educational opportunities." Good literatures, arts and sciences: These still seem to be the hallmark of the traditional academic institution. After advocating the spirit of free inquiry and open expression, the 1997 revision of the mission statement makes soft mention of an impact on students' lives after college: "Harvard expects that the scholarship and collegiality it fosters in its students will lead them in their later lives to advance knowledge, to promote understanding, and to serve society" (Harvard College, 2012b). That statement carries a whiff of civic engagement, and could be read as suggesting a deep institutional commitment to experiential learning. But on careful reading, one realizes that the means by which it "expects" to promote leadership and social service center on "scholarship and collegiality" rather than on direct experience in the larger world. That expectation, of course, stands as an article of faith rather than of empirical demonstration; no one, to my knowledge, has ever shown that students exposed to scholarship and collegiality in the university ultimately display a greater commitment to serving society by virtue of that exposure.

Recently, however, the Harvard faculty revised its common requirements, moving to a General Education (GenEd) program that seeks explicitly to "connect a student's liberal education...to life beyond college" (Harvard College, 2012a). The core, like the mission, mentions preparing students for leadership and civic engagement after they graduate. That rhetorical commitment sounds like a deep recognition of the institution's responsibility to the larger world, and might be thought to imply a significant shift in curriculum and teaching. But implementation of the GenEd program does not specifically speak to those goals. Rather, it simply requires that students pass one letter-graded half-course in each of eight academic categories: Aesthetic and Interpretive Understanding; Culture and Belief; Empirical and Mathematical Reasoning; Ethical Reasoning; Science of Living Systems; Science of the Physical Universe; Societies of the World; and United States in the World (one of these courses must engage substantially with the study of the past). The courses that fulfill those requirements need not—and in fact typically *do* not—engage students in activities outside the classroom, library, or laboratory.

That is, the statement about preparing leaders who are civically engaged reads like a rhetorical device, a nod to the real demands of twenty-first-century life, rather than as a determination to create practices and programs that make it happen. The ABL courses described earlier certainly do seek to realize those engagement goals. But recall that in the six years since the ABL program was created, a total of 30 courses have been offered a total of 80 times, with an aggregate enrollment of 1,600. Admirable and worthwhile as those efforts are—and I believe they are both—they constitute a drop in the proverbial bucket of the overall Harvard curriculum, and materially affect a vanishingly small portion of the college's graduates—and do not appear to have created a movement among faculty across the college to incorporate experience into their courses. As a result, the bulk of the experiential learning and civic engagement done by Harvard students falls in the realm of the extra- or cocurricular, through organizations like Phillips Brooks House, rather than in the credit-bearing curriculum.

Similarly, Amherst College's mission statement articulates the goal of educating students to "seek, value, and advance knowledge, engage the world around them, and lead principled lives of consequence" (Amherst College, 2011a). The phrase "engage the world around them" has the virtue of being inspiring and current at the same time that it obligates the institution to nothing specific or concrete. Certainly the CCE represents a serious and meaningful effort to implement the mission's principle—but, like Harvard's ABL program, it directly affects rather a small and self-selected cohort within the student body, and an even smaller portion of the faculty. Without spending a great deal of time embedded in the Amherst community, it would be difficult to determine the extent to which the worthy idea expressed in the mission statement shapes the thoughts and actions of the faculty and students. Moreover, the specific mission of the CCE—"To prepare engaged citizens to foster democracy and work together to develop communities where everyone thrives, by identifying and facilitating high quality opportunities in the community" (Amherst College, 2011b)—speaks only to the civic-engagement/service-learning version of experiential education philosophy and practice; it says nothing about the importance of learning from and through work, or about the value of experience as a source of learning more generally.

Another symptom of the status of experiential learning in the academy can be found in the location of these programs in the various colleges and universities. The ABL program at Harvard resides in the Derek Bok Center for Teaching and Learning, which is located institutionally not in any of the academic departments or directly under the provost, but under the dean for undergraduate education. This is not at all to suggest that the college doesn't take the center seriously, but rather that the program sits slightly off the main academic path of the university. Few of the scholars in the various departments of the Faculty of Arts and Science, I imagine, think often of the ABL program; it exists on the margins of their consciousness and typically does not intersect their work.

In many other institutions, community-based learning enterprises reside not under academic affairs, but in offices related to student activities, career services, or external relations. The organizational reporting patterns are often byzantine, but reveal something about the institution's sense of where out-of-classroom learning fits. My own institution, New York University (NYU), for example, recently combined the Office of Community Service and the Office of Federal Service Programs into the Office of Civic Engagement, which oversees such student volunteer programs as America Reads/America

Counts, Jumpstart, and the Public Service Corps. (Notice that *civic engagement* has become the term preferred over *service-learning* in the field over the past decade; cf. Jacoby, 2009.) Significantly, the civic engagement office falls into the portfolio of the vice president for government affairs and community engagement, who reports to the senior vice president for university and public relations—not to the provost (NYU, 2011a). Students can locate other service opportunities—on-campus, off-campus, or through one of the university's many global sites—through the Center for Student Activities, Leadership and Service, whose director reports to the vice president for student affairs (NYU, 2011c). (He also oversees such operations as the college radio station, the club and fraternity systems, and student government.) Although that vice president reports to a senior vice provost who reports to the provost, the connection of the service-learning opportunities to the school's academic program—to courses, to faculty, to research—is tenuous and distant. Community service, in the institutional mind of NYU, falls more in the realm of student activities than in the realm of credit-bearing study.

What work- or career-related experiential programs exist at NYU outside the professional schools are found primarily in the career services office. They offer a large database of noncredit internship opportunities for undergraduates, who find information and advice through a website called "Jobs + Internships" (NYU, 2011b). The joining of employment with internships signals the underlying functions of the program. There *are* a number of course-related, credit-bearing internships at NYU—in the Gallatin School's Community Learning Initiative, in the Metropolitan Studies Program, and in several departments in the College of Arts and Science, as well as in such professional schools as education, public service, and social work—but most are basically civic engagement or service-learning courses, and there is no centralized oversight or facilitation of those efforts. Instead, they have been generated either by departments or by individual faculty members with an interest in experiential learning. None of these observations is intended to criticize these programs—they serve important functions with care and quality—but rather to indicate that my own university, like many other mainstream institutions of higher education in the United States, relegates most forms of experiential education to the margins of its institutional structure, far from the academic units regarded as fulfilling the university's core educational mission. By and large, the faculty of the university is not involved in these experiential programs, and many would resist such involvement and question its scholarly integrity and quality. And yet, as a reflection of standards in the field, in 2006 this degree of activity earned NYU a rating from the Carnegie Foundation for the Advancement of Teaching as a "community engagement" institution (Carnegie Foundation, 2012).

Of course, Harvard, Amherst, and NYU are not necessarily representative of the entire spectrum of American colleges and universities, but a review of perhaps 50 school websites suggests that most resemble those three in their construction of experiential learning efforts: a few small islands of passionate and committed work surrounded by a sea of more traditional versions of the academic enterprise.

So colleges do offer students and faculty opportunities to engage in experiential learning, and nod to these possibilities in their mission statements and recruitment materials, but they typically marginalize these options in terms of scope, funding, organizational location, and, most important, integration into the core educational practices of the institution. This paradox raises a number of important questions that I propose to address in this book. Some of these issues can be formulated in relation to a hypothetical situation that I have posed before (cf. Moore, 2010): Imagine a college student who is enrolled in a course in organizational sociology, and is reading Max Weber's classic work on bureaucracy; at the same time, she is engaged in an internship at the New York City Department of Education (DOE), one of the world's great bureaucracies. Several layers of issues are embedded in that scenario. First, there are *epistemological* questions: In what sense and to what extent is the knowledge that she encounters in reading Weber related to the knowledge she engages in her work for the Department of Education? Do Weber's concepts and theories map onto her experience at the DOE? Do they inform her understanding of that situation and enlarge her capacity to act intelligently in it? And vice versa, does her experience at the Department shape her comprehension and use of Weber? More broadly, do the kinds of knowledge encountered in the so-called real world intersect sufficiently with the kinds of knowledge engaged in college studies to render them mutually intelligible and beneficial?

Assume for the sake of argument that there is in fact a meaningful and potentially productive relationship between the academic knowledge and the experiential knowledge this student encounters. On the work or service side, how is the student's activity in the work setting organized in such a way as to make learning possible as a naturally occurring process (cf. Billett, 2001; Nijhof & Nieuwenhuis, 2008; Raelin, 2008)? Does the social organization of the newcomer's experience give her access to a substantial array of knowledge valued by the academy? On the school side, what is the role of the educator (instructor, coordinator, adviser) in enhancing her understanding of and use of that learning and in connecting it to academic knowledge? What can the teacher do to squeeze additional learning out of the experience, to add educational value beyond the natural experience? If the university were to take the student's experience-based learning seriously, what would their resultant practices look like? These questions are *pedagogical*: They relate to the social processes by which the student's learning is generated, organized, enlarged, and assessed both within and beyond the work or service site itself.

Finally, there are *institutional* issues stemming from the narrative. Does the university have any business operating at the intersection between academic and experiential forms of knowing and learning? What is the proper purview of the college in terms of the kinds of knowledge it generates, disseminates, uses, and valorizes? What does this role mean in terms of the proper relationship between the faculty mentor and the student? More broadly, how does this practice speak to the special role of the university in society and in the communities it inhabits?

These questions—the epistemological, the pedagogical, and the institutional—constitute the core elements of this book, and give shape to the sequence of chapters. Each will be addressed as a series of challenges and opportunities for higher education: pitfalls and possibilities in the strategy of using experience as a serious source of knowledge and learning in the academy. They speak to the nature and efficacy of engagement as an educational process, as a mode of experience in which putative learners participate in activities outside the traditional classroom, laboratory, and library.

These observations and speculations about the role of experiential learning in higher education are based on several kinds of sources. First, extensive scholarly literatures address these questions from empirical, theoretical, and professional perspectives. Some emerge from studies of internship and civic engagement programs by people who identify themselves as experiential educators: their forms, missions, practices, and outcomes. Some come from other scholarly traditions and disciplines, and do not directly speak to experiential education practices; rather, they seek to answer questions about such matters as cognition, organizational life, and situated learning.

Second, I will be drawing on my own research conducted over a period of more than 30 years. I have led or participated in three large-scale research projects related to internships and experiential education. The first focused on students in an alternative high school that gave academic credit for direct experience in an amazing array of workplaces and organizations in a big city: English credit for writing for a community newspaper; history credit for guiding tours in a local museum; science credit for processing blood samples in a hospital. My research assistants and I visited 35 different sites multiple times, observing interns as they interacted with coworkers and performed their various tasks; we also interviewed the students and their supervisors, as well as their school-based advisers (Moore, 1981a,

1986, 1990). The second study, based in the Institute on Education and the Economy (IEE) at Columbia Teachers College, examined work-based learning as a kind of educational reform. Once again, we did ethnographic observations of student-interns as they worked in hospitals, legal offices, hotels, and other sites; we interviewed them, collected related documents and artifacts, and spoke to their school instructors (Bailey et al., 2004). Finally, I turned my attention to the school-based component of the experiential education process, and interviewed students and faculty about their conception of the relation between work-based experience and school-based learning (cf. Moore, 2004). More recently, I interviewed a number of experiential educators about their programs, their philosophies, and their practices.

While I will draw on these observations and interviews at various points in this book, I will *not* be attempting to *prove* anything about students' experiences. Instead, I will use them to illustrate points I am trying to make about engaged learning. The stories I tell will put flesh on the theoretical bones of my analysis of learning from experience, but should not be regarded as definitive or dispositive in any way. Indeed, some of them will be composites of two or more actual students' experiences, true to the spirit of the enterprise, but not true in the strict empirical sense. Still, I will discuss experiential education in more detail and closer to the ground than most treatises on the subject do, in the interest of making concrete the sources and implications of my argument.

A caveat on the scope of this book: I want to acknowledge that there are many forms of experiential or engaged learning—work-related internships, service-learning, community-based research, study abroad, student-driven research, and so on—and that to some extent they entail different kinds of knowledge and different kinds of social processes. The solo intern working at a business does not encounter the same kinds of experiences as a student participating in a class-based research project on an urban neighborhood. I direct most of my attention to work-based internships and some to group-based service-learning. That is partly because my own interest has focused more on work as a dominant site of experiential learning, and partly because (as I will show) a great deal of scholarly work has already been done on civic engagement and service-learning; I want to add a corollary perspective to that literature. Moreover, I spend far more time on experiential programs in liberal arts colleges than in professional schools, primarily because the connection between classroom learning and field-based learning seems intuitively obvious in the latter—though, in fact, my own experience many years ago as a social-work student doing three days a week in field placements and then trying to process the work in graduate courses suggests that the synergy is not inevitable. In any case, not all of my observations and arguments will extrapolate neatly to all formats.

Now a word on the structure of the book: Following this introduction, chapter 2 makes a case for a particular theoretical and methodological perspective on the problem of understanding how people learn from experience in work and service sites, and how that learning is shaped (enhanced, directed, assessed) by pedagogical practices back at school. Much of the scholarly and professional literature on experiential learning operates from a set of principles and premises different from the traditions within which I work, and this chapter will explain the theories that I believe best illuminate the things I have seen in the field.

The remainder of the book will divide into three related parts, as mentioned above. Part one examines the epistemological and (in a certain sense) curricular issues in experiential education. Building from the framework sketched out in chapter 2, chapter 3 proposes ways of talking productively about *what* students learn from their experiences in work and service settings; it draws on several authors' frameworks for describing the *content* of learning. Chapter 4 addresses the question of how field-based forms of knowledge map onto the kinds of knowledge encountered in college. If, as some of the theorists whom I will introduce in chapter 2 argue, knowledge is defined and used differently in different social contexts, then a crucial question in this field arises: whether and how the forms of knowledge engaged in work and service sites can be seen to interact productively with the knowledge encountered in college classes. In some ways, this part of the book is an adventure in applied epistemology, an attempt to use specific lived examples to explore the ways knowledge is defined, distributed, and used in different settings.

Part two moves on to the pedagogical questions, issues about *how* the learning happens in these different contexts. Chapter 5 proposes a specific conception of pedagogy different from the one normally encountered in educational studies, which assumes a teacher and a student rather than a worker interacting with coworkers, customers, and supervisors, or a volunteer or organizer providing services to clients or partners. Much of the chapter suggests a framework for understanding what I have called the *pedagogy of experience* (Moore, 1981a): the naturally occurring social organization of activity and resources that makes it possible (or difficult) for learning to occur. The chapter analyzes a number of specific learning situations to clarify the dimensions of naturally occurring pedagogy and how it works as an educational process. Chapter 6 goes on to examine the similarities and differences between naturally occurring pedagogy and teaching methods used in the university, to determine whether and to what extent they coincide or conflict. Chapter 7, in turn, explores the experiential pedagogies used by educators back at school to get student-interns to reflect on and elaborate their experiential learning, and investigates several difficult issues facing this practice: the *transfer of learning* problem, or the question of how knowledge from one situation is (or is not) carried into another; the *reflection* problem, or whether experience requires sustained, critical, or guided reflection in order to generate learning; and the *politics* problem, or the issue of the educator's goals in terms of revealing and transforming power relations in the workplace, the school, or the larger society. The chapter identifies several pedagogical models that constitute useful approaches to these questions: workplace learning (cf. Billett, 2001; Raelin, 2008), meaning-and-work programs (cf. Flyvbjerg, 2001; Sullivan & Rosin, 2008), and feminist and critical pedagogies (cf. Fisher, 2001; Freire, 1970; Giroux, 2011; Shor, 1992; Simon, 1991). Driving the discussion will be the issue of whether and how experience can be processed in educationally productive ways, of how engagement transforms into learning.

Chapter 8 investigates the *institutional* challenges and opportunities related to engaged learning programs. One aspect of that chapter is an analysis of the mission of the university, from its founding to the present, as it is represented and described both in college literature and in critiques by various commentators. The differences of opinion about the functions of the academy have a profound bearing on questions about the role of experience as a source of knowledge and learning within that institution. Some positions, I will show, are incompatible with experiential learning philosophy and practice; others are apparently more consistent, but begin to deconstruct under close scrutiny. Yet other conceptions of the nature of higher education lend themselves perfectly to experiential education. These differences are not easily described on a spectrum from conservative to liberal, as the title of a recent book by Stanley Fish, no conservative, demonstrates: *Save the World on Your Own Time* (2008).

In the concluding part of chapter 8, I propose an answer to the question of whether experiential learning should be practiced in the academy. At the risk of destroying the dramatic tension in the book, I will reveal now that the answer is, *it depends*. I will argue that experiential learning might be used as a tool for profound transformations in the functions and operations of the academy, transformations that I believe are progressive and positive; but I will also argue that these changes will not happen if experiential pedagogies are half-baked or half-hearted. In the absence of a real commitment to their far-reaching implications, experiential education and community engagement not only will *not* change higher learning for the better, but will threaten the quality and integrity of that practice as it has developed over the past several hundred years. Done right, experiential education can be a wonderful thing for the academy. Done wrong, it may be more trouble than it's worth. The intervening chapters will, I hope, provide a framework through which the reader can understand what factors or dimensions the answer depends upon, and provide the terms by which she can make a decision for herself.

CHAPTER 2

A Theoretical Framework

Before proceeding to a discussion of specific issues related to engaged learning at the college level, I want to lay out the theoretical point of view that informs the later chapters on epistemological, pedagogical, and institutional challenges and possibilities in experiential education; in addition, I will explain my take on several concepts helpful in the later analysis. The question addressed here is this: What conceptual tools will most effectively build our understanding of what goes on when a newcomer engages in activities in an out-of-classroom setting, whether a work-related internship or a community-based service project? The approach described in this chapter draws on an eclectic but (I believe) productive body of theory and research on the nature of knowledge-use and learning in situated experience. It differs in some ways from the common conceptions of learning found among both mainstream and experiential educators—especially in terms of its degree of specificity—but is, I will argue, more compatible with the fundamental premises and goals of engaged education.

To the extent that experiential educators cite theoretical foundations for their work—which is generally not a lot (cf. Sweitzer & King, 2004)—they typically rely on three pillars, each of which will be elaborated and critiqued below: a philosophy of experience based in John Dewey (usually his 1938 tract, *Experience and Education*); a more-or-less constructivist psychology of learning based in Jean Piaget (1967) and sometimes Jerome Bruner (1973); and, perhaps the most commonly cited theory among internship and service-learning educators, David Kolb's (1984) notion of learning cycles and learning styles. In most professional writings and discussions, these ideas remain undeveloped and under-theorized, as in the following excerpt from a recent guide to service-learning:

> This approach to knowledge creation fits with the perspectives of George Herbert Mead, William I. Thomas, and Charles Horton Cooley, all part of the Chicago school of sociology from the 1890s onward. More recently, the pragmatism of John Dewey and the learning-theory model of David Kolb follow this intellectual heritage. (Kronick, Cunningham, & Gourley, 2011, p. 3)

That is as far as these authors go in articulating their theoretical perspective. Now, each of these sources represents a reasonable and productive contribution to a theoretical framework for engaged learning—in fact, I will use several of them—but they are not developed here fully enough to be truly useful. Particularly for practitioners (who outnumber theorists in the field by a huge margin), the understanding of experience-based learning emerges from, well, experience and a bit of intuition. The common wisdom suggests that there is knowledge somehow contained in organizations and practices in the world, and that when the student enters those settings, she acquires what is there. That is, the site presents an array of knowledge and skill, and the newcomer engages it and learns it.

Again, this intuitive conception of the experiential learning process makes sense in many ways, and forms a reasonable foundation for pedagogical practice. But it oversimplifies some elements of the phenomenon, and assumes greater stability and uniformity than actually obtain. It tends toward an over-psychologized vision of the learning process, one which assumes that any intern, with sufficient initiative and effort, can get access to what knowledge there is in the setting, and that personality (or, sometimes, "chemistry") typically determines the success of the learning experience. That vision underestimates the power of social factors: organizational structures and processes, culture, power dynamics. The claim that personality and individual effort shape experiential learning is not incorrect—it is just not the whole picture. In this chapter, I propose a conceptual framework that extends, deepens, and complicates that picture.

These ideas derive only partly from studies of school-based experiential education. More of them come from the fields of adventure education (Kraft & Sakofs, 1982; Kraft & Kielsmeier, 1995; Roberts, 2012; Warren et al., 2008), workplace education (cf. Billett, 2001; Raelin, 2008), and adult education (Fenwick, 2003; Knowles et al., 2011). Among the several versions of experiential education based in colleges and universities, service-learning and civic engagement are the most highly theorized (cf. Butin, 2010; Eyler & Giles, 1999); work-related internships and cooperative education practices have not received nearly as much attention—which is why this book looks more often in that programmatic direction.

This framework draws not so much on research about explicitly educational practices as on theories generated in such academic disciplines as psychology, sociology, and anthropology with no particular attention to engaged learning programs in schools. These are woven together to provide a basis for my approach to answering the kinds of questions addressed in the rest of the book: How can we identify and understand the process by which student-interns learn as they engage in out-of-classroom activities? What kinds of things can they be said to learn through that experience? How is that process socially organized in such a way as to make the learning possible (or difficult)? In what senses is the process compatible or incompatible with the learning that takes place in school? In this chapter, I will first describe the theoretical sources of the framework I propose to deploy in this book, and then will lay out several basic concepts on which later chapters will proceed: knowledge, learning, curriculum, and pedagogy.

Theoretical Sources

To begin, a few words about philosophical and social-scientific stances that do *not* seem very productive for a theory of experiential learning. On one level, that theory rests on a foundation of philosophy: a general conception of what constitutes knowledge, where it comes from, and how people come to have it. Of course, philosophers have been debating these questions since before Socrates, arguing about whether experience functions as a legitimate and reliable source of knowledge, whether it "counts" as a constituent of the learning process. Platonists have argued that true knowledge, knowledge of the Forms, derives not from experience but from reason and dialectic (Jay, 2005; cf. Plato, 1984). Cartesians have similarly maintained that our senses are susceptible to false impressions and mistaken inferences, and that only a method of radical doubt and reason can lead to truth (cf. Descartes, 1960). Some contemporary scholars of the history of higher learning argue that this fundamental reliance on reason over experience continues to inform academic inquiry even today (Illeris, 2009; Reed, 1996)—a point to which we will return later in the book. In any case, the tradition called rationalism regards reliable knowledge as universal, certain, and decontextualized, and sees experience as too particular, contingent, and variable to yield serious knowledge directly without the conscious exercise of reason.

British empiricism took a contrary stance toward the question of experience as a source of knowledge, maintaining that the human mind at birth is a blank slate (*tabula rasa*) and that all ideas and knowledge emerge from sense experience and the mental associations it produces (cf. Locke, 1996). American behaviorism, a descendant of empiricism championed by such scholars as John Watson (1998) and B. F. Skinner (1965), regarded experience as determining human behavior: A person acts in ways conditioned by prior experience and its consequences. The learner is essentially passive in this model, and philosophical concepts like freedom and dignity are thought to err in their implication that the person has agency and chooses to behave in certain ways (Skinner, 1972).

Forms of social theory that emerged in the late nineteenth and early twentieth centuries took a more rigorous look at the social context of behavior, thought, and learning. Emile Durkheim (1915), for example, regarded knowledge as embedded in a basically stable form in a basically stable society, a social system in equilibrium. What makes social order possible—and this was always Durkheim's fundamental question—is the transmission of core social knowledge and norms from one generation to the next, ensuring sufficient consensus among members to allow institutions and practices to persist. That is, learning to him was essentially a matter of socialization and acculturation, of initiating the neophyte into a body of socially approved knowledge and skill. That process finds its expression, of course, in experience—but experience is primarily shaped by and serves the needs of social institutions and forces. Talcott Parsons's functionalism, which dominated American sociology in the mid-twentieth century, conceded the importance of experience to the individual, but also saw experience as sculpted by social forces serving the functional needs of institutions. To explain social action, Parsons argued, was to locate the ways in which individual actors were led to perform certain kinds of action by being socialized into and controlled by the norms, roles, and sanctions of their social systems. Thus, he regarded experience as a legitimate source of knowledge primarily in the sense and to the degree that it embeds the person in a stable, institutionalized system of relations and actions (cf. Parsons, 1964; Turner, 1998).

For the experiential educator, I maintain that these philosophical schools constitute a dead end. The Platonic and Cartesian perspectives treat experience as a largely unreliable source of knowledge—not real in the former case, subject to doubt and error in the latter. The extent to which either school of thought dominates American higher education is a question open to debate; clearly, though, these ideas have influenced the status of experience in the academy. Empiricism and behaviorism, for their parts, leave the learner in a passive state, stripped of agency. Even Durkheimian and Parsonian social theories tend to emphasize the social fact over the individual actor, regarding behavior and thought as shaped by social processes and requisites beyond individual control. None of these theories offers a solid ground for an educational practice that takes firsthand experience seriously: the rationalists because they consider it unreliable; the empiricists, behaviorists, and structural-functionalists because they would need to engineer any out-of-school experience carefully to ensure that it transmitted the desired lessons—and clearly that strategy fails the test of feasibility.

As a final element of this section on less-than-productive approaches to learning from experience, I want to say something about the theorist whose ideas have most thoroughly permeated the thinking of experiential educators: David Kolb, whose *Experiential Learning* (1984) is cited in nearly any work that purports to examine that phenomenon (now including this one). My position on Kolb smacks of ambivalence, because on the one hand I believe his work makes a substantial contribution to the field, but on the other I regard it as a somewhat misguided distraction.

Drawing especially on Dewey (1910, 1938), Jean Piaget (1967), and Kurt Lewin (1951), Kolb defines learning as "the process whereby knowledge is created through the transformation of experience" (1984, p. 38)—a definition that works well so long as one avoids the question of what constitutes knowledge. If, as some epistemologists argue, knowledge is "justified true belief" (cf. Feldman, 2003), experience runs into trouble as a source of that knowledge, since in experiential contexts both justification and truth are up for grabs. More on this problem later. In any case, Kolb describes learning structurally in terms of two intersecting dimensions, each with two polar opposites:

- the dimension of *grasping* experience either through apprehension (*concrete experience* [CE]: "reliance on the tangible, felt qualities of immediate experience") or through comprehension (*abstract conceptualization* [AC]: "reliance on conceptual interpretation and symbolic representation");
- the dimension of *transforming* that experience either by intension (*reflective observation* [RO] on experience) or extension (*active experimentation* [AE] on the external world) (1984, p. 41).

This two-dimensional, four-pole scheme identifies four "elementary forms of knowledge":

- *Divergent* knowledge results from experience grasped through concrete experience and transformed through reflective observation (CE/RO);

- *Assimilative* knowledge results from experience grasped through abstract conceptualization and transformed through reflective observation (AC/RO);
- *Convergent* knowledge results from experience grasped through abstract conceptualization and transformed through active experimentation (AC/AE);
- *Accommodative* knowledge: experience is grasped by concrete experience and transformed by active experimentation (CE/AE) (1984, p. 42).

Kolb describes these four stages of handling experience as a *learning cycle*—a process that leads in turn from concrete experience to reflective observation to abstract conceptualization to active experimentation—and observes that individuals tend to favor one or another of the four forms of knowledge, depending on their preferences for grasping and transforming experience, that is, their *learning styles*.

Kolb's notions of the learning cycle and of learning styles have been appropriated by many experiential educators in the United States. Many of them administer his Learning Styles Inventory (1985) to their student-interns, and get them to think about their own learning styles and the way they interact with people with other styles.

While there is a certain elegance to this theory, while Kolb does address many complexities in the learning process, and while he certainly draws on useful precursors, the scheme is problematic in a couple of ways. First, educators have interpreted it as a description of an actual sequence of moments in a learning process: You start with a concrete experience, then you think about it, then you formulate abstract concepts about it, and finally you test it out in action; then you move on to a new experience, or to the "same" experience somehow transformed by your new insights. That cyclical format (even with its upward-spiraling amendment) works as a pedagogical tactic: Instructors can walk interns through this sequence intentionally and systematically as they process their workplace experience; and they can encourage students to identify and understand their own and others' learning styles. But Kolb is strangely mute on the ontological and phenomenological status of the learning cycle idea. He discusses individual learners in terms of their styles, but does not describe scenes in which learning actually happens in this particular sequence or form. The scheme does not really capture what happens in the world.

Bente Elkjaer (2009) offers a telling critique of Kolb's theory when she notes that his four moments of the cycle appear, in structuralist fashion, to constitute distinct elements in the world, separate "things." Although Kolb claims Dewey as an intellectual source, Dewey avoids this kind of structural distinction among phases and forms of learning and acting. Elkjaer notes that the stages in Kolb's learning cycle are not connected with each other in an organic way, and that the scheme negates his claims about a dialectical tension between the experiential and the conceptual, "since dialectic logic would show how experience and conceptualization are necessary for and condition each other... From the vantage point of pragmatism and Dewey's definition of experience, Kolb distinguishes between action and thinking rather than seeing them as united" (2009, pp. 85–86).

These moments in the learning cycle, in fact, are not actually separated in time and activity: People do all four, though not necessarily in the stated order or to the same degree or with the same consciousness, in many kinds of circumstances. Rather than being distinct forms of learning or knowledge, they intersect and interact as people make sense of their situations. Kolb uses a structuralist framework to explain a dialectical process—and it doesn't quite work.

Second, and perhaps more crucially, where are context and culture in Kolb's framework? Surely different cultural situations privilege and reward certain kinds of learning styles and constrain others. In some contexts, for example, exercising initiative is regarded as a good thing, handsomely rewarded (think hedge fund manager), while in others it constitutes insubordination (think second violinist in an orchestra). In some contexts, taking time to think is a viable strategy, where in others lightning-fast decisions are expected. Educators need to be aware of both elements of the learning transaction: the person *and* the situation, as they shape each other (cf. Billett, 2011). Kolb's theory is strong on the first (at least in a typological sense), but not on the second; his theory focuses on individual learners more than on learning situations. Using Kolb as a guide to understand types of learners and generic aspects of the learning process, that is, makes sense; but understanding the content of actual students' actual learning demands a more elaborate model.

The theoretical perspective on the question of engaged learning that I find most productive for American higher education synthesizes a number of complexly related traditions: pragmatism, constructivism and constructionism, interactionism, cultural-historical theory and activity theory, situated and distributed cognition, theories of practice, communities of practice, and organizational culture. No one of these schools of thought fully addresses the issues raised by this phenomenon, and none of them speaks directly to experiential education as a pedagogical practice, but together they constitute a set of conceptual tools through which we can comprehend what goes on when people learn. Most importantly, they draw attention to the details of experience, and resist simplistic assertions about the learning consequences of general environments.

In taking this synthetic stance, I share a concern with Knud Illeris in *How We Learn* (2006): that it will be derogated as "eclectic," meaning incoherent and without a well-defined foundation. But as Illeris argues, "It is impossible to arrive at an adequate understanding of the complex field of learning [experiential or otherwise] without relating to the results achieved in so many scholarly approaches" (p. 7). In that spirit, I will try to demonstrate that these disparate fields and theories share at least some core assumptions and concepts about the way learning occurs.

This framework rests most distantly on an idea from Kant (1998): that human beings perceive reality in an active process, not a passive one. Contrary to Descartes' claim that God puts ideas in the mind, and contrary to Locke's assertion that there are no innate ideas, Kant argued that our minds are (to use an anachronistic term) hardwired to grasp the external world in terms of such categories as space, time, and causation. We cannot know noumenal reality, things independent of our perceptions and cognitions; we can know the world only as phenomena constructed by the mind. This idea suggests that people are not simply passive recipients of percepts and ideas through experience (as the empiricists would argue) or creatures of a determinate God (as Cartesians would have it) (cf. Gardner, 1999). Rather, we actively construct our worlds and our concepts. The issue for a theory of experiential learning, of course, is what role experience plays in the particulars of that process.

The more proximate foundation for a theory of experience comes from American pragmatism. Charles Sanders Peirce first articulated what he called the pragmatic maxim: One's conception of any object resides in the effects one conceives that object to have. The meaning of a proposition—or more broadly a claim about knowledge—lies in its practical consequences, in the difference it makes in the way the world works, in its implications for actual practice in a problem-situation. In opposition to what might be called a spectator view of knowledge as impersonal fact, Peirce insisted that we construct these meanings as active participants, not as passive observers (Peirce, 1877; cf. Magee, 1998).

William James, the American psychologist-philosopher, built on Peirce's ideas when he argued in 1899 that one learns best through one's own activity; that sensory experience is basic to learning; and that effective learning is holistic, interdisciplinary, and specific (James, 1981). He later illustrated the distinction between this experience- and practice-oriented philosophy and more conventional philosophy with a story about a student of his who

had always taken for granted that when you entered a philosophic classroom you had to open relations with a universe entirely distinct from the one you left behind you on the street. The two were supposed, he said, to have so little to do with each other, that you could not possibly occupy your mind with them at the same time. The world of concrete personal experiences to which the street belongs is multitudinous beyond imagination, tangled, muddy, painful and perplexed. The world to which your philosophy-professor introduces you is simple, clean and noble. The contradictions of real life are absent from it. (James, 1981, p. 8)

This quotation captures the spirit of pragmatism better than a careful rehearsal of the subtle arguments among its various advocates, which continue to this day (cf. Goodman, 1995)—and it articulates vividly the challenge of using experience in the academy. The essential message of the pragmatists for our purposes is that knowledge (perhaps better termed *knowing* or *knowledge-use*) is something that we *do*, a practical activity in the actual world and not merely packets of information stored between our ears. This position aligns perfectly with the premises of experiential education.

Probably the philosopher most frequently associated with experiential learning, of course, is John Dewey. Building on the pragmatist conception of meaning, truth, and knowledge, Dewey made several points that advance our understanding. First, his conception of experience focused on the transaction between the person and the environment; he situated experience not simply within individual heads, but in a process of living. For one thing, this notion took experience and learning out of the discrete realm of minds and placed it in a social context. For another, it suggested that experience was not simply about knowledge in the cognitive and informational sense, but also entailed emotions, volition, aesthetics, and ethics; that is to say, learning from experience goes beyond the mere accumulation of knowledge (cf. Elkjaer, 2009, p. 74).

Dewey proposed two major elements of experience as a learning process: *continuity* and *interaction*. In his classic *Experience and Education* (1938), he argued that "every experience both takes up something from those which have gone before and modifies in some way the quality of those which come after" (p. 35). Experience is not momentary or transient, not something that merely happens at a specific point in time; nor is it a steadily growing repository of stable, decontextualized knowledge-items ready for deployment at the appropriate times. Rather, it is an ongoing process in which each moment shapes the next. And the process is not strictly internal to the person, but entails interaction between the person and the environment. Dewey wrote, "An experience is always what it is because of a transaction taking place between an individual and what, at the time, constitutes his environment"

(1938, pp. 43–44). The environment, then, is material, it is social, and it is historical. These dimensions take us far beyond the mentalistic conception of experience and learning suggested by Plato and Descartes and beyond the behaviorist conceptions of Watson and Skinner.

Instead, in a pragmatist vein, ideas, concepts, and thoughts become instrumental, tools used by the person—in fact, the people, plural—who confront meaningful problems in their situations. Thinking is not simply intracranial ratiocination, but the process by which people engage in inquiry, in Dewey's sense (1910; cf. Elkjaer, 2009). Phillips and Soltis (2004) find these elements consistently in Dewey's conception of inquiry-driven experience:

> Thinking always gets started when a person genuinely feels a problem arise. Then the mind actively jumps back and forth—struggling to find a clearer formulation of the problem, looking for suggestions for possible solutions, surveying elements in the problematic situation that might be relevant, drawing on prior knowledge in an attempt to better understand the situation. Then the mind begins formulating a plan of action, a hypothesis about how best the problem might be solved. The hypothesis is then tested; if the problem is solved, then according to Dewey something has been learned. The problem solver has learned about the connection between his or her action and the consequences. (p. 39)

This quintessentially Deweyan description of the learning process serves almost as a template for accounts of students engaging new learning situations, and is at the heart of Kolb's (1984) theory of experiential learning.

More than being a mere spectator observing activity in the world, Dewey argued, the experiencing-learning person is fundamentally a participant, one with a vital interest in the solution to the problem, and knowledge is a "mode of participation" in those activities (1916, p. 393). This notion of knowledge as a mode of participation clearly moves Dewey's consideration of knowing and learning beyond the image of atomistic bits of information or skill being deposited in the head and retained in the mind (cf. Freire, 1970, on the "banking model" of education). Rather, knowledge resides in the process by which people grapple with the meaning of experience, by which they bring their previous knowing to bear on their current situations, by which they pose and pursue questions in a process of inquiry that leads to new insights and understandings, by which, as Dewey claimed, they make the indeterminate experience determinate. And it brings attention to the conative (desire, volition) and affective aspects of learning as well as the cognitive (1938).

George Herbert Mead, a Chicago psychologist of the early twentieth century, moved the pragmatist conceptions of mind and thought further toward their social contexts. In *Mind, Self, and Society* (1934), Mead argued that the mind and self emerge from communication among participants in social interaction, that the individual mind can exist and operate only insofar as it shares meanings with other selves. Consciousness is not simply affected by action, interaction, and joint action: It is integrated into all of them, and generates its contents and its practices from that social process. Similarly, Mead argued, the self is not a distinct, ideal substance in some transcendent realm separate from social interaction; rather, it is constituted in and by that interaction, in a process that social theorist Charles Horton Cooley had earlier called the looking-glass self (Cooley, 1922). It entails taking the role of the other, putting oneself in others' positions in order to understand how they perceive and make meaning of various things—not merely as a question of empathy, but as a way of informing one's comprehension of the world and of one's place in it.

Herbert Blumer (1969) drew on Mead's social behaviorism in creating symbolic interactionism, a school of thought in the general realm of sociology dependent on several premises: (a) that human beings behave toward things (people, objects, events, etc.) on the basis of the meanings those things have for them; (b) that those meanings arise in the course of interactions with others; and (c) that those meanings demand interpretation, sense-making, rather than simple and automatic understanding. This interpretivist conception of social interaction contributes to a strong foundation for a productive theory of experiential learning.

In addition to a pragmatist foundation, a theory of experiential education can lean toward phenomenology—not so much in the highly abstract and universalist approach of Edmund Husserl (cf. 1973) as in the more socially oriented theories of Alfred Schutz (1970), and especially in the version developed by Peter Berger and Thomas Luckmann in *The Social Construction of Reality* (1966). The latter pose this fascinating question: How is it that human beings experience as objective a world that they have subjectively created? That is, if one accepts the Kantian premise that the world as we know it emerges from phenomena created in and by our minds, rather than through direct contact with the noumenal world, then one must confront the phenomenological fact that we *experience* the world as ontologically real, as existing apart from our minds. Their ingenious solution to this problem lies in their description of a dialectical process in which we interact with others around meanings socially generated and shared, externalize those meanings, and then internalize them as if they came from outside. We participate in what they call a social stock of knowledge: a shifting body of ideas, concepts, customs, interpretations, habits, typifications, and metaphors that are to some extent shared and that function as the basic agreements constituting social order. Even though we perpetuate and realize this social stock of knowledge in the course of our joint activities with others, we regard it as having facticity, the ontological quality of being factual, and we tend to take it for granted, to assume it as a basis for our actions and thoughts. Berger and Luckmann's theory once again places the mind and meaning in social context.

Erving Goffman, though not strictly a symbolic interactionist, produced a series of books that inform the analysis of experience in everyday contexts. In his classic *The Presentation of Self in Everyday Life* (1959), he used a dramaturgical metaphor to examine the ways participants in a given social encounter manage the impressions others have of them. In *Frame Analysis* (1974), he showed how people's experience is shaped by their common conceptions of society, of social roles, of interactions: that is, by their frames. Goffman's analytical tools explain the situated dynamics of experience more effectively than they locate those experiences in a larger system of social relations and power. But they do help the experiential educator trying to understand her students' engagement in real-world activities.

If this theory of experiential education favors the philosophical method of pragmatism (with a touch of phenomenology) and the sociological method of interactionism, it leans toward constructivism as a psychological theory of knowledge and learning. In general, this school of thought argues that human beings do not simply acquire or absorb ideas or concepts, taking them into their minds whole cloth (or, in Descartes' scheme, having God place them there), but rather they construct those ideas through an active process of mental operations. They organize, interpret, transform, and elaborate concepts in ways drawing on but not determined by experience.

Perhaps the major progenitor of constructivism was, of course, the Swiss genetic epistemologist Jean Piaget. While his theory of developmental stages in cognitive operations does not have much bearing on the issues in this discussion (because by the time they reach college, students have generally achieved the stage of formal operations and are capable of abstract thinking), his description of the processes by which learners incorporate and manage new knowledge does. Piaget (1967) argued that individuals organize their thoughts, concepts, and behaviors into schemas, mental structures representing various aspects of the world, of experience, and of ideas. One schema, for instance, might be about physical space, and contain notions like dimension, extent, and boundary. Another might organize conceptions of other people, drawing on such variables as gender, age, and ethnicity. As a person experiences the world, Piaget said, new information enters the mind and has to be processed somehow in relation to the already-existing schemas. If the new experience basically conforms to the terms of one or more of those schemas, a process called assimilation takes place: The new information is tucked away into that schema as one would place a folder in a file cabinet. If, on the other hand, the new experience somehow resists categorization in the existing system, accommodation occurs: The person may create a new schema, substantially alter an existing one, or completely ignore the disturbing information. Although the concept of the schema has sometimes been interpreted in too mechanical and stable a manner, it provides a useful tool for analyzing the thinking (and learning) done by interns and service-learning students: Understanding their learning means (partly) tracking changes in their store of schemas.

Constructivist inquiry has also been extended into the realm of moral development (Kohlberg, 1981), and elaborated to account for gender differences in development and the nature of knowing (Belenky et al., 1997; Gilligan, 1982). Common to all these approaches is a conception of the knower-learner as an active, agentic participant in the learning process, and of that process as entailing an engagement with, a working on, experience. A limitation is that they also tend to focus on the person, the individual, as the unit of analysis.

Though working from a perspective that was recognizably constructivist, the Russian psychologist L. S. Vygotsky, a contemporary and sometime critic of Piaget who died in 1934, created an approach to learning and development that situated those processes squarely in their social, historical, and cultural contexts. Among American educators, he is best known for his concept of the Zone of Proximal Development (ZPD): "the distance between the actual developmental level [of the learner] as determined by independent problem-solving and the level of potential development as determined through problem-solving under adult guidance or in collaboration with more capable peers" (Vygotsky, 1978, p. 86). Although that idea will reappear in our later discussion of pedagogy for experiential learning, the more significant element of his theory for our purposes is his insistence that thinking and learning must be understood as embedded in—not merely related to or affected by, but inextricably bound up in—sociocultural and historical activities, contexts, and relations. The thinker-learner utilizes various resources in the context—social relationships, cultural traditions, language, technologies such as writing and the computer—to make sense of situations, to construct meanings, to define and solve problems, and to participate in activities. That is, Vygotsky argued that all cognitive work is mediated by the larger sociocultural context within which it occurs. This developmental approach makes two principal claims: that "higher mental processes in the individual have their origins in social processes," and that "mental processes can be understood only if we understand the tools and signs that mediate them" (Wertsch, 1985, pp. 14–15). And since the individual achieves the capacity to engage in more complex forms of cognition by interacting with more-advanced others in a meaningful social context (back to the ZPD idea), we reach an important implication for experiential educators: Sometimes the learner participates in a social activity that manifests a higher-level cognitive process *before* actually mastering or understanding that process. The common rhetoric in experiential pedagogy about "applying" concepts and skills first acquired in the classroom may get that sequence wrong.

This line of work, expanded into activity theory by Vygotsky's colleagues and students such as Luria (1976) and Leont'ev (1979; cf. Wertsch, 1981), became influential among American scholars during the 1980s and 1990s, and reinserted the thinking-learning individual into a sociocultural and historical framework. These principles informed many studies in cross-cultural psychology, all based on the premise that cognitive processes vary across and are embedded in social and cultural contexts and in situated activities (cf. Cole & Means, 1986).

Some scholars use a similar term for a school of thought that is close to constructivism but not quite identical: social constructionism (cf. Gergen, 2009). The descendants of Piaget tend toward the former, and focus primarily on the insides of heads, but the adherents of the latter insist, like Vygotsky, on the importance of the social and cultural elements of the process of knowing and knowledge-use. Burr (2003) identifies some common characteristics of social constructionism as a theory: a critical stance toward taken-for-granted knowledge; a belief in the historical and cultural specificity of thought and action; the claim that knowledge is generated, sustained, and altered by social processes; antiessentialism, the principle that people, actions, and institutions have no essential properties; the notion that groups of people jointly construct conceptions of the world based on their experiences of particular standpoints or perspectives.

During the 1980s, this line of inquiry moved into anthropology when Jean Lave formulated a dialectical conception of the social nature of thinking and learning. In *Cognition in Practice* (1988), she analyzed the ways in which apprentice tailors in Liberia, grocery shoppers, and members of Weight Watchers solve mathematical problems in what she called activities-in-setting: the emergent relations between the thinking person, the activity in which the person is engaged, and the context in which that activity appears. As an example, imagine a shopper pushing a cart through the aisles of a supermarket, trying to make decisions about which items to purchase. Her thinking processes must be understood within several cultural-historical domains: the "arena" of the store as a more-or-less stable material and organizational resource, in which the array of goods is shaped by competitive market forces, corporate policies, and profit motives; her personal situation as a member of a family, as a consumer, and as an eater; the media environment of advertisements and product placements on TV, and so on. So her decisions are driven partly by the push of the store, partly by the pull of her family's food preferences, partly by media-driven images and desires—all in dialectical interaction. Taking the analysis to a more fine-grained level, imagine that she needs to compare prices of similar items. Lave showed that the shopper's calculations are done not algorithmically in ways learned in math class, but in complex mental processes particular to the situation, yet no less effective for decision making (1988; cf. Lave & Wenger, 1991). Here is an interesting point that actually reinforces the cultural-historical perspective on grocery shopping: Since Lave's study in the 1980s, technological changes in the arena of the supermarket—price-comparison labels on shelves, mobile scanners available to shoppers—have radically reshaped the cognitive work done by shoppers: no more price calculations, no more keeping mental track of cumulative expenses. Some of the cognitive demands of shopping, that is, have been off-loaded onto new technologies. That fact radically reconfigures the supermarket as an environment for thinking and learning.

Another useful branch of this school of thought focused on the concept of working intelligence (cf. Scribner, 1986), called practical intelligence by Sternberg (1986): the capacity for thinking and problem-solving in such everyday contexts as the workplace. Scribner studied the thought processes and problem-solving of workers in a commercial dairy, showing, for example, how the pre-loaders (who assembled batches of goods to be loaded onto delivery trucks) used visual cues rather than arithmetic calculations to decide how to rearrange items in crates so they could minimize their physical effort (Scribner, 1986). An anthology edited by Rogoff and Lave, *Everyday Cognition* (1984), presented a number of studies of the processes of thinking and learning in such quotidian situations as ski slopes and dinner tables. In the years since then, this line of inquiry has explored the sites of a vast array of everyday experiences to discover the ways in which cognition is shaped by culture and context.

John Seely Brown and his colleagues (1989) were among the first scholars to use the term situated cognition, arguing that knowing and thinking are inevitably, inextricably, and fundamentally embedded in emergent social situations, that learning and cognition cannot be separated from the activities in which knowledge is developed and deployed. According to this premise, conceptual knowledge functions as a set of tools created, framed, and distributed by the community that uses them.

An influential theory even more related to experiential learning appeared in 1991 when Jean Lave and Etienne Wenger wrote in *Situated Learning*:

Learning viewed as situated activity has as its central defining characteristic a process that we call *legitimate peripheral participation*. By this we mean to draw attention to the fact that learners inevitably participate in communities of practitioners and that the mastery of knowledge and skill requires newcomers to move toward full participation in the sociocultural practices of a community. (1991, p. 29)

This concept has been interpreted both radically, as implying that learning occurs in social systems and not inside heads (Hanks, 1991), and moderately, as suggesting that learning and cognition are simultaneously (in fact, dialectically) social and intracranial processes (cf. Salomon, 1993a). In any case, the situated learning concept has been widely used (and occasionally criticized) in such fields as adult education (cf. Fenwick, 2003; Merriam, 2001) and workplace learning (cf. Billett, 2001; Malloch, et al., 2011; Rowden, 2007).

The ideas of situated cognition and situated learning have been elaborated in the literature on distributed cognition, which maintains that cognitive activity is not only situated, but also shared. That is, the work of thinking, problem-solving, and learning is often stretched across a complex system of social actors and resources, not performed fully by a single actor (Perkins, 1993; Resnick et al., 1991; Salomon, 1993b). To be sure, these theorists argue, individuals think and learn, but the nature and meaning of those processes must be regarded as embedded in a larger system of activity, social relations, and technologies. In the real world, cognitive work is often divided among participants, and even among technologies. A classic formulation of this idea can be found in Edwin Hutchins's "Learning to navigate" (1993), which describes the way a team of sailors led by a quartermaster collaborate in navigating a ship out of a river into the ocean. The cognitive and technical work of the navigation is distributed among six sailors in intricate and complex ways; some of the work is also performed by machines (sextants, computer programs). This concept helps us understand college interns, who usually perform only a segment of organizational work, and rely on colleagues, supervisors, and technologies to contribute to the task performance as well.

The notion of community of practice, first mentioned in Lave and Wenger (1991) and later expanded by Wenger (1998), gives us yet another vocabulary for analyzing experiential learning: "Communities of practice are groups of people who share a concern, a set of problems, or a passion about a topic, and who deepen their knowledge and expertise in this area by interacting on an ongoing basis" (Wenger et al., 2002, p. 4). The earlier formulation of the idea sparked a good deal of imaginative and productive thought among scholars and practitioners in the field (cf. Fenwick, 2003; Malloch et al., 2011; Rainbird et al., 2004), but lacked detail and raised troubling questions (Billett, 2001; Cairns, 2011; Hughes et al., 2007). It worked from a more-or-less commonsensical image of a group of people— Liberian tailors, Mayan midwives, members of a Weight Watchers group— who share practices, activities, and what Lave and Wenger (1991, p. 98) called a "lived-in world." The legitimate-peripheral-participation conception of learning implied that this community has something like a center, toward which neophytes gradually move as they learn (1991, p. 29). As critics have pointed out, this notion, though quite evocative, runs the risk of portraying the social stock of knowledge in a community as given and static, rather than as dynamic and expansive (cf. Fuller, 2007).

Wenger's (1998) later treatment of the communities of practice idea offered greater detail and rigor in the conceptualization of practice, which is a crucial tool in the analysis of engaged learning:

> The concept of practice connotes doing, but not just doing in and of itself. It is doing in a historical and social context that gives structure and meaning to what we do. In this sense, practice is always social practice. Such a concept of practice includes both the explicit and the tacit. It includes what is said and what is left unsaid; what is represented and what is assumed. It includes the language, tools, documents, images, symbols, well-defined roles, specified criteria, codified procedures, regulations, and contracts that various practices make explicit for a variety of purposes. But it also includes all the implicit relations, tacit conventions, subtle cues, untold rules of thumb, recognizable intuitions, specific perceptions, well-tuned sensitivities, embodied understandings, underlying assumptions, and shared world views. Most of these may never be articulated, yet they are unmistakable signs of membership in communities of practice and are crucial to the success of their enterprises. (Wenger, 1998, p. 47)

This notion of practice will translate in the next chapter into a conception of the curriculum of experience. These are the kinds of things people learn as they engage in situated activities.

A community of practice, according to Wenger, arises, grows, and achieves coherence when people are (a) mutually engaged in (b) a joint enterprise whose meaning members negotiate with each other and which they carry out through (c) a shared repertoire of "routines, words, tools, ways of doing things, stories, gestures, symbols, genres, actions, or concepts that the community has produced or adopted in the course of its existence, and which have become part of its practice" (1998, pp. 73–82). That is, the community of practice exists at the intersection of social relationships, joint activities, and shared knowledge. So learning, in this scheme, is not simply a matter of an individual's acquiring some piece of knowledge or skill used by the community, but rather one of the group members' changing and expanding participation in these negotiated activities. Thus, when Wenger refers to learning, he is not talking specifically and exclusively about individuals or their knowledge; he is talking about the evolving, negotiated practices of a group, about knowledge-use as embodied in the joint actions of the community. This concept seems useful for analyzing the learning experiences both of individual students in work settings and of groups of students collaborating with community members in a civic engagement project.

The community of practice idea resembles in some ways the learning organization concept popularized by such theorist-consultants as Chris Argyris and Donald Schön (1978, 1996) and Peter Senge (2006). These authors look for the ways in which organizational practices and structures contribute to the likelihood that members will learn; they argue that an organization that promotes and facilitates learning will succeed where a more rigidly hierarchical and static organization will fail to meet the challenges of the market and the environment. But their conception of learning is less social, less collective, more rooted in conventional images of knowledge-units being created and disseminated.

Similarly, the communities of practice idea bears a passing resemblance to the concept of organizational culture, whose proponents argue that social interaction in any situation is made possible by the participants' shared understandings of purposes, structures, activities, norms, and values—that is, by culture. This particular version of cognitive anthropology, which dates back to such theorists as Goodenough (1957) and Spradley (1972), locates culture in knowledge, and thus shows how learning is made possible. This idea has been applied at the level of the organization by such anthropologists as Applebaum (1984), Martin (1992), and Hamada and Sibley (1994). The latter made the intriguing point that anthropologists and management theorists conceptualize organizational culture in very different terms: the former as a naturally occurring feature of social interaction in particular contexts, the latter as a variable that can be manipulated in the interest of corporate efficiency and productivity (cf. Deal & Kennedy, 2000; Kanter et al., 2003).

Other theoretical models worth attention from experiential educators include action science (Argyris, 1994) and reflective practice (Schön, 1983). In their earlier work, Argyris and Schön (1974) developed the concepts of reflection *in* action and reflection *on* action to describe the processes by which professionals think about their work in theoretical-actional terms both during and after the actual performance. One of their important insights was that theory informs practice as it occurs as well as in a post-activity reflection process. As thinkers as long ago as Marx have argued, separating theory from practice (as Kolb tends to do in his learning cycle model, but as Dewey does *not* do in his conception of experiential learning) is both descriptively inaccurate and strategically ill-advised. Schön (1983) also insisted that reflective practice entailed not just technical knowledge but artistry, a form of knowledge-use that is creative, not rule-governed or algorithmic, that works from a sense of the problem-space rather than from strict definitions and metrics (cf. Crawford, 2009, on work as "soulcraft").

This brief review of the literature on experience, knowledge, and learning contains a great many elements, none of which completely captures the framework that I will deploy in this book. Many of the ideas reported here will be elaborated in later chapters, and new ones will be added. The framework so far also neglects, for the moment, consideration of some factors crucial to an understanding of situated learning. Not least among them is *power*. Any effective analysis of how newcomers in a social context (a workplace, for example) come to participate effectively in its relationships, its activities, and its stock of knowledge has to account for the ways those things are shaped by the fact that some participants, some practices, and some structures carry more power than others (Moore, 2008). That issue raises questions not only about the relations among participants in a situation, but also about larger systems of power in society (cf. Foucault, 1980, 1995; Giddens, 1986).

This review also invokes concepts and theories that have been discussed in other ways, using other terms. For example, where Jean Lave uses the term *arena* to denote the persistent, more-or-less stable organizational context of a kind of experience (e.g., the supermarket), Pierre Bourdieu (1977) might prefer the term *field*. Similarly, the concept of *social stock of knowledge* in Berger and Luckmann (1966) might be compared to Michel Foucault's (2010) notion of the *discursive formation*, although the latter tends to operate at a higher level of generality than the former. There are subtle differences between the two sets of concepts—Foucault tends to attribute less agency to individual actors than Berger and Luckmann do, for example—but these will be addressed in later chapters only if they illuminate our basic problematics. Like Illeris (2009), I am not dogmatic about specific terminology, not wedded to one specific theory.

For now, suffice it to say that the framework used in this book implies a set of commitments to an understanding of human experience, to a vision of what is going on when a student-intern engages in work at a company, or a group of students takes part in a community service project. In that vision, individuals work at making sense of their situation as they participate in activities; they do not simply absorb knowledge, skill, or "the way we do things here," but rather identify and try to solve problems, to understand and use the language and the social codes, to present themselves as competent, legitimate participants. They perform mental operations, sometimes following algorithmic procedures, sometimes engaging in problem-solving and executive functions. Sometimes they share those processes with other actors in the situation, but inevitably (though variably) they are enmeshed in social relations and cultural practices that give substance and form to their thinking and learning. They have agency—they can choose ways to think and behave—but they also operate within a system of institutional, social, political, and cultural constraints and affordances. That system has features both local and societal (Erickson, 2004). Their experience unfolds within an arena, a field, a discursive formation, a culture; but it is also shaped by their individual personalities and beliefs. To theorize experiential learning, we need to take all these elements into account.

This framework recognizes and attempts to grasp the incredible subtlety of the social and psychological dynamics of the learning process. It rejects a simple set of assumptions about what and how an intern or community activist learns. It resists the temptation to consider a particular site—say, a business office or a government agency—as a unitary, predictable, controllable domain within which any student will have access to any and all knowledge; it avoids such easy claims as, "well, there's all sorts of interesting stuff going on here—it must be a good internship placement." The fundamental (if frustrating) premise of this theory, its answer to the generic question about whether someone learns something from a particular experience is, well, it depends. These theories provide a foundation against which the observer and the educator can analyze, assess, and (perhaps) guide the learning process. The following section will offer several more specifically education-related concepts to flesh out that approach.

Basic Concepts

Using these theoretical perspectives as a base, this section will focus on several key concepts for the analysis of experience-based learning. In the five chapters that follow, I will explore these terms in greater depth, both theoretically and empirically, identifying subtle elements of their use and illustrating their utility in making sense of situated experiences. These terms sit at the heart of my argument about the challenges and possibilities of engaged learning at the university level. They are *knowledge*, *learning*, *curriculum*, and *pedagogy*.

To repeat, these terms refer not to distinct phenomena, but to different ways of analyzing the same basic phenomenon. They are lenses, perspectives, heuristics, not things in themselves.

Knowledge

A lengthy disquisition on the concept of knowledge would consume too much of this book, so I will begin by saying that my use of the term emerges from the traditions of pragmatism, interactionism, and constructivism described earlier in this chapter. Knowledge resides in the complex set of informational, material, and social resources and processes that people use to make sense of and act in their worlds. In part, those resources take the form of representations, models, scripts, and schemas in actors' minds. In part they exist in activity structures, sociocultural practices, and material tools, and are manifested in the ways people accomplish their individual and joint purposes. Knowledge, that is, consists in the capacity to act effectively in the world in respect to some situated goal, to recognize, to apprehend, to understand, to make sense, and (perhaps most significantly) to do things with intelligence.

The term capacity, of course, has an elusive quality: It has both a potential and a kinetic sense, captured in the distinction between knowledge and knowing (or knowledge-use). Some theorists treat knowledge as a possession: something a person "has," usually "in mind." If I can retrieve from my memory the fact that the Erie Canal opened in 1825, then that little nugget is part of my store of knowledge. If I understand Weber's concept of bureaucracy, then I "have" a complex Piagetian schema somewhere in my head, and can haul it out when I need it. Other theorists prefer to treat knowledge as an activity, as something one "does"; that is the sense in which *knowing* is the more effective term. The Erie Canal factoid represents knowing in the sense and to the extent that I *use* the information effectively and appropriately in an actual situation.

The kinds of things I know, as we will see in greater detail in the next chapter, might take different forms: facts; concepts and theories; procedural skills; social relations; styles of inquiry, justification, and explanation; worldviews and values, and so on—the terminology is less important than the fact of formal diversity. The ways one uses these different kinds of knowledge vary even more substantially: to solve a problem, to maintain a relationship, to establish or exercise power, to fashion a material object, to tell a story, and so on—and on and on. This intersection between the potential form of (stored, available) knowledge and the kinetic practice of knowing (active, purposeful) constitutes what Simon et al. (1991) called working knowledge, the kinds of stuff one knows and uses at work; referring to a wider range of contexts, Sternberg (1986) called it practical intelligence, and Lave (1988) called it cognition in practice.

On the debate over knowledge-as-possession versus knowing-as-activity, I straddle the fence: There are benefits to approaching learning processes from both perspectives. Knowledge can exist in potential form, stored somewhere and accessible for retrieval (I am not qualified to discuss the neurological processes entailed here, nor do I think they are terribly germane to this analysis), and does not wholly disappear between the occasions of its use. Obviously, whether one *has* the knowledge matters when the next appropriate occasion pops up. The more consequential state of knowledge, however, is knowledge-in-use, or knowing: It shapes, enables, and contributes to the ways in which people make sense of, take part in, and carry out situated activities.

Another crucial question about knowledge is where it resides, or where it is manifested and used—and here my position departs from the mainstream. Whereas most philosophers and psychologists regard knowledge as something that resides in heads (brains, minds, "between the ears"), as something possessed and utilized by individuals, I want to argue that knowledge and knowing are features of *activity systems*: one or more persons engaged in socially meaningful and purposive action mediated by one or more cultural tools. (Lave [1988] refers to this concept as activity-in-setting.) The notion of the activity system combines the actor-participants with their activities, and adds the resources they utilize in carrying out those activities, including such tools as language, computers, books, databases, and objects. We will examine several activity systems in later chapters. The point is that activity systems, not just individuals, display, use, and alter knowledge.

Learning

Given that conception of knowledge, the notion of learning follows rather neatly: It is the construction, acquisition, modification, enhancement, or reorganization of knowledge and/or knowledge-use by an activity system. Clearly, then, learning is a process, not a product; saying "she *has* a lot of learning" conflates learning with the potential form of knowledge, with knowledge as a possession. Rather, learning comprises changes in knowledge-use by the activity system.

That process may be productively analyzed at two related levels: the collective or systemic, and the individual. Despite my somewhat unorthodox strategy of locating learning in the activity system and not just in the individual mind, I certainly have no objection to the commonsense assumption that individuals learn; in my terms, their participation in the system's use of knowledge changes (cf. Lave & Wenger, 1991). But I also argue the less popular assertion that activity systems themselves learn, that knowledge-use changes in significant ways across the work group, the community of practice, the organization—"significant" both for the way the system accomplishes its collective purposes and for the way its individual members learn.

From this perspective, I need to ask several different kinds of questions. Who or what is doing the learning? What kinds of knowledge-changes occur? What new knowledge is created by or injected into the system? How is knowledge-use restructured? What does the learner or the system *do* in the process of learning? Through what activities and cognitive reorderings does the learning occur? How does the activity change as the learning takes place? These questions are compatible with Lave and Wenger's (1991) conception of situated learning: They focus on social practices and the ways in which people—especially but not only neophytes—participate in these practices. In addition, they inquire into the ways in which these practices evolve and change (Moore, 2004).

As we will see in detail in later chapters, we can examine the process by which an activity system generates, uses, and reformulates knowledge. The individual persons who participate in the system bring various kinds of (potential) knowledge to the activity. Other kinds of knowledge are embedded in some of the tools through which the activity is carried out. In most settings, the knowledge-use at work is neither stable nor algorithmic: It shifts—expands, gets reorganized, changes focus or content—during the course of the activity, and especially across time and additional activities. In that sense, and to that extent, the system learns. Of course, the individual participants can reasonably be said to have learned, as well, in different ways and about different things.

Curriculum

Given these conceptions of knowledge and learning, we can venture a working definition of the term curriculum. In most conversations about education, that term traditionally denotes a phenomenon located in schools: a plan, often written, for exposing students to particular bodies of information, for teaching them skills, for ensuring that they learn what the institution wants them to learn (Beauchamp, 1975). Some definitions focus on the "subject matter"—the informational, conceptual, and actional content of the plan, or the desired outcomes of the classroom process (Lewis & Miel, 1978)—while others attend to the experience children have when they are exposed to that content (Pinar, 2004; Tipper, 1982). In any case, the curriculum concept generally refers to the intentional, planful aspect of the educational process in schools.

By contrast, I want to argue that a version of the concept can also be a useful tool for analyzing the knowledge that students and other newcomers engage when they participate in work sites or community service projects. Rather than a plan for students' learning, the naturally occurring curriculum of experience resides in the socially organized stock of knowledge utilized in the situated activities of a community of practice. The basic claim embedded in the term is that knowledge-use is not haphazard or random in these situations, that participants generate, share, enact, validate, and privilege particular forms of knowledge. In any given context, members define, distribute, and use knowledge in varied and particular ways. Some things count as knowledge while others do not. Moreover, some people get access to some forms of knowledge, while others do not; sometimes that access is a graduated process by which some members move progressively into certain bodies of knowledge, demonstrating greater and greater mastery, and sometimes access is a function of organizational position. The situated curriculum in this sense is not a static body of information and skill that could be adequately represented in, say, a training manual. Rather, in a sense consistent with the theoretical framework developed in the first part of this chapter, it is an emergent cultural production, an aspect of the lived experience of a community of practice (cf. Moore, 2004; Wenger, 1998).

The curriculum lens, that is, provides a perspective on two analytically distinct levels of the organization and use of knowledge in a setting: the collective and the individual. First, the analyst can examine the forms of knowledge-in-use in a particular situation, focusing on how they are socially organized—the categories, the contents, the scripts and rules, the sequencing, the relationships, the access—as well as on how they change over time in terms of organization and participation. Second, the lens can be used to identify the aspects of the social stock of knowledge with which a particular learner engages.

Again, this lens is distinct from the pedagogical lens (which will be explained in a moment, and in later chapters) only in an analytical sense: These are two ways of looking at the same knowledge-use process. In the next chapter, I will use the curriculum concept both to identify some of the components and forms of curriculum as a situated phenomenon, and to examine some examples of the kinds of curricula that appeared in some of our research sites. That is, we will investigate the kinds of claims made for and about experiential education as answers to the question, What do students learn? The fourth chapter will address the question of whether and how the curriculum of experience contributes to the curriculum of the college.

Pedagogy

Finally, we can articulate a working definition of pedagogy. The term typically denotes the teaching strategies and methods used in schools by educators (Bain, 2004; Pascarella & Terenzini, 2005; Svinicki & McKeachie, 2010), and sometimes refers to the philosophical premises underlying those methods (Leamnson, 1999, p. 7). In contrast, I find the concept useful as a gloss for a more general phenomenon, one not limited to school settings: Namely, pedagogy is the social organization of the process by which an activity system or any of its constituents learns. As they organize themselves to accomplish their joint purposes, whether in workplaces, in households, or on playing fields, activity systems structure their interactions in part by utilizing the social stock of knowledge in the setting. When they encounter problems of various kinds, glitches or snags in the operation, they find ways to adjust and improve that knowledge-stock: add to it, amend it, reorganize it, pare it down for the sake of efficiency, or distribute it differently among members. Certain aspects of the relationships among the system's elements—its human participants, its material, informational, and social resources—and certain kinds of actions make that learning more or less likely, more or less effective. That is what I mean by pedagogy. It has structural features—the persistent relations among elements; and it has process features—the ways things get done in the system. And, as I will show in a later chapter, it is shaped by a variety of factors within and outside the setting.

Sometimes the structures and processes are designed explicitly and intentionally to enable learning to happen. Someone may occupy the role of "teacher" and someone else the role of "learner"; or the learner may set about trying to teach herself, to learn independently. On the other hand, sometimes the learning process takes shape as a by-product of members' trying to accomplish other purposes: play a game, produce a magazine article, lead a museum tour, have a dinner-table conversation. The existence of pedagogy as a feature of situated activity, that is, does not depend on the intentionality of its participants, on someone's harboring the explicit goal of enabling learning to happen. Rather, the questions driving the analysis of pedagogy are, first, whether (and what) some or all of the activity system learns, and second, if so, how that learning is made possible by the way the system does things and uses things. Chapters 5 and 6 present a framework for answering those questions.

With these basic concepts in place, we can now proceed to a closer investigation of engaged and experiential learning in the academy.

CHAPTER 3

Analyzing the Curriculum
of Experience

The theoretical position sketched out in chapter 2 provides a foundation for addressing the first element of our central problematics: How can we best describe, analyze, and explain the kinds of things student-interns learn as they engage in work or community service in the real world, outside of school? How do experiential forms of learning map onto the things they learn in academic classrooms? Are the two forms of knowledge-use compatible, complementary, additive, synergistic, or are they in tension or, at least, in separate worlds?

This chapter and the following one will deal with the *what* of the learning process, with what might be called the curriculum of experience (Moore, 2004). The next part will deal with the *how*, what I have called the pedagogy of experience (Moore, 1981a). But to be clear, the distinction between content and process, between curriculum and pedagogy, is purely analytical and heuristic. It does not suggest that these are two different things in the world. Rather, they constitute distinct lenses through which we can examine one basic phenomenon: learning-in-action. Dividing the analysis into chapters should not create the false impression of separate elements of experience, when the terms are in fact just different category systems for looking at one thing. Moreover, the notion of content implies that there is "stuff" that gets deposited in someone's mind, as suggested in Paulo Freire's (1970) critique of the "banking model" of education. Given the conception of knowledge and learning discussed earlier, that "coins in a piggy-bank" image needs to be resisted and dismissed—although I will certainly not deny that individuals carry knowledge around in their heads, and can retrieve it in some usable form at appropriate moments. Learning, as we have seen, is as much about participation as it is about content. That fact makes the what/how distinction even more sketchy—though I will utilize it for heuristic purposes.

In the last chapter, we briefly developed the idea of the curriculum as flowing from a conception of knowledge and learning; that idea obtains both in school classrooms and in non-school, experiential settings. This chapter, building on that general notion, first examines a number of types of knowledge-use that represent possible claims for forms of learning in internships and civic-engagement projects. Then it identifies some important features of experiential curricula, and some factors that shape them. The next chapter goes on to compare the ways these forms of knowledge-use and learning proceed in work and service settings to the ways they appear in academic classrooms. Finally, I will address the question of whether experiential learning contributes to the kinds of learning sought in college.

One of the central arguments of this chapter—indeed, of the whole book—is to challenge what I call the *rhetoric of application* among advocates of experiential education: the claim that students learn something in the classroom and then "apply" it in the real world. A corollary of that claim can be found in an early definition of experiential education: "learning activities that engage the learner directly in the phenomena being studied" (Kendall et al., 1986, p. 1). Both versions of that rhetoric assume the isomorphism of knowledge across social contexts: "Learn it here, use it there," or "Study it here, experience it there." A simple expression of the present argument is this: "It" is not the same thing in school and in the rest of the world. The relationship between an academic curriculum and an experiential curriculum proves to be more complex than the rhetoric of application suggests.

For purposes of illustration, I will focus primarily on three student-interns and one community-based service project taken loosely from my teams' research. These portraits are not meant to correspond precisely to what we saw happen, but rather are adapted to make analytic points. The descriptions are realistic, but not necessarily scrupulously accurate representations of our observations. I am not trying to "prove" anything with the narratives, but to raise important issues. Here are the four:

Heather, a junior who interned as a tour guide in a state history museum, led groups of elementary-school children through the facility. The tour normally proceeded through several steps: The guide greeted the class at the door and escorted them to the auditorium, where she gave a brief introductory speech about the museum, showed them a film about, say, colonial life in the area, and then displayed and explained certain household artifacts (candlestick molds, bed warmers, etc.) from a cart; then she led them through several exhibit halls, discussing the displays and setting up a short exercise (say, drawing forms of transportation in the colony).

Roberto, a junior majoring in urban studies with a minor in design and architecture, worked in the enforcement division of a federal agency charged with protecting employees' legal rights. He conducted intake interviews with new complainants and gathered basic information for cases. Under the close supervision of the chief of the investigative unit, he made recommendations about whether the agency should pursue a particular complaint based on his understanding of employment law.

Lisa, a senior journalism major, interned in the features department of a well-known fashion magazine. In addition to performing basic clerical work—photocopying and proofreading articles, preparing press kits—she developed a database system for compiling "look-books," collections of photos from fashion shows and design firms that had been commented on by various editors and staff members. She also did background research for writers preparing articles on celebrities and new fashion trends (cf. Moore, 2007).

Finally, a civic-engagement class at a large urban university engaged in a Participatory Action Research (PAR) project (McIntyre, 2008): In collaboration with residents and small-business owners in a gentrifying neighborhood, 12 students conducted a study of the economic and social impact of the possible replacement of locally owned shops by upscale, national chain stores. They worked with community activists to design the study; interviewed and observed shopkeepers, their employees, and their customers; tracked employment and consumption patterns, and met with government officials and real-estate developers. At the end of the semester, they presented the results of their study at an open meeting at the local community center, and their local collaborators made recommendations for ways to preserve the social and economic vitality of the neighborhood.

Forms of Curriculum Content

The first aspect of the curriculum of experience that I propose to describe is the forms of knowledge-use that appear in the situated activities of a community of practice. As a broad analytic scheme, the concepts addressed here refer to particular ways of talking about the social stock of knowledge in a scene. The framework has an etic character: These are terms that might be germane to nearly any site, that an outside observer might look for wherever experiential learning is purported to be happening. From an insider's emic perspective, the terms might be configured variably, mean somewhat different things, carry different weights. For our purposes here, as a device for identifying an important element of the curriculum, I will organize the discussion around the etic terms, but I will illustrate them in more emic terms by invoking specific examples. Again, these concepts are heuristics, not ontologically distinct forms of knowledge; they might be useful as pedagogical devices—an internship instructor could use them as ways to structure journal assignments, for example—but here we will use them for analytical purposes.

Facts and Information

One obvious form of knowledge is consensually agreed-upon "facts" about the situation, the arena, the activity, and the larger context: statements and claims about things (objects, persons, events) in the world of practice or beyond, which claims are accepted by participants as straightforward and incontrovertible. In some respects, this form of knowledge is what insiders refer to when they mention the "stuff" a newcomer learns. Embedded in the practice of tour guides in the State History Museum, for example, were certain kinds of historical facts: the names of colonial governors, or the types of transportation vehicles used in the nineteenth century. Heather's supervisor expected her to display a repertoire of this textbook-like information as she gave the auditorium talk, answered student questions, or led the exhibit-hall exercises—and to invoke it correctly. Indeed, the supervisor herself displayed these facts in her own tours, as well as in her sessions with the intern; she referred to them as "things you've got to know."

Roberto, in the fair-employment office, took as factual the content of employment laws and procedures: For example, employers are required to give a specific number of days' notice in advertising a job. Some elements of the law, of course, were open to interpretation, but some were regarded by lawyers on both sides as matters of settled fact. Lisa, at the fashion magazine, needed to know which celebrities had worn which designers' gowns at recent awards ceremonies; she exhibited this kind of insider's knowledge in casual conversations in the office as well as at editorial meetings. Students in the PAR class discovered certain facts that even pro-gentrification developers would accept: for example, the average household income of residents in the district.

Interns learn that facticity claims are invoked for certain purposes by certain actors in certain kinds of interactions, and that they are sometimes open to challenge. That is, newcomers not only learn the facts, but also learn *about* the facts. The PAR researchers reported that community residents relied on local shops for a specific percentage of their purchases; economists for the developers' group proposed a different figure, and a struggle ensued over the competing assertions. For Roberto and the equal-opportunity lawyers, a specific provision of the law might be regarded as a fact; for attorneys defending employers, the meaning of that provision might be contested. On the whole, however, the curricula of most work sites include at least some facts over which there is no argument. What such facts *mean* in the context within which they appear, on the other hand, the weight they are accorded and the uses to which they are put, vary enormously across situations. I will address that feature of situated knowledge in a later section.

Concepts

The notion of information seems somewhat particulate, rather like marbles one might collect in a box: the name of the last Dutch governor of New York, the content of a labor law, or the designer of the dress Gwyneth Paltrow wore to the Oscars. Somewhat more molecular, more systemic, is the *concept* concept: the idea of a connected set of impressions and ideas, inferences and representations, with its implication of typicality and taxonomy, with the reference to categories of things and their relations (Murphy, 2002). One can picture concepts as the product of the thinking mind—certainly the individual person makes inferences, reaches generalizations, organizes ideas—but they are (at least) as often generated by social processes. Culture, as Clifford Geertz (1977) eloquently declared, is the "webs of significance" through which we make and use meaning—and that process involves the social construction and cultural transmission of organized concepts (1977, p. 5; cf. Berger and Luckmann, 1966).

Part of the internship experience, then, entails becoming familiar with and using concepts embedded in the practices of the organization. On one level, that means learning the language, mastering the vocabulary of the community of practice. (Some would invoke Foucault's [2010] conception of discourses or discursive formations here; I want to reserve that more holistic perspective on interns' learning for a discussion of that idea later in this chapter.) On another, it means building the capacity to utilize those words competently; to recognize their appropriate domains and their implications; to exploit their utility in the variety of situations in which they play a part; to comprehend their weight, their relations, and their underlying logics—to *participate* in the use of the concepts that constitute that culture. Gumperz and Hymes (1986) refer to this learning as the development of communicative competence. Psychologists use a variety of terms to denote different levels and forms of concepts: schemas, representations, scripts, plans—all refer to socioculturally organized modes of apprehending the lived world.

So Heather not only acquired informational nuggets about state history, but she also engaged a number of concepts common to the community of tour guides and docents in the museum. Some of those concepts, for example, related to the items on the artifacts cart: household management, domestic production, living conditions. She had to mobilize those concepts in producing the conversation following the film in the auditorium, elaborating on them in ways meaningful to the students in the audience. That meant she had to construct relational concepts meaningful to herself, to build foundations from which she could generate stories, spin out responses to kids' questions, and conduct further research in the museum library: "Oh, yes, this bed warmer was one of the tools people used to stay warm during the long winter; they were the responsibility of the women and girls in the household—just as making the candles was. These items show how women and girls in the colonial family had different chores from men and boys." Other concepts were about the visiting children and teachers: about forms of behavior ("This group is well behaved"), about developmental stages ("These kids are not ready for a discussion of arguments over slavery in the colony"), and about instructional styles ("This teacher runs the class like boot camp!"). Still other concepts organized her thoughts about the museum as a social institution: about kinds of actors (curators, security staff), about physical design and its impact on use (visitor flow), about the distinctions among such missions as "conservation" and "education."

Similarly, Roberto engaged concepts above the level of the content of statutes. He came to use legal concepts like due process (certainly an idea open to varied interpretations and applications), as well as taxonomic ideas about types of complaints, some justified like "age discrimination" and others as flimsy as "slacker employees annoyed at their bosses." He could formulate his own principles and taxonomies by treating the case documents as raw data and exercising decontextualized reason on them, but he was far more likely to take on those of the community of practice, especially through his conversations with his supervisor, during which he absorbed the vocabulary by which he could communicate with his colleagues. For her part, Lisa took part in a community of practice whose concepts were softer-edged—what do they mean by "hot," or "out," or "wannabe"?—but no less important in terms of the ongoing operation and her growing competence and identity as a participant. The PAR students engaged concepts with a more overtly political cast: gentrification, community, organizing. In all these cases, concepts played a major role in students' learning—but the nature of those concepts, as we will consider in the next chapter, varied substantially between school and action.

Skills and Competencies

Another form of situated knowledge, one more intuitively suited to discussions of internships, can be found in the things learners *do*, in the procedures through which they perform certain manual or conceptual operations (Bailey et al., 2004). The notion of skill has a long history of debate over such issues as where it is located and how stable it is. In one version, the concept is straightforward and commonsensical: Skill is the general term used to denote knowledge that a person has of the procedures for carrying out a specific task or a more generic type of operation. In that reading, a skill resides in the individual person (whether in the mind or the body), and is applied in appropriate situations where that operation needs to be performed. This image of skill can be found in official policies like the School-to-Work Opportunities Act of 1994, or in *What Work Requires of Schools*, a report of the Secretary's Commission on Achieving Necessary Skills (SCANS, 1991), which identifies the "fundamental skills and workplace competencies" required by the workplace of the future: generic basic skills such as reading, writing, math, speaking, and listening; thinking skills like creativity, decision-making, and problem-solving; and the ability to work with a variety of technologies and information (cf. Casner-Lotto, 2006).

But some psychologists and sociologists have challenged this common view of skill as an objective set of attributes or capabilities acquired by the individual and applied across different settings. Situated cognition theorists, for instance, argue that tasks abstracted from the situations in which they are performed cease to resemble skills in the real world; that is, real skills are situated, concrete, grounded in the circumstances of their use (Attewell, 1990). Ethnomethodologists, for their part, reject the notion of skills as intracranial, stable, unitary, and transferable, and argue that skills are more like situated performances than like individual traits or capacities (Garfinkel, 1967; Mehan & Wood, 1975). Vallas (1990) regarded skill as a property not of the individual but of the job, of the situation; Spenner (1990) agreed, suggesting that skills are socially constructed and defined, as well as situated. In general, these critics maintain, the notion of generic skills seems flawed, and does not capture the complexity of skills actually embedded in organizational practices.

More recently, Raelin (2008) criticized the basic premises of what he described as the competency movement, the effort to identify and develop "specific, observable, and verifiable" behavioral markers of competent workers. Human resource managers and trainers who believe that generic competencies apply to entire classes of practitioners across organizations and positions fail to realize, Raelin argued, that only organic competencies applied to specific jobs and tasks are meaningful categories of work (p. 43). Raelin evaded the location-of-skills problem by changing the key term to competency—clearly a feature of the person rather than of the situation, although the personal features that qualify as indicators of competence certainly vary across settings. His argument begs an important question, however, for advocates of experiential learning in higher education: If organic skills and competencies are always deeply embedded in the contexts of their use, and if the concept of generic skills lacks explanatory and practical power, what function is played by the kinds of skills learned by college interns in particular work and service environments? Are they appropriate content for the university curriculum? This question raises the issue of transfer of learning, which we will consider at a later point.

In any case, members of the case-study organizations (as well as their teachers) did talk about skills and competencies, and regarded them as appropriate learning matters for interns. The *kinds* of skills displayed in the 60 internship sites and community projects that we studied took nearly infinite forms. Some were procedural: the capacity to carry out a multistep task. A student in a hospital surgery department, for example, learned to set up an anesthesia machine (the "red cart") by connecting particular tubes in a particular order, placing the needed materials in their proper locations, and checking certain pressures. Other skills were cognitive: the capacity to carry out certain mental operations, to solve certain problems. These varied in the degree to which the solutions were algorithmic, amenable to predetermined, if-then procedures, rather than open to improvisation. Roberto had to interpret the facts of a presented case in terms given by employment law, to determine what sort of case it was and forward it to the appropriate section. At the ambiguous cusps of the category system, where cases could be more than one thing or the details did not fit easily, he had to exercise substantial judgment—or at least learn to. Sometimes the cognitive skill went beyond problem solutions and into problem formulation, recognizing an issue not previously addressed by the work group (cf. Scribner, 1986). One student who worked in a city councilmember's office noticed that the member spent an inordinate amount of time tracking down information about where a particular bill was in the legislative process. He volunteered to construct a database system that tracked every bill in the pipeline.

Finally, some skills were social: The student had to do something with or relate to other people in a way that demonstrated certain traits or accomplished certain results. One form of social skill often claimed in the literature on civic engagement (cf. Eyler and Giles, 1999) is the ability to work with others, especially diverse groups of coworkers, clients, or customers: to recognize, appreciate, and handle difference. In a more instrumental vein, this skill has been labeled as teamwork: working cooperatively toward a shared goal, playing one's part effectively and supporting others in playing theirs. Leadership—the capacity to motivate, guide, and organize others—is yet another skill sometimes claimed for community engagement (cf. Longo and Shaffer, 2009).

Heather needed to display the skill of public speaking as she welcomed the classes to the museum in an introductory talk. Lisa demonstrated competence at internet searches; she became the go-to Google person at the fashion magazine. Some members of the PAR class became adept at constructing GIS maps to capture and analyze demographic data about neighborhood residents, while others enhanced their interviewing techniques. The variety of skills deployed in our research sites was staggering.

Social and Organizational Knowledge

Another element of what people need to know and learn in the course of an internship or civic-engagement project revolves around the relationships among members of the setting: structural matters like roles, hierarchies, and organization charts; how people are organized in terms of production processes; cultural matters like styles of behavior and dress, appropriate expressions of respect and deference; political matters like the distribution and exercise of power.

Every social system operates with certain structural characteristics. An organization chart, in the case of a workplace organization, describes the system's more or less stable, identifiable, and official roles and the relationships among them. The phrase "more or less" should be taken seriously: These roles and relationships are never written in stone, absolutely clear and persistent; rather, they are emergent, enacted, situated, negotiated, and contested. I am not engaging in a traditional form of structuralist analysis. Still, there is generally some degree of regularity in conceptions and performances of various roles—and that is part of what the newcomer-intern usually learns (cf. Hatch, 1997).

In the education department of the history museum, for example, the role structure was relatively simple and flat: A director oversaw the general programming and work; an administrative aide maintained the files and correspondence; the bulk of the members were docents, tour guides who worked part-time on a volunteer basis leading groups on visits to the facility. Among the docents, there was no formal hierarchy: All of them basically did the same thing; although some veterans were accorded greater respect and admiration for their considerable knowledge and skill, the job descriptions were identical.

The employment-law office, at least the part open to Roberto, comprised several types of actors: supervising lawyers who assigned cases, formulated strategies, and oversaw decisions; staff attorneys who pursued resolution of the cases through negotiations among the parties or through court prosecutions; investigators who received basic descriptions of the complaints and collected information about them; intake specialists who received the complaints and solicited additional information and documents to pass on to the investigators; clerks who maintained the files and produced the correspondence and other official materials. The process flow (another structural element of the organization) moved from the original complaint through the intake stage, to the investigation stage, to the determination and execution of a strategy for handling the case. Each actor carried out specific aspects of the process and then passed the results on to the next person; sometimes they consulted each other, but more often the work was divided across participants. So the role structure was far more differentiated than the education department's in the museum: Intake specialists did not prosecute the cases, file clerks did not gather information. Part of the curriculum in the agency, that is, centered on knowing who did what, who reported to whom, and how the resolution process moved forward. Again, this role structure represented a curriculum in the sense that it constituted an aspect of the situated definition and distribution of knowledge and a system by which participants entered, engaged, and moved through the stock of knowledge.

But notice that no one participant encountered or engaged all of the knowledge comprising this system. The curriculum here, as in any complex organization, was not identical for every participant; the concept of distributed cognition works here. The file clerks knew how to organize the flow and storage of the case documents, but did not know how to produce those documents or generate the information contained in them. The intake specialists were familiar with some of the basics of employment law and knew what data needed to be entered into the forms, but understood only in general terms how the investigators gathered the information necessary to pursuing the cases. The investigators knew the law just enough to determine what kinds of evidence needed to be collected from what sources. The lawyers, for their part, understood the law and its application to the specifics of a case, and could formulate strategies appropriate to those particularities. This division of labor seems obvious on one level, but it strongly shaped the actual curriculum experienced by the intern.

On a cultural level, participants in a workplace need to know such things as how to dress appropriately, how to interpret various behaviors, what to make of a person's being five minutes late to an appointment (is that an insult, or does it meet the customary standard of punctuality?), and what language is appropriate to which situations and relationships. A colleague of mine in a social welfare agency years ago once casually dropped the term "mind-fuck" in a staff meeting, and a pall descended upon the room: She had violated the linguistic norms of the work group.

The micropolitics of the workplace (cf. Moore, 2008) also constitute an element of the situated curriculum of experience. Participants come to know where real power resides, how to get things done, who needs to be mobilized in order to gain support for a position or a strategy. These matters rarely appear in the formal organization chart, but those with organizational savvy master them and use them to their advantage. Lisa learned that if she had a certain idea for a story, she would do better pitching it to a particular editor who she knew was more positively disposed to that kind of journalism. Roberto came to understand that he needed to express a degree of deference to his supervisor in their weekly meetings, conceding points even when he might be tempted to argue. He realized—he learned—that this supervisor wanted to be treated as the boss, and to wield power in the determination of strategies and resolutions.

Another vocabulary for analyzing this element of the curriculum of experience draws on theories and concepts from postmodernism, particularly from Michel Foucault. In *The Archaeology of Knowledge* (2010) and other texts, Foucault advanced the idea of discursive formations: complex systems of institutional practices and relationships that arrange what can be known and said, and what remains unsaid; modes of speech, writing, and other communication that structure—give reality and shape to—the interactions among participants. On the local level, discursive formations may also include standards of dress, social uses of space, and other communicative channels. One advantage of these terms is that they provide a language for situating the specific organizational settings of student-interns' experience in the larger system of power relations and discourses constituting the greater society within which they exist. On the other hand, I have chosen not to rely overmuch on Foucauldian concepts because they tend to be more revealing about large-scale historical and social processes—for example, his analysis in *Discipline and Punish* (1995) of the emergence of discipline as a cultural feature of modern European society—than about situated activities; they lend themselves more to "Big-D" (systemic, societal) than to "little-d" (situated, enacted) discourse analysis (cf. Erickson, 2004, pp. 128–129). Moreover, Foucault tended to acknowledge less individual agency than the present analysis assumes. As Anthony Giddens (1984, p. 157) famously declared, "Foucault's bodies have no faces."

Similarly, one could deploy Pierre Bourdieu's (1977, 1992) notions of *habitus* and *field* in this analysis. Habitus, the "sense of the game" that informs actors' behavior and thought, and field, the particular social and physical ecology within which the game is played, are certainly evocative ideas. Like the term discourse, they lend themselves to considerations of the relations between power and knowledge, which are crucial in the analysis of engaged learning. Like Foucault, however, Bourdieu operates at a higher level of abstraction than does the framework advocated in this book. The schemes described in chapter 2 seem more productive in generating insightful interpretations of students' actual situated experiences.

Personal Development

Another type of knowledge-claim about internships focuses on students' learning about themselves, their growth in terms of handling their own emotional and thought processes and their relations with other people. Howard Gardner's (2006) concept of interpersonal intelligence provides one vocabulary for describing some elements of this curriculum, particularly those associated with capacities located in the individual worker-intern. Gardner defines interpersonal intelligence as a "capacity to notice distinctions among others—in particular, contrasts in their moods, temperaments, motivations, and intentions" (p. 15). In some ways, the social knowledge discussed earlier is objective, a matter of fact embedded in structures and practices. On other levels, however, the use of this knowledge requires a subtle reading of others, an ability to infer their motives, feelings, and intentions. Gardner's implication in his Multiple Intelligences (MI) theory is that these capacities are inherent in individuals, that if I am good at reading others in one setting I will be good at reading others in another situation. While I will concede that some individuals are generally better at doping out others' moods and motives, I will also argue that (a) the clues available for that reading are not a matter of universal, decontextualized intelligence, vary across settings, and thus need to be learned; and (b) the weighting of those issues also varies: It is more important to pick up on your boss's mood in some situations than in others, and one has to learn the difference. That is, while some people enter a setting with a greater general capacity for reading people and understanding social rules and customs, the judgments and actions arising from those interpretations are different across situations—and constitute part of the curriculum of experience.

Gardner also included intrapersonal intelligence in his MI theory: the capacity to read and manage one's own emotions and reactions. Daniel Goleman (2006) later combined interpersonal and intrapersonal skills in the concept of emotional intelligence: the ability to identify, assess, and control the emotions of oneself, others, and groups (cf. Mayer et al., 2004).

Whether one opts to distinguish these two forms of personal intelligence is, for our purposes, not so important as to acknowledge that part of what an intern learns is how to read and handle feelings and emotions, both others' and her own.

Lisa, for instance, once failed to produce a report for her supervisor by the established deadline, and her boss harangued her loudly for ten minutes. The intern had to suppress her own anger and humiliation during the event, rather than break into tears or yell back. Learning to do that was a rough lesson. Roberto, in doing intake at the employment-law agency, came to understand that he had a tendency to sympathize with complainants and overlook pertinent information that might work in the employer's favor. In an expression of growing emotional intelligence, he learned to make a point of asking about that material.

Again, the term intelligence generally refers to a trait of the individual and not to the social situation, but both dimensions are clearly at work in these events. Different sociocultural settings permit or prefer different kinds of emotional displays. Look, for example, at the differences in funeral behavior across ethnic groups: the stolid German Lutherans, the keening Irish Catholics. Even within single organizations, plenty of variability in emotion appears to be allowed: Sometimes one manager in a company is prone to violent outbursts of temper against his subordinates while another is calm and mild in response to similar provocations. So there is a generic ability at stake here—being able to understand and control one's emotions—but there is a situated knowledge element, as well: the need to read the (variable) social rules for allowable displays of emotion.

Another form of personal-development claim can be made for the educational impact of experiential learning: constructing an identity. In this process, the learner engages with a social system in which she comes to play a role and be recognized (and recognize herself) as a member, performing certain kinds of actions and displaying certain kinds of characteristics. Wenger (1998) highlights the construction of social identity as one of the key elements of increasing participation in a community of practice (cf. Lave and Wenger, 1991)—that is, of learning. Clearly, identity formation represents one aspect of the curriculum of experience, manifesting itself both in one's internal conception of oneself and in the recognition one receives from other members of that community.

Heather gradually moved into the role and identity of the museum tour guide. The chapter on pedagogy will describe the *means* by which that happened, but here we can examine the *content* of her evolving position. Part of what qualified a volunteer (or intern) as a guide was the competent performance of the tasks constituting the role: greeting the class, showing them the film in the auditorium and doing the artifacts cart, leading them around some of the exhibits and explaining what they were seeing. But there was more: the growth of an ineffable sense of being a member of that community, an insider. Heather's conception of her own social identity in relation to other tour guides changed: They increasingly treated her as "one of us," reflexively acknowledging and constructing her insider status by such acts as including her in back-office conversations, pulling her into a group photograph, making suggestions for sources of historical information or for teaching techniques, and even asking her thoughts on how to handle a certain kind of behavioral problem.

Even though Lisa stayed in a relatively peripheral role in the magazine office, she appeared to move toward a social identity consistent with the overall social configuration of the place. Nobody, including Lisa, ever considered her fully "one of us": She was temporary (both in the number of days per week she worked and in the duration of her placement); her functions were marginal to the operation; she never quite built the close working relationships that a full-blown member would have. And yet by virtue of her participation in certain kinds of activities and processes, she began to evince rudimentary qualities of the social identity of an insider. Her clothing conformed more closely to the unspoken expectations of the editors, writers, and staff; she piped in with comments and suggestions when people were casually discussing celebrity sightings and new fashions, using jargon familiar to the group; she displayed greater comfort in approaching other members of the team with information and questions. Although Lisa cannot be said to have assumed the full-scale identity of a fashion-magazine staff member, she became increasingly familiar with the dimensions and subtleties of such an identity. That learning has to be regarded as part of the curriculum of experience in that site. In fact, it represents one of the main goals college students have for internship experiences: to find out "what it's like" to work in such and such a place or profession.

Values and Ethics

A final constituent of the curriculum of engagement claimed by experiential educators (cf. Sweitzer and King, 2004; Warren et al., 2008) is the conceptions of the good and the bad, the right and the wrong, the worthwhile and the insignificant that are shared, enacted, and enforced by participants in a community of practice. This dimension of knowledge centers not merely on facts or skills, but on judgments about actions, ideas, people, relationships, properties, and possessions. It assumes that those things are not simply things, but matters of shared valuation. It highlights the point that members of a social domain regard some kinds of behavior as right, just, and good, and others as despicable and wrong. Where those lines are drawn varies wildly by context, but virtually any set of social interactors work from *some* conception of values and ethics.

Sometimes these values are expressed explicitly and directly in situations within an organization; sometimes they are even formulated as codes of ethics, or rules and regulations. In Roberto's office, for instance, the actions of lawyers and investigators were governed not only by office policy but also by statute and by a professional code of ethics. A lawyer who violated the rules could be disbarred; an investigator who overstepped his bounds could be arrested. But their general approach to the work was informed by underlying values, as well, implicit conceptions of justice and fairness that motivated not only the promulgation of law but the actions of staff members. Many of them could have made higher incomes in nongovernmental legal practices, but chose to work in labor law out of a deep commitment to those principles. Part of what Roberto learned, therefore, was the content and power of those values. Of course, there were moments as well when he learned the opposite: something about the impact of cynicism and fatigue on professional behavior, when the lawyers expressed impatience with complainants or doubts about the functioning of the legal system.

The PAR students learned about the ethics of social research, both because their project had to be cleared by the university's human subjects committee and because neighborhood participants raised certain concerns. The students discussed these issues in class sessions led by the instructor, who included readings on ethics in the syllabus. But the more memorable learning stemmed from occasionally bristly conversations in which local activists called the students on their positionality as members of an elite and sometimes exploitive institution. They had to confront questions about reciprocity, respect, and the distribution of power.

Lisa's learning centered not so much on overtly ethical issues as on what the editors and other staff members at the magazine valued: the fashionable, the trendy, the snarky. In conversations as well as in the written product, she encountered symbolic expressions of these values in the derision a writer showed toward a particular celebrity, in the envy and awe another displayed toward a US$12,000 handbag. These messages took both stark and subtle forms, but in either case constituted part of Lisa's curriculum.

The claims about students' learning of values and ethics appear somewhat more often in the writings on service-learning and civic engagement (e.g., Butin, 2010; Eyler & Giles, 1999) than on those about work-related internships and cooperative education (cf. Linn et al., 2004; Ryder & Wilson, 1987). The very concept of service implies an explicitly ethical mission and a values-laden stance toward activities and relationships. But there are also arguments for attention to the ethical elements and challenges of work practices and organizations that confirm that matters of morality and integrity are not confined to service-learning settings (cf. Sullivan, 2004; Sullivan and Rosin, 2008).

Features of Curriculum

In a general sense, then, the curriculum of experience can be described in terms of various elements of the socio-cognitive task demands that engaged learners encounter in their work or service activities: what knowledge and skill they are being asked to display, what sorts of relationships they are expected to sustain, what kinds of value commitments they need to demonstrate. Each of these curriculum components has been analyzed in terms of its content. In this section, we will consider some general features of those knowledge-forms, dimensions on which they might vary in ways crucial to the student's learning.

Modes of Thought

One variable in the constitution of the curriculum of experience can be found in the different ways students (and other participants) are expected to think, to define and solve problems, to organize information. The psychologist Jerome Bruner (1996b) identifies several "frames for thinking": modes of cognition that operate on the basis of different styles, principles, and procedures. One such mode of thinking, he argues, is *actional*: "a form of meaning making [that] is concerned with relating events, utterances, acts or whatever to the so-called arguments of action: who is the agent of what act toward what goal by what instrumentality" (p. 96). In the world of business or government or community service, thought is usually structured around action and its results. Some other social interactions manifest a mode of thought Bruner calls *narrative*: telling stories to achieve intersubjective connections and purposes (cf. Bruner, 2003). Stories make the point that particular events or personalities are in fact instances of broader types, that they have meaning beyond their specificities. Finally, Bruner identifies a third important mode of thought, the *propositional*, in which "meaning making is dominated by the rules of the symbolic, syntactic, and conceptual systems that we use in achieving decontextualized meanings" (p. 98). This kind of thinking entails the formal procedures of logic—deduction, induction, and abduction—and is more cautious, more rule-driven, more systematic than the other modes. Here we have the scientist, the lawyer, the engineer—and, for our purposes, the scholar, the academic. Claims made in this mode are taken to follow rules of inference and argument, to apply to a wide array of formally defined situations, to aim toward nomothetic rather than idiographic analysis.

These distinctions in thought processes are important partly because some theorists—including Dewey (1910)—claim that people in everyday life "think like scientists," reasoning from evidence to theory and back. But Diana Kuhn (1989) and others have shown that this assertion does not in fact reflect what people normally do. Rather, people often fall prey to such fallacies as confirmation bias and naive realism—even in academic settings where the culture favors scientific thought, but especially in the rest of the real world.

So one of the things we can do in the course of analyzing the curriculum of experience is to identify and trace the kinds of thinking and argument participants engage in as they work to accomplish their joint purposes. The modes-of-thought concept has a dual character in this curriculum-analysis enterprise: It constitutes one of the things members learn to do—effective storytelling is not an innate skill, but is something one acquires or develops as one interacts with storytellers and listeners—and it represents one of the variables through which learning can be described.

As an example, imagine Heather "doing the artifacts cart" in the state history museum. She picks up a bed warmer and, when none of the children recognizes it, tells a story: "In the winter, when you want to get in bed, you discover that the sheets are too cold, so you take this pan downstairs to the fire and get some coals. When it's hot, you rub it on the sheets using this long handle." Her narrative captures the attention of the youngsters better than a formal disquisition on the history of household appliances. Or picture Lisa chatting with the feature editors at the magazine, recalling the previous night's Oscars ceremony. Some of what they do is pure narrative—storytelling, dishing—but some of it is actional: considerations of the way they might turn some of the stories into publishable articles. On the other hand, Roberto might engage in propositional thinking as he follows a decision-tree algorithm to determine whether the facts of a complaint fit under this or that legal provision.

The level or type of thought demanded by a particular task or activity can also be described in terms of Bloom's taxonomy of educational objectives (Bloom et al., 1956): knowledge, comprehension, application, analysis, synthesis, or evaluation. Is the student-intern being asked simply to retrieve information ("the Erie Canal opened in 1825"), to construct an analysis ("the current residents of this neighborhood will not be able to afford to shop in the new chain stores"), or to evaluate something ("this story about movie stars' dresses at the Oscars seems like the kind of thing our readers like")? (Marzano and Kendall [2007] have produced an updated version of the taxonomy; the point applies to their framework as well.) A number of such analytic devices might yield interesting observations about the modes of thought appearing in the curriculum of experience.

Pragmatics

A second variable in the analysis of that curriculum is the social meaning of the learning activity in the context in which it occurs—its pragmatics. That dimension can be examined in several ways. One is to identify the *centrality* of the activity: the relative importance of various kinds of knowledge-use in the overall operation of the activity system. Some forms of knowledge advance the core mission of the organization, while others bear on incidental, ancillary, or support functions, and some have no utility at all. Heather, for example, performed a central role in the museum, one without which the education department could not exist. A second criterion is *demandedness*: the extent to which the activity system requires (rather than hopes for, or doesn't really care about) competent performance of the knowledge-task. The magazine editors expected Lisa to do online research for the writers, but her work on the look-books was completely optional. A third dimension is *prestige*, the degree to which performing a task or possessing knowledge either depends on or confers a certain status to the intern. The PAR student who was selected to present the group's findings to the community meeting had already acquired a solid standing in the class, and her competent performance enhanced that status.

Trajectory

Given these elements of the curriculum of experience, we can describe an individual student's learning trajectory in terms of changes over time in the content, complexity, and importance of her work, and in the degree of autonomy and status that she achieves. Heather began the semester simply tagging along with a veteran tour guide, watching what she did. After a couple of tours, she was asked to work with a few children on the drawing exercise in the transportation hall. Next she was unexpectedly assigned to do the artifacts cart when the lead docent was called away. Over time, she engaged and mastered all of the constituent tasks of the tour guide. That is, her trajectory was strongly upward in terms of all our variables. Another intern-subject worked in a rural veterinary clinic. On the last day of the 30-week internship, Fred was doing the same things that he did the first day: answering phones, setting up equipment for operations, and cleaning cages. His learning trajectory was essentially flat (cf. Bailey et al., 2004; Moore, 1986). The learning trajectory might also be analyzed in terms of the emergence of expertise. Clearly, no careful observer would claim that a 14-week part-time internship can provide a college student with sufficient engagement with work-based knowledge to turn her into an expert in almost anything, but as an analytic device the notion of expertise does at least identify the dimensions along which a person occupying a particular organizational role might develop in order to move in that direction.

A copious literature on expertise has grown over the years examining the distinctions between the knowledge-use of novices and that of experts (cf. Chi et al., 1988; Dreyfus and Dreyfus, 2005; Flyvbjerg, 2001; Hoffman, 1992). Glaser and Chi (1988) summarized some of the key characteristics of experts' performance on tasks: They perceive large, meaningful patterns or chunks in their areas; they have superior short- and long-term memory; they are faster than novices; they see and represent a problem at a less concrete, more principled level; they analyze problems qualitatively rather than simply apply algorithms; and they monitor their own performance regularly and rigorously (pp. xvii–xx).

Bereiter and Scardamalia (1993) shifted the focus a bit, investigating not the traits of experts but the process of performing skillful activities. They suggested that the relevant contrast is not between experts and novices, but between experts and experienced nonexperts. The important difference between those two groups is not technique or knowledge, but approach: Experts address problems whereas experienced nonexperts carry out practiced routines; the expert continually grapples with the constituents of the problem, reconceiving and reorganizing them, whereas the nonexpert seeks to apply known solutions even to novel problems (p. 11).

A powerful conception of the path to expertise was developed by Hubert and Stuart Dreyfus (1988), who identified five phases or stages in the learning of skills:

- *Novices* learn general rules for action, and behave as if they apply across situations;
- *Advanced beginners* start to recognize relevant features of the context in which the skill is executed, though they still attempt to apply general rules;
- *Competent performers* begin to take responsibility for their actions and decisions rather than relying upon the rules; they exercise some degree of interpretation and judgment;

- *Proficient performers* are deeply involved in their actions, and have constructed their own approaches based on prior actions and experience; they exercise greater judgment, and account for subtle elements of the situation in deciding what to do; their actions begin to look not so much like careful deliberation on the problem as it relates to the rules, but like intuition;
- *Experts* do not so much solve problems and make decisions as they "just do what works"; their actions are intuitive, holistic, based in deep understandings of situations, alternative strategies, and vast experience. (cf. Flyvbjerg, 2001)

This progression represents a challenge to the experiential educator. If the intern occupies a role that confronts her with tasks of a substantial degree of difficulty and complexity, she is likely to move no further than competence over the course of a 14-week semester. She may learn the rules, looking for socially prescribed methods for performing tasks and solving problems; she may begin to notice patterns and similarities across situations—but she is unlikely (again, if the work is demanding) to achieve proficiency or expertise. That is not to denigrate the experience or the learning—certainly achieving competence warrants time and effort (college credit may be a tougher call)—but only to raise the possibility of limits. Still, examining the dimensions on which the expert operates in that context can round out an analysis of the curriculum of experience.

Heather's learning trajectory as a tour guide moved her along the expertise spectrum—but not all the way. The constituent skills of her role were not as measurable as winning chess games, but her supervisor could see her progress. For example, in her first performance on the artifacts cart, Heather finished discussing five household items in five minutes; her boss chuckled and whispered to the researcher, "That would have taken me half an hour!" By the end of the term, Heather could stretch out her talks to five minutes per item: She moved toward expertise. When the PAR students first started crunching the demographic data on shopping patterns in the neighborhood, they took a long time and frequently consulted the instructor; toward the end of the term, they could produce charts quickly and without help.

Ordering

The curriculum can also be described in terms of the sequence in which the newcomer gains exposure to its various components. One aspect of that organizing process is called classification by Basil Bernstein (1975): the extent to which knowledge is divided into rigidly defined categories (e.g., sales, marketing, and operations in a corporation; chemistry, sociology, and philosophy in a university). This concept will turn up again in the chapter on pedagogy, because it shapes the social organization of the student's exposure to knowledge. But it also represents a way of analyzing the organization of that knowledge itself. Some settings divide knowledge into finely distinguished categories, while others treat their stock of knowledge as a syncretic heap. The museum, for example, regarded the tour guide's knowledge as of a piece. The magazine, on the other hand, drew significant lines between knowing how to lay out a page of pictures and knowing how to write an article.

Then there is the question of the order in which the student gets access to the various components of the knowledge-in-use. Jean Lave (2011), who studied apprentice tailors in Liberia, noticed that they learned to sew before they learned to cut. That sequence was a persistent feature of the situated curriculum of the community of practice of tailors. Heather engaged the various components of the tour-guide role in a predictable order: observing a veteran docent, working with kids on a drawing exercise, doing the artifacts cart, performing the welcoming speech, putting them all together. Because the PAR project was based in a college class, the instructor organized the training in research methods in a specific order, from foundational to advanced. On the other hand, Lisa engaged tasks and their associated knowledge as they arose in the production process, not according to some sort of educational logic.

Factors Shaping the Curriculum

Several factors shape the situated curriculum of a workplace or other setting (cf. Moore, 2004). These factors also shape the pedagogy, as we will discover in chapter 6. Whether theorizing about learning from experience, designing an experiential program, or evaluating students' experiences, educators ought to take these matters into account. They fall into three general categories:

Personal Features of the Participants

The curriculum emerges in ways shaped by the individual learner's educational history, previous knowledge, and experience. This point reflects Dewey's (1938) notion of continuity: What you already know shapes present learning. Obviously, a person well versed in computer skills will enter a computer-related role more smoothly and quickly than one with no experience. As it happened, Heather's parents had taken her to a number of museums over the years—including this one—and she was familiar with the layout and the content of the institution. Her internship there was, not coincidentally, more successful than that of a classmate of hers who was not already museum-savvy.

But there are also effects from the individual's learning style (Kolb, 1984) and personality. Someone willing to take risks and exercise initiative will learn differently from another person who hangs back, waiting for direction and validation. Lisa, although she enjoyed dishing about fashion, was not particularly self-confident or assertive. Partly as a result, she did not carve out new tasks or roles at the magazine; she stayed rather on the periphery of that community of practice.

Internal Features of the Organization

The curriculum of experience takes shape as well from the negotiated structuring of roles and processes in the setting. An outfit with a highly differentiated organization chart, with many divisions and layers, distributes knowledge in ways different from one that looks flat and nonhierarchical. A production process with many distinct and sequential operations distributed across a complex role system creates a curriculum very different from one in which members all work on one major process. Bernstein's (1975) notion of classification provides a device for analyzing this dimension of the curriculum, as well. The Fordist assembly line, where each worker performs a discrete operation on the product as it passes by, is a classic instance of strong classification. Roberto's curriculum at the fair-employment agency resembled the factory in terms of the degree of knowledge-specialization. Certainly lawyers performed tasks different from those handled by investigators; in fact, even among the attorneys there were specialties. The museum, on the other hand, displayed weak classification: The knowledge base for docents was quite permeable, flexible, and shared.

The culture of the particular workplace shapes the curriculum of experience, as well. The particular culture of a work organization constitutes something the newcomer not only learns *about*, but also learns *through*: It creates frames of mind, promotes discourses, establishes norms, and tells stories that shape the ways in which the neophyte comes to engage in activities, use knowledge, and participate in communities of practice (cf. Applebaum, 1984; Hamada & Sibley, 1994). A workplace with a culture of intense competition represents a learning environment very different from one with an ethic of collaboration. Among our cases, the history museum favored a collaborative, learning-driven style of interaction and relationship, whereas the culture of the fair-employment agency was more no-nonsense, results-oriented, and hierarchical.

External Environment of the Organization

Finally, several aspects of the larger environment within which the organization works affect the definition and use of knowledge in the situated curriculum. Market relations, for instance, become something that the member needs to know about, but they also shape the nature of the available knowledge: A highly competitive market environment generates different kinds of knowledge—crisper, more distinct—than one where the organization faces little opposition. Lisa's fashion magazine was struggling to maintain its market share in a cutthroat industry, and may for that reason have given her fewer opportunities to engage new tasks and encounter new knowledge.

Technological changes—the invention of new tools and procedures—clearly affect the nature of knowledge-use within the organization. Imagine the possibilities that opened up to the PAR students because of the invention of SPSS (formerly Statistical Package for the Social Sciences) and GIS programs. Regulations, whether from the government or from unions, also constrain knowledge-use; certain things are permitted, certain things are not. Roberto's work was driven in part by such regulations.

Moreover, the external environment encompasses more general cultural and social factors, as well: social class, popular beliefs and trends, historical forces, and the like. These influence the shape of the situated curriculum in powerful, if distant, ways. Organizations peopled by, say, upper middle-class, college-educated, professional workers, for instance, may be more likely than working-class organizations to express knowledge in forms that sound abstract, decontextualized, and propositional (cf. Bernstein, 1975). The readers of the fashion magazine may have differed in their tastes, for example, from the people who visited the history museum, yet both organizations could be sensitive to temporary enthusiasms among their constituents. For example, the museum's curators responded some time ago to the public fascination with the television mini-series *Roots* by mounting an exhibition related to slavery in the colonial period. The magazine staff focused on dresses at the Oscars right after the awards show aired.

Challenges for Situated Curriculum Analysis

This chapter has proposed a set of concepts and terms for analyzing the curriculum of experience, the things internship and community service students learn through their engaged activities. It is important, however, to acknowledge some limitations of that approach. Theories of situated cognition and learning, chapter 2 notwithstanding, do not capture the whole content of the learning process; they beg some perplexing questions. Some commentators on situativity theory point out several flaws in the approach. Bereiter (1997), for example, argues that it devalues decontextualized forms of learning that, in fact, have been quite productive in human history:

> The situated actions of just plain folks come off as flexible, adaptive, and elegant—in a word, intelligent—whereas action based on formal procedures and principles comes off as brittle, plodding, insensitive to nuance—in a word, stupid. It is time, therefore, to look at the other side. Although non-situated cognition may not be very good for guiding a robot in a game of tag, it has proved capable of guiding a space vehicle to Mars. Surely there is a lesson for us in that. (pp. 286–287)

Bereiter notes that situated learning theory raises the problem of transfer, the question of whether knowledge acquired or constructed in one context can be useful in another. If one takes a radically situationist stance on that issue, one paints oneself into a corner: The learner would need experience in every conceivable situation in order to gain competence for each one. Clearly, that is not the case. The curriculum analyst needs to determine (a) whether participants in a situated activity are importing and using knowledge from other situations, inside or outside the present arena, and (b) whether the knowledge they use in the current encounter gets exported into other scenes. The first part of that challenge is methodologically easier than the second. One can watch for signs of improvisation and innovation, for people doing things in ways they haven't done them before; one can simply ask, "Where did you get that?" On the other hand, the second part raises a problem of longitudinality: How long, and where, would you need to observe participants to inquire about the utility of situated knowledge in other, subsequent settings?

In either case, it is worthwhile to examine knowledge-use in specific settings to see whether it is likely to have been transferred from or to be transferred to other situations. Perkins and Salomon (1992), Bransford et al. (2000), and Ormrod (2007) all suggest that transfer is more probable when, among other things, the knowledge-in-use bears structural and substantive similarities to knowledge used in other settings that the participants are likely to encounter. So the analyst can check for that feature of the knowledge: whether it bears resemblance to thinking done in other situations, or conversely whether it is highly specialized and narrowly applied (cf. Cree & Macaulay, 2001; Mestre, 2005). (The transfer problem will receive more attention in the chapters on pedagogy.)

Bereiter (1997), Hughes et al. (2007), and others also suggest that situated learning theory doesn't handle innovation well: If participants learn only from the way things are done (and have been done) in a specific context, then how do they do something new? Obviously, Lave and Wenger (1991) do not argue that communities of practice simply reproduce their knowledge base over and over again—but they do not explain the sources or dynamics of innovation, either. Imagine, for instance, that one of the docents in the history museum gradually realizes that children are not responding to the artifacts cart in the same way—kids increasingly find the bed warmers and candlestick-makers boring. Now, the guide could simply pull from a bag of well-practiced teaching tricks to reinvigorate the discussion, but she might also conclude that she is dealing with a new generation of elementary-school kids—more tech-savvy, accustomed to pulling up information on their iPods and smartphones; more prone to jumping around in their attention and activity—and that she needs to revise her conception of the learners and the learning process and come up with a wholly new approach to engaging the kids in thinking about colonial life. That means that she—ultimately, the education department as a community of practice—has to innovate. Where does that come from?

Another problem with situated learning theory, related to the innovation problem, stems from the notion of the legitimate peripheral participant's movement from the margins to the center of the community of practice. That metaphor tends to suggest that the learning process entails absorbing, reconstructing, and organizing already-existing forms of knowledge, rather than expanding outward into new knowledge. Engestrom (2001, 2008), in particular, has developed this line of inquiry in his conception of expansive learning, something that goes beyond participation (legitimate, peripheral, or otherwise) in a community of practice.

These critiques (cf. Cairns, 2011) pose important (though, I believe, not fatal) challenges for the analyst of the curriculum of experience. The innovation problem suggests that determining what a person is learning in a given activity or encounter requires an effort to find out whether any of the knowledge being used there is new, whether participants are expanding, revising, redirecting, or otherwise changing their solutions to situated problems, or whether they might even be discovering or formulating new problems. The transfer problem raises the question of whether, how, to what extent, and under what conditions knowledge from one situation migrates into another. If that didn't happen in either direction, experiential learning programs would be pointless.

So the curriculum of experience emerges in highly particular ways from highly particular encounters and activities. It manifests a dizzying array of knowledge-forms, used in varied ways by varied actors with varied purposes, styles, and personalities. One cannot simply point to an environment—a museum education department, a legal office—and say, "Here is what the intern will learn." Rather, as the theorists from chapter 2 insist, the curriculum is an emergent feature of the interaction between the person and the environment, between the activity system and the larger domain within which it operates. In chapter 4, we will consider the ways in which that process might be similar or different in college classrooms, and the goodness of fit between school-based learning and experiential learning.

CHAPTER 4

Comparing Curricula—Academic and Experiential

Without a doubt, students engage a vast array of knowledge in out-of-school sites, and we have analyzed their learning processes in terms of the curriculum of experience. This chapter will move on to address the question posed earlier: To what extent and in what ways does the curriculum of experience coincide with, supplement or, conversely, conflict with or undermine the curriculum in higher education? Of course, there is no unitary curriculum of higher education, even within single institutions—the learning content of an organic chemistry class is obviously different from that of a seminar on political protest in the 1960s—but using the framework developed in chapter 3, we can identify and analyze the points of contact between the natural curriculum of internships and civic engagement and the intentional curriculum of the academy.

In 1987, Lauren Resnick delivered a presidential address to the American Educational Research Association in which she identified several dimensions of the in-school/out-of-school distinction. She was talking primarily about elementary and secondary schools, but the terms seem appropriate to college-level education as well. Schools focus on individual cognition, she noted, whereas thinking outside of school is generally shared (Resnick was an early leader in the "shared cognition" movement; see Resnick et al., 1991). Schools promote pure mentation—that is, thinking without the support of such tools as calculators—whereas people in the world outside of schools utilize all sorts of tools in conducting their mental activities. In the real world, cognitive work is fundamentally contextual: People often use situated objects and events directly in their reasoning, without necessarily using symbols to represent them; school learning, by contrast, is mostly symbol-based, a matter of manipulating abstractions. Finally, she argued, school-based learning is general and decontextualized, while thinking in the world calls for knowledge that is particular and situation-specific (Resnick, 1987).

In a similar vein, the psychologist Sylvia Scribner (1986) identified some of the features of working intelligence that distinguish it from school-like cognitive skills and knowledge. Drawing primarily on a study of workers at a dairy plant, she noted that out-of-school work entails several kinds of thinking rarely found in schools:

- *Problem-formation*: People at work have the opportunity, sometimes even the requirement, to define as well as to solve problems; in school, teachers generally pose problems, and students solve them.
- *Flexible modes of solution*: Workers sometimes employ diverse approaches to solving a problem, Scribner observed, depending on the fine-grained character of the situation; schools typically demand more standardized or algorithmic solution procedures.
- *Using the environment*: People in real-world situations incorporate elements of the task environment into the problem-solving system; the environment is not simply the arena within which the problem is solved, but becomes part of the tool set for that solution.
- *Effort-saving*: In most instances, she argued, people in the real world try to expend as little mental or physical energy as they can in solving a problem, whereas the more mandatory procedures in school attend far less to effort.
- *Forms of representation*: Most school-based thought is essentially symbolic, whereas people in the world represent their problems in a variety of ways fitted to the occasion.
- *Cognitive teamwork*: Anticipating Resnick's later work on shared cognition (Resnick et al., 1991), Scribner noted that, in the real world, thinking is distributed across members of an activity system, whereas in school the cognitive work more often has to be performed by an individual. (Scribner, 1986; cf. Bailey et al., 2004)

Bent Flyvbjerg (2001) provides a third perspective on the college/real-world distinction. In the service of arguing for a new conception of the social sciences, he identifies some key features of inquiry and thinking in the academic arena. Natural scientists, he notes, generally produce knowledge that they can validate as explanatory and predictive. Working largely from a scientific method that tests hypotheses against evidence, they aim at knowledge claims that are universalistic, decontextualized, abstract, and theoretical. Social scientists, on their part, have often (unfortunately, Flyvbjerg argues) emulated the natural scientists, seeking to generate similarly abstract theories and laws describing social behavior. By comparison, scholars in the humanities—literary studies, history, philosophy—deal primarily with texts, images, and ideas, not (usually) in a nomothetic or law-seeking mode, but still largely focusing on the theoretical and abstract. On the other hand, he maintains, people in the practical world exercise a form of intelligence not adequately described as abstract rationality. They encounter and grapple with concrete, situated problems; they take context into account, and look for solutions that serve their interests rather than meet the demands of pure reason. This perspective echoes Bruner's (1996b) analysis of modes of thought: the propositional, the actional, the narrative. Their basic point is that academic knowledge tends toward the theoretical, the universal, and the necessary, whereas real-world knowing tends toward the practical, the particular, and the contingent.

The insights from Resnick and Scribner became part of the conceptual foundation of situated cognition theory (cf. Illeris, 2009); Flyvbjerg's ideas have sparked considerable debate among social scientists (cf. Schram & Caterino, 2006). I propose to incorporate them into my own analysis of the distinctions and complementarities between in-school and out-of-school knowledge-use and learning, but to add some concepts as well. In both cases, my discussion of this issue will be adapted from observations of students in actual internships, including the ones highlighted in chapter 3, but adding a few other settings: a rural veterinary clinic, a small investment firm, the charter-school office of a big-city department of education. Given the premises outlined earlier about how to understand learning from experience, these reality checks are necessary for a solid analysis of the compatibility of experiential learning and academic learning in higher education.

In some respects, the in-school/out-of-school dichotomy distorts the nature of learning processes in the different social settings. The reality is that almost every kind of school-like learning can be found in some form of non-school setting or other. Testing, that paradigmatic academic practice, happens in apprenticeship programs (cf. Hamilton, 1990); known-answer questions—questions that a teacher asks a student even though she knows the answer—show up in on-the-job training as well as in school, although they are admittedly odd in most situations involving adults (cf. Darrah, 1996; Kusterer, 1978); every professional in a high-powered consulting firm knows about homework—at least about taking work home, which may not be quite the same thing. What is more, the claim that school-based problem-solving tends to be standardized or algorithmic while real-world problem-solving takes more flexible forms overlooks the myriad out-of-school production processes that are quite algorithmic—hence, for instance, the methods and procedures manuals in the phone company where I once worked—and it underestimates the ways in which thought may be creative, unexpected, and non-algorithmic in school, especially at the higher levels and, it must be said, in the more elite institutions. That is, my purpose here will not be to identify clear and persistent distinctions between learning in school and learning in the workplace or service setting, but rather to discover those areas where academic and experiential curricula might be similar, where they might be complementary, and where they might be wholly distinct or even in conflict.

Curriculum Content

One dimension of the in/out comparison focuses on the question of content, the *what* of the learning process. Clearly, this section cannot take on the entire array of content addressed in college courses: the procedures for solving derivation problems in calculus; the competing historical theories about the shift in power away from Rome and toward central Europe; the emergence of Cubism in the early twentieth century; experimental methods for testing the impact of personality on intimate relationships—the list could go on ad infinitum, as it could for descriptions of experience-based learning. Instead, we will consider an analysis based on the terms laid out in the previous chapter; another part will introduce additional variables.

Facts and Information

To be sure, there are times when the information disseminated and used in a work or service site looks like it could appear in schools, as well. Certainly the historical information that Heather encountered in the museum had a school-like cast to it in some respects: One can easily imagine an American history class discussing the building of the Erie Canal; one can even picture a quiz posing its opening date—1825—as a question. Similarly, one can imagine a law-school course with a reading list that included federal statutes on equal employment opportunity. In the Institute on Education and the Economy (IEE) study (Bailey et al., 2004), we observed an intern at a veterinary clinic, where among other things he encountered information about the anatomy of a cat's tail. All of these tidbits have the appearance of school-like information.

But they rarely carry the same meaning in the workplace as they would have in school. In the world outside of classrooms, knowledge of information can never be divorced from the nexus of socially constructed meanings within which facts are generated, consensually validated, and, importantly, used. Factual knowledge always has the property ethnomethodologists call indexicality: Its meaning is not found in the index at the end of a book, or in a glossary or a timeline, but rather is constructed in the contexts of its use. Heather's encounters with state history, for instance, differed even at the level of facts from the way she would have engaged similar material in school. Even presuming that she encountered the building of the Erie Canal in her American history class, she would have learned the opening date as one particle in an extensive list of dates and names, or possibly as an item in a coherent historical narrative articulated by her instructor, or as a multiple-choice question on a test. In the museum, on the other hand, she experienced the date as a device in a conversation with school children, as a tool for directing and fleshing out the substance of an activity she was leading. The different function of that historical nugget in her work, I venture to speculate, may have enhanced her retention of the date; it certainly played a role in the construction of her identity and the display of her competence as a tour guide.

Similarly, Roberto would have processed the content of employment statutes differently in law school than he did in the fair-employment office. On a cognitive level, remembering the content so that he could reproduce it or answer questions about it on a test is one thing; organizing the content so that he might make decisions about what to do with the factual details of a real case is quite another. In many law schools and at least some undergraduate law-related classes, students learn through a case method in which stories are told about how the law has actually been applied in specific situations, and that process may produce mental schemas somewhat like those used in the decision process in the office. But even then the facts of the case in school are not so rich or so authentic as they are when one is sitting with an actual person who displays actual emotions about being mistreated by her actual employer. That realism makes the learner understand that the "facts of the case" presented on the course handout do not capture nearly all the complexity and nuance of the situation. Different kinds of facts have different ontological statuses; authentic, instrumental facts are experienced differently from decontextualized ones.

In a rural veterinary clinic, a student named Fred happened to observe an operation in which a cat's tail had to be amputated (Bailey et al., 2004). On a whim, perhaps because he was interested and perhaps because he was being observed by a researcher, Fred asked the vet if the tail was "bone all the way down." That question had a situated but fragmentary quality to it: It had meaning in the situation in which it appeared, in contrast to a diagram of a cat's tail in an anatomy text; at the same time, it was not preceded by a more comprehensive or systematic exposure to information about the feline skeleton, so it stood on its own as an interesting but solitary factoid. Fred may well have remembered the response to his question in the future, but he would have been hard-pressed to place it in a larger context: He knew little about other aspects of the cat's anatomy. This is not to minimize the significance of the factual content of his learning—or Heather's or Roberto's—but to say that even these school-like tidbits carried meanings very different from what they would have borne in a classroom.

Far more often, however, the factual content of interns' experiential curriculum did not look at all like what they were learning back in school. In the magazine office, for example, Lisa encountered little items about, say, the name of the designer of Gwyneth Paltrow's dress at the Oscars. That item might have shown up in a discussion in a fashion class, had she taken one, but probably not in any of Lisa's liberal arts courses. Nor would the gossip about celebrity hook-ups or the yachts of billionaire entrepreneurs. (Of course, I could be wrong about that. Classes in popular culture these days are steeped not only in highly abstract, postmodern theory but in references to current events and personalities like Lady Gaga and *American Idol*. Still...)

In the course of several research projects, we witnessed interns using a myriad of such specialized and nonacademic facts. A student in an investment bank had to locate particular corporations' price/earnings (P/E) ratios for the previous year; a feature writer at a community newspaper witnessed the performance routines of department-store Santas in Brooklyn; a worker in a municipal department of education tracked charter-school test scores. Now, one can imagine each of these facts being used by a professor in a discussion of some theory, concept, or issue: the corporate earnings figures for a class in financial analysis, the charter-school test scores in a course on educational reform. But that is not how they were being used in the internships. Rather, they were tools utilized in problem-solving or even problem-formulation: the P/E ratios as one device for determining whether to invest funds in a particular business, the Santa performances as a human-interest story based in the local community, the charter-school scores as a criterion for recertifying (or potentially closing) experimental schools.

Academics can turn almost any factoid into grist for a theoretical discussion; in some respects, that ability constitutes an argument for the compatibility of in-school and out-of-school learning. But a great deal of the work we saw interns performing entailed knowledge of facts that would make for pretty thin lessons: what equipment and supplies to lay out for an operation on a cat's tail; the critics' ratings of the best-dressed and worst-dressed at the 2011 Oscars; even the name of the last Dutch-speaking governor of New York. (As it happens, the last item could be placed in an interesting historical context: That governor, Rip Van Dam, played a role in the John Peter Zenger trial, which led to the principle of the freedom of the press in America. See, an academic lesson! But that lesson did not play out in Heather's experience at the museum.)

The particularity of the information encountered by interns at work does not ipso facto disqualify it as a component of an academic or more broadly educational practice. There are other aspects of that information, though, which I will discuss in a bit, that make that its use challenging and problematic.

Concepts

While the specific information-bits engaged in work and service sites might be turned to pedagogical use in school (a possibility that I will cite in my argument about the efficacy of experiential learning in higher education), the kinds of concepts organized by the communities of practice in various internship settings appear even more different from the kinds typically studied in school. Again, some of those situated concepts *sound* academic: Heather's engagement with transportation developments (such as the opening of the Erie Canal) in nineteenth-century New York State could well have become the genesis of a paper for a history class. But her construction of and relation to those concepts would have been different in that enterprise. The predominant mode of thought in the museum was narrative—the docents told stories to the kids, and did not spin out theories or explanatory schemes—whereas the more propositional mode in school would have favored using the facts in developing a theory about, say, the impact of infrastructure changes on economic conditions in the state, about how the Erie Canal shaped New York politics during its heyday, before the advent of railroads as freight carriers. Docents and school children in the museum could have considered those theoretical concerns—but the fact is that they didn't, despite the fact that the museum's charter makes it an explicitly educational institution, where such concerns might be more natural.

Similarly, the concept of due process, which does show up in law-school classes, surely informed the work Roberto and his colleagues performed for the fair-employment agency—they had to follow certain rules in order to make a valid case around a complaint—but it was an instrumental tool rather than a jurisprudential principle. Even the lawyers, who had studied the concept in law school, were not interested in spinning out its theoretical contents or ramifications, or in addressing subtly varied interpretations or challenges—unless that cognitive work advanced their functional strategy. Similarly, corporate P/E ratios have a conceptual structure in finance classes somewhat different from the one they have in an investment bank; certainly investment bankers *use* the concept differently. What is more, at Sunil's level as a college intern at the firm, the knowledge-use around P/E ratios was largely mechanical, not conceptual: He calculated them or, more often, dug them up online and reported them to his supervisor; he did not analyze them for decision-making purposes, much less think about a theoretical explanation for their relation to corporate success. He did consider that issue in a finance class, but even repeated encounters with the P/E concept at work did not deepen his understanding on that front.

Similarly, a student named Myisha, who collected statistics for a charter-school recertification visit by board of education staff, was reminded of the debate over the value of such schools as a tool in educational reform, an issue she had encountered in a college class. But the situated meaning of those statistics (test scores, attrition rates, attendance rates, etc.) was found in the department's judgment about whether a particular school should be allowed to stay open. The larger, more abstract question about whether charter schools represent a positive development in public education could be—and generally was—ignored by the staff.

Again, I have been discussing work-based concepts that have at least *some* degree of similarity to ideas used in school. Far more commonly, the situated concepts would be odd ducks indeed in academic settings. Lisa's work at the magazine revolved around such concepts as look-books, press-kits, and fashion shows. An academic—say, a sociologist of culture—*could* have made interesting theoretical comments on the work at the site, but staff members themselves did not think in those terms. Rather, their work was driven by the need to generate stories that would attract readers and therefore sell advertising. All concepts, as Dewey (1910) argued, are tools, instruments for the doing of something, so I do not want to say the magazine staff use their concepts as tools and the academics do not—but certainly the two camps used them for different purposes: the editors as devices for putting out a profitable magazine, the media-studies faculty as the foundation of abstract explanations of a complex and general social phenomenon.

Skills and Competencies

Perhaps the easiest, most intuitive claim to make about the curriculum of experience is that it connects school-based instruction with field-based work around skills. As it happens, I am interested less in professional education—schools of education, business, social work, and so on—as a site of experiential learning than I am in liberal arts colleges; I think the issues related to educational reform are more powerfully drawn in the latter. But it is still worth examining the compatibility of the skills learned in the field with those learned in school, because even that seemingly obvious claim is more problematic than one would expect. The common rhetoric about the process of skills acquisition suggests that students (a) learn job-related skills in school and then (b) apply them in their internship sites, thus reinforcing and extending their capabilities and preparing them for later careers. Is that so?

Well, to some extent. In preprofessional areas like accounting and engineering, certainly, students in school learn principles, concepts, and procedures that give them a leg up on people without such training in the domains of application. An accounting student whom we observed working in the accounts payable department of a public relations firm had taken classes in the fundamentals of double-entry bookkeeping that at least got her started in the workplace. But even in this relatively straightforward case, the relation between the school-derived knowledge and the work-related skill was not seamless. Although there are professional standards for accounting practice, each firm has its own variant of that practice, its own way of doing things; it divides the labor and interprets the standards in its own manner (within broad legal and professional bounds). Our student had to learn the firm's particular methods. That learning gave her a new perspective on the standardized version she got in school: She came to understand the variability of accounting practice, at least the version in her company, thus decentering the authoritative model presented in her classes. Learning that general principle is a good thing, something that professionals-in-training virtually always have to come to terms with: There are the rules, and then there are the ways things actually get done. The distance between the two may be small or large, but the school-based practices rarely map perfectly onto reality. Of course, although she got the larger message, the intern encountered only one variant of the standard model at the PR firm; the company also used some very specific procedures at which she became skillful, but which she most likely could not transfer to other job settings in the future.

Interestingly, even in relatively technical professions like accounting and engineering, prospective employers often claim to value more generic employment skills—teamwork, written and oral communications, initiative, and so on—over more specific skills. Their basic philosophy seems to be that they can teach their way of doing things to newcomers with the appropriate basic skills and capabilities. In fact, some say they would *prefer* to have new employees who have not learned procedures and rules that do not function in their settings; they do not want newcomers to have to unlearn skills (Casner-Lotto & Benner, 2006).

The compatibility problem poses still greater difficulties for students in the liberal arts, and even in the less technical professions like social work and business. The skills they acquire in their internship sites frequently take such a specific, situated form that it is hard to argue that those skills will transfer or serve them in future employment, much less in academic classes at school. The problem here is the extent to which one can extrapolate from such situated skills to develop insights and abilities applicable in a wide range of settings. Even if that extrapolation is theoretically possible, the fact is that student-interns rarely get a chance to practice it either in their work sites or back in school. Because they are not typically given instruction or support in that process, their ability to derive broader, more widely applicable skills from specific experiences is probably only marginally greater than that of students who work at part-time jobs not related to their studies.

Many of the skills we witnessed in our research took highly site-specific forms. Earlier we met a young woman in a health-careers program who learned to set up an anesthesia cart in the operating room of a hospital. The likelihood that she would be doing that same job in the future was minimal; even if she did, her employer would probably be using different brands of equipment, and so she would have to learn a new technique anyway. In a consumer research firm, another student learned to use a proprietary tool for eliciting information from focus groups; the general nature of focus-group research might have been transferable, but she was actually forbidden to use the specific tool in other corporate settings. This is not to argue that learning situated skills in college internships is never worthwhile, just that claims about their value must be scrutinized carefully.

In any case, internships generally build skills different from those engaged in college. Academic skills tend to revolve around abstract reasoning: identifying literary devices in a novel or short story, constructing an argument about the economics of gentrification, solving a mathematical problem underlying string theory. Some academic skills do resemble practices found in some workplaces: internet searches (recall Lisa's facility with that process), writing memos (although relatively few of our student-subjects ever wrote anything of the sustained, propositional nature of a term paper), analyzing social dynamics. Like facts and concepts, however, situated skills typically do not map neatly onto those found in schools. They are instrumental in a different way, and they are often carried out in teams, so the functions (and the attendant knowledge) are distributed more widely.

The profound issue for experiential learning in liberal arts institutions is this: Does acquiring the skills used in specific work or service environments constitute the kind of learning college students are meant to do? What does a student in media studies gain by working at a record label collecting sales data on new releases? How does serving food in a soup kitchen enhance a sociology major's understanding of the dynamics of poverty? There are reasonable answers to those questions, but they are not in themselves strong justifications for experiential education programs.

Social and Organizational Knowledge

Certainly an internship or service-learning placement affords a college student the opportunity to experience a wider range of social and organizational contexts than she has encountered in school, and (potentially, at least) to reflect on that experience in ways that generate new insight and understanding. For 13 or more years, the student has been embedded in a social system with a limited and by now quite familiar array of roles, settings, and activities: teachers and students; classes, clubs, and cafeterias; lectures, discussions, and science fairs. Now, as an intern, she becomes a "legitimate peripheral participant" (Lave & Wenger, 1991) in a highly complex system organized into different units and engaged in all sorts of unfamiliar activities: hierarchies with far more layers than a school has; sales, marketing, and production divisions; long-range planning processes, supervision meetings, training sessions, and so on. The culture of the corporation, an example of a placement site, looks in some ways very different from that of the school (cf. Deal & Kennedy, 2000; Deal & Peterson, 2009). Unless the college student has had broad experience in a variety of part-time, volunteer, and other jobs, she will run into new dynamics, new structures, new customs in the internship—and that presents tremendous opportunities for learning.

The issue is whether the school wants to promote and enhance that kind of learning, to push that element of the curriculum of experience. To be sure, there are many courses in the university devoted to the analysis of organizations and their dynamics. The hypothetical I posed in the first chapter—the student taking a class in organizational sociology and reading Max Weber on bureaucracy while doing an internship at the department of education (DOE)—raises some of those issues here. Certainly one can argue that the two forms of knowledge about organizations—the theoretical and the experiential—are complementary: They are *about* the "same" thing. Just as clearly, they are *not* actually the same forms of knowledge: They evoke different cognitive perspectives and logics, focus on different concepts and problems, and rely on different criteria for validity. Theoretical-academic knowledge, though often based on empirical study, is usually meant to be decontextualized and explanatory. Experiential knowledge is generally meant to be contextual and instrumental. Again, that difference does not mean that the two forms cannot complement one another. Under certain conditions, Weber *can* inform our student's understanding of her experience at the DOE; and vice versa, her experience *can* enrich (and/or challenge) her grasp of Weber. That possibility, in fact, represents a central claim about the value of experiential education—but its realization demands a longer discussion of the pedagogical issues in this practice, which will come in a later chapter.

Other aspects of the social-organizational knowledge that an intern encounters seem less clearly related to ideas and skills that the college promotes. Emotional intelligence (Mayer et al., 2004) and interpersonal intelligence (Gardner, 2006) certainly play a role as personal and cultural traits in workplaces: They matter in the way things happen and people get along. As theories, however, they attract little attention, especially outside the circle of human resource managers. Similarly, being culturally competent—knowing how to dress appropriately and what kinds of language to use in various situations, for instance—clearly improves a person's success in the work setting. But the constituents of that competence normally remain beneath consciousness; one rarely studies up on the details of language rules for staff meetings—one simply picks them up. These social forms of knowledge tend to be tacit, beneath the level of conscious awareness (cf. Polanyi, 1974). Nonetheless, these ideas and experiences do seem complementary, capable of informing one another under certain pedagogical conditions.

On the other hand, we have observed a curious characteristic among interns as learners in their placement sites: Unless they are pushed, they tend *not* to see very far into their organizational settings. I have frequently been surprised—indeed, stunned—by the lack of knowledge my own student-interns have had about the structures and dynamics of their larger organizations. As the instructor of an internship seminar, I have asked students to draw organization charts depicting the hierarchy of roles and reporting relationships that surround them—and most often they can't go more than one or two steps past their immediate field of vision. A student in one of my classes worked for the housing department in a large city, and didn't know exactly which unit she was attached to until I encouraged her to find out. The reason for this tunnel vision, for this failure to take in the dimensions of the larger organizational environment, I came to believe, is the newcomer's anxiety about saving face by just doing the job: She needs badly not to look stupid, to get along, and therefore basically does what her immediate supervisor asks her to do, without inquiring into the larger system within which she works. In any case, we cannot assume that playing a role within a large social system necessarily implies that a person comprehends the dimensions and dynamics of that larger system. The social and organizational knowledge gained experientially by the intern may be no more extensive than the theoretical knowledge she garners from a mere skimming of Weber on bureaucracy. Once more, though, this form of knowledge, when it teased out and examined, seems potentially compatible with a college-level curriculum.

Values and Ethics

New workers and interns almost inevitably absorb some of the value positions of their communities of practice. They come to understand, at least on an intuitive level, the preferences and priorities of the people they work with. Heather could not avoid hearing about the commitment of the docents in the museum to the study of history and to educational quality; they talked about it in the break room, they displayed it in their tour performances. Roberto had conversations about cases with his supervisor and coworkers in which they used language that reflected their curious combination of a belief in justice and fairness in employment, and a degree of cynicism and fatigue in the pursuit of those goals. On the one hand, they wanted the complainants to be treated well and to find redress of their grievances. On the other, they found the regulatory and judicial system to be sluggish and sometimes incapable of meeting those needs. In that quandary, they sometimes gave short shrift to their work on behalf of certain individuals when they thought their chances of success were slight; they preferred (understandably) to maintain their sanity and save their energy rather than bang their heads against the wall in a lost cause. That lesson was not lost on Roberto. Although it seems different from an ethics lesson in a law class, the two do at least seem complementary.

On occasion, interns face serious ethical issues: They are asked to do something slightly less than moral; they experience sexual harassment, or witness pilfering or other wrongdoing by employees. They struggle with these problems as any worker would. The educational question is whether and to what extent they do, can, or need to analyze and resolve the problems by means of academic, intellectual forms of ethical inquiry. Most of them have not studied Aristotle's *Nichomachean Ethics*, Kant's categorical imperative, or Rawls's theory of justice. Even if they have, they are not likely to invoke those theories in struggling with their situations. Here, then, is another area where advocates of experiential education rightly claim benefits for this practice: These ethical dilemmas can be examined rigorously and out of the context where they arise, thus lessening the danger entailed in raising them at the site (Eyler, 2009).

This issue is partly pedagogical—in which sense it will be addressed in a later chapter—but partly curricular: It is about the complementarity of forms of knowledge and thought regarding ethical and value questions. Clearly, people think about and resolve ethical problems in different ways in school and at the work or service setting. Contextuality, specificity, practical and personal consequences: These dimensions of situated ethics make them substantially different from abstract speculations. Just as clearly, however, the modes of ethical inquiry practiced in schools do have something to say about those in the real world. In this sense, at least, the curricula of the academy and the practical world once again seem potentially complementary.

Self and Identity

People learn about themselves in all sorts of contexts, from dinner-table conversations to lecture halls to sidewalk encounters. The range of self-learning experiences interns have in their work and service sites is probably no greater, on the whole, than what they encounter in the rest of their lives. But it *is* broader—and less familiar—than the experiences they have in school classrooms, laboratories, and faculty offices. By the time they enter college, students have already had many years of negotiating the self in academic settings: of dealing with the spotlight put on them when teachers ask them questions about assigned readings, of seeing how they respond to competitive moments like facing down a line of adversaries in a high school debate contest, of suffering from anxiety in high-stakes exams from standardized third-grade tests to the SATs. Going through developmental changes from childhood to adolescence to early adulthood (cf. Erikson, 1963, 1994), they have constructed different conceptions of themselves over time—but the nature of school as an institutional, interactional context has remained largely familiar.

Most students have had part-time or summer jobs before or during college, and therefore have encountered the particular demands of the work world: having a boss, working in functionally diverse and sometimes contentious groups, interacting with a range of role types and individuals. But the internship role differs from the part-time job in some ways, not least because the student is encouraged to reflect on the experience in ways more rigorous than one applies to a normal job. Particularly if the school asks her to think about what she learns about herself through the internship, she may discover things about how she handles pressure, how she deals with authority, how (un)comfortable she feels interacting with people very different from herself, how hard she likes to work or the conditions she finds most conducive to commitment and satisfaction...and on and on.

These issues rarely arise in college classrooms; they are not a part of the standard curriculum. The typical college professor shows little interest in helping students learn about themselves; she wants them to learn about

English literature of the nineteenth century, or about organic chemistry, or about Foucault. She considers self-revelation a distraction, a waste of effort and time—and a source of discomfort. That stereotype, of course, distorts as much as any such simplistic portrait: There are many college teachers these days who do in fact care about their students' learning about themselves, who express care and concern for issues of self-development. But many of those academics tend to approach those issues outside of the formal curriculum, in their office hours or over a beer at the student center. The exception may be those who practice a form of feminist pedagogy (cf. Fisher, 2001; hooks, 1994). Whether the self-knowledge derived from experiential learning counts as an element of the content of higher learning, whether it plays a role in college education, is thus a matter of judgment—and not a simple one at that.

The process of identity-formation described by Wenger (1998) and other social theorists may be somewhat more compatible with the curriculum of mainstream higher education. Becoming a member of a community of practice, as he describes it, entails not only the "soft" matters of feelings and self-concept, but also the acquisition and use of knowledge of the types discussed earlier: facts, concepts, skills and competencies, even values and ethics. What it means to be an architect, or a high school English teacher, or a financial analyst involves moving along the novice-expert scale, developing modes of thought, repertoires of performance, and skills of problem-solving that are in many ways compatible with the curriculum of the academy.

But identity consists in more than those knowledge and skill sets: It entails the assumption of a kind of persona that functions in a particular social setting. It means being "one of us." In Heather's case, it meant not only guiding a tour, but *being* a tour guide. For Lisa, it meant not only knowing about celebrities, but also *being* the kind of person who can dish with the best of them. The curricular question confronting experiential educators, then, is whether and to what extent that sort of identity-formation belongs in the university. Certainly it represents a natural extension of the knowledge-related aspects of the professional identity constructed in an internship, but the claim that it should be addressed in school arouses some contention (Fish, 2008). One dimension of difference between school-based identities and workplace- or community-based identities is that the former tend to focus on individuals and the latter on groups.

Curriculum Features

On the level of content, we have seen that situated knowledge-use in workplaces and community action projects differs substantially from the forms of academic knowledge encountered in the university, but I want to argue that the two sets might be complementary under certain pedagogical conditions. Clearly, Heather's engagement with historical information in the museum, while superficially "about" similar things (dates, names, trends), entailed cognitive processes different from those which she used in college history classes. Nonetheless, a good teacher might exploit the tenuous relations between those knowledge-forms to promote rich learning. We will explore those possibilities in the section on pedagogy.

Dimensions of the curriculum of experience other than content, however, pose challenges for the practice of experiential education in the university. There are certain ways in which the encounter with knowledge in the work or service setting differs importantly from the encounters with academic knowledge in school. We can compare the two settings in terms laid out in chapter 3.

Sequence

As we have seen, one feature of any curriculum, whether experiential or academic, is the sequence in which the learner engages its various elements. At the level of the single course, knowledge in schools typically finds order in the syllabus, the professor's plan for the topics, readings, and activities that will constitute the semester's investigations, as well as the specific and general learning goals she wants to accomplish (cf. O'Brien et al., 2008). One obvious and persistent feature of the syllabus that distinguishes it from the curriculum of experience is that it is organized explicitly and exclusively around students' learning, whereas the latter gives priority to production processes, using such principles as efficiency and profit, service and achievement.

The syllabus also emerges from the teacher's reasoned conception of the structure of knowledge in the topic domain, on her judgment about the order in which things ought to be encountered and learned (cf. Bruner, 1966). The specific sequence might be based on any of several principles:

- *Foundational concepts* of the discipline: There might be things you need to know before you can make sense of subsequent facts, concepts, and theories. In chemistry, for example, you may need to know about the structure of atoms before learning how they combine into molecules; in sociology, you might want to understand role theory before approaching conflict theory.
- *Chronological order*: In some disciplines, certain things happen or appear before other things. In your medieval history course, you learn

about Charlemagne before you hear about the Crusades; in philosophy, you need to know Nietzsche before wading into Heidegger.

- *Thematic structure*: Facts, ideas, or theories might be organized around several core themes which the instructor regards as useful for shaping the students' learning. A course on the concept of community, for instance, might distinguish communities based on location, interest, and activities.
- *Difficulty*: Sometimes the course materials are ordered according to their degree of difficulty, so the students build confidence and skill as they work toward the more challenging ideas and operations.

Even educators who subscribe to a constructivist, learner-centered view of teaching and learning—for example, O'Brien, Millis, and Cohen in *The Course Syllabus* (2008)—acknowledge the importance of the professor's constructing an orderly and rational sequence of activities for the class based on her conception of the substantive structure of the issue, theme, discipline, or period under examination. One virtually never runs across courses in higher education (dis)organized on the model of A. S. Neill's plan for Summerhill, the radically democratic, child-centered school in England (Neill, 1984). When I taught in an alternative high school in Philadelphia many years ago, I once co-facilitated a course called "The Learning Cell," based on the radical proposition that the group would spontaneously and democratically generate the substance and goals of their learning, that the teachers would not impose a syllabus on the class but rather would enable the students to figure out collectively what they wanted to learn and how they wanted to learn it. Aside from a session when we cooked up some fine spaghetti, the experiment bombed.

The same point about sequence can be made at the level of the discipline or major. If a student elects a major in economics, for instance, the faculty of that department will have determined not only a general content of the curriculum, but a sequence. At NYU, one takes introductory macroeconomics before microeconomics, for instance, then moves on to more advanced courses in those areas, as well as classes in substantive areas like international economics and econometrics. The important point here is that the order of the student's engagement with the discipline comes from the faculty's decision about a logical sequence, not from a production process.

By contrast, the curriculum of experience generally emerges not from the instructor's rational analysis of the sequence by which learning best happens, but from the structure of roles and activities in the community of practice. The sequence in which a newcomer might encounter and engage various kinds of knowledge is not even determined strictly by the order of steps in the production process—"first we do this, then we do that, so first learn this"—but by other aspects of the organizational system: the role structure, the politics and prestige of knowledge-use, and the stake the organization has in each of the tasks that make up the process. Jean Lave (2011) suggests an example of a factor in the sequence in which learners encounter particular tasks: error cost. Using the example of apprentice tailors in Liberia, she notes that neophytes learn to sew before they learn to cut fabric, despite the fact that the order of actually producing a garment moves from cutting to sewing. That is because the cost of an apprentice's mistake is far greater in the latter than the former: One can remove bad stitching, but one cannot restore a poorly cut bolt of cloth to its original condition. This feature of the learning process will be addressed more fully in the chapter on pedagogy. Suffice it to say here that the curriculum of experience finds its shape in reasons far beyond the learning needs of the newcomer.

Heather's first real task in the history museum, for instance, was to work with one or two children on a drawing exercise in the transportation hall: She sat on the floor with them and made suggestions and comments as they sketched carriages, sleighs, and horses. That exercise occurred toward the end of the tour, not the beginning, but it represented an opportunity for her to do something with relatively low socio-cognitive demands and low error cost: If she made a mistake (discouraged a child, or misstated the use of a vehicle, for example), the museum did not suffer much in terms of client satisfaction, expense, or time.

In fact, the curriculum of experience is shaped deeply by the *need to know*. Once the intern's role has been established, she is often given access only to the knowledge necessary for performing the related tasks. In the college classroom, by contrast, the teacher assumes that every student needs to learn everything. Roberto, whose role in the fair-employment office entailed complaint intake and referral of cases to the appropriate investigators and lawyers, needed to know just enough about employment law to make that determination. He spent the first few days at the site reading through the relevant statutes—but only at the level at which he could say, "This is an A; that is a C," and refer the case along. He did not need to understand the history of the laws, or their deep underlying principles, or the grounds on which they might have been challenged in the past; he merely needed a basic taxonomic scheme for gathering initial information and sending the documents to the next station in the process. Nor did he need to know how the agency's budget was formulated, or what factors went into human resource policies, so he never encountered that stock of knowledge-in-use in the organization.

The curriculum of experience might appear haphazard and illogical from the perspective of an educator, but in fact there is a powerful logic at work: the logic of organizational process and interest. For the organization's purposes of efficiency, reputation, and success, the learning sequence generally works well: The right people come to know the things it needs them to know. There are, to be sure, corporate internship programs that pull students out of the production process (often in an orientation at the beginning of the term, sometimes in weekly workshops) to expose them systematically to broader information about the larger organization, but they are the exception.

Coverage

Although this term carries a bad reputation in higher education—it sounds too mechanical, too rote—it does raise the important question of what and how much information and knowledge the instructor intends to expose students to in the course. College students say about their classes things like, "We're covering American labor history from 1880 to the formation of the AFL-CIO; next semester we'll cover from the mid-1950s to the public union battles in 2011." That is, the course syllabus provides a rationale and a structure for encompassing a specific domain of knowledge, and attempts to be reasonably comprehensive in that approach. Once the domain has been identified—American history before 1865, for instance, or the nineteenth-century French novel—one can ask how thoroughly the student engages the material in that area. Of course, the instructor has to make choices of content—she cannot do *all* the novels written in France during the nineteenth century—but there is generally a reason for the selections: representatives of a limited array of genres, examples from the major authors, and so on.

The same cannot be true of the curriculum of experience. Exposure to knowledge in the domain of the activity system is necessarily and inevitably episodic and fragmentary. Here is where the need-to-know principle affects the intern's learning. In the context of a particular activity system—say, Roberto's community of practice in the fair-employment office, comprising the lawyers, the investigators, the clerks—a vast array of knowledge was used in the performance of the core mission: ensuring that violations of equal-employment laws were either prevented or punished. But no one player within that community needed to know, or in fact had the opportunity to know, all of those facts, ideas, and concepts. Here we are brushing up against matters related to the pedagogy of experience, which will be addressed in the next two chapters, but the point is clear: Even by the selective standards of the Nineteenth-Century French Novel class, Roberto did not enjoy comprehensive coverage in the realm of employment law. Rather, he got to learn only what he needed to know in order to do his job. Moreover, during his brief stint in the office, certain kinds of cases appeared more often on the docket than others, and his exposure to the rarer issues was slim to nonexistent. A class on employment law would have been far more extensive and systematic in content coverage.

Similarly, the fashion magazine where Lisa worked historically took on a wide range of topics and produced an enormous variety of stories: about changes in the popularity of hats, or about costume history in the film industry, or about yet another diet fad. In her 14-week internship, Lisa encountered only a few of those topics. One could argue that all the processes she witnessed in production fell into one of a very limited array of categories, and therefore that her coverage on that front was complete—but even that was not the case. Between the time she spent gearing up to use the software programs in the office and the time she spent on ancillary tasks like compiling the look-books, she actually had exposure to very few substantive elements of the production phase. She was asked to do online research for a few articles, and so both improved her skills in that kind of tool-use and learned a few things about specific celebrities. But those items were, in the first case, not deeply situated (online research is done in many different settings) or, in the second, highly fragmentary, not connected to any other significant knowledge. On the whole, her exposure to knowledge about both the production of a fashion magazine and the world of fashion and celebrity was "a little of this and a little of that." Fred, the veterinary intern, learned about the anatomy of a cat's tail, but not about the rest of the feline skeleton. In both settings, the knowledge coverage was quite limited.

Classification

Bernstein's (1975) concept, mentioned earlier, provides another intriguing tool for comparing the curriculum of college courses and the curriculum of experience. It raises the issue of the ways in which knowledge is divided into categories and the extent to which those categories intersect. In general, college courses and majors display strong classification: Disciplines stake out their particular knowledge turfs and struggle (often unsuccessfully) to protect their boundaries through departments, professional associations, peer-reviewed journals, and curriculum guidelines (Abbott, 2001). Course titles reflect a firm and relatively narrow conception of the domain within which the class will operate. The chemistry department guards its bailiwick from incursions by the biology department, and certainly it would never be mistaken for the English department. To be sure, this situation is changing: One of the features of the postmodern university is the increase in interdisciplinary and multidisciplinary programs like biochemistry and cognitive science (Klein, 1990; Moran, 2010), so the classification of knowledge is a matter of some contention and redefinition.

On some levels and in some situations, the classification of knowledge in some production and service organizations seems to be as strong as it is in the academy. In the fair-employment office, for example, lawyers had one kind of knowledge (which was different from the knowledge of attorneys in other kinds of settings, like corporate tax firms) and investigators had a different kind. To some extent the division of cognitive labor stemmed from the need for efficiency in the production process, and to some extent it supported the professional turfs of the respective actors. The investigators harbored certain professional secrets, ways they found information that they would not want the lawyers to know.

By contrast, other work organizations practice a kind of weak classification, letting different sorts of knowledge mix together in one activity. For instance, the tour guides in the history museum utilized a substantial variety of information, concepts, and skills: about dates and characters in state history, about types of children and their behavior, about public speaking, and so on. Not only were those knowledge-forms all utilized by the same actors—the docents—but they were also used simultaneously, as in "doing the artifacts cart": The guide had to recall useful information about household implements while attending to the signals coming from the fourth-grade class in front of her, while remembering to speak in a style sensible to those kids. One could argue that college teachers (at least good ones) perform the same multimodal knowledge-displays as the tour guides; indeed, the guides were regarded as educators, and in fact many of them were former public-school teachers. But in modern and postmodern work environments, that intersection of knowledge-forms—that weak classification—is relatively rare: Modernization often implies specialization.

If this analysis seems to be vacillating on the issue of whether the curriculum of experience differs from the curriculum of the college classroom on the dimension of classification, that is because it *is*. The answer to the question, "Are the two different in that way?" is, "Well, it depends. Sometimes they are and sometimes they aren't." Ironically, interdisciplinary inquiry has been gaining strength in the university while specialization grows in such fields as medicine, law, and computer design. College faculties organize themselves into discipline-based departments, but their classification of knowledge— their definition of their respective turfs—has increasingly blurred over the past 25 years (Moran, 2010). Meanwhile, corporations organize themselves around practices—sales, human resources, planning, and so on—and practices are always based in knowledge, and generalists seem to be less common in the postmodern economy, though the topography of specialties is shifting.

For present purposes, the issue is this: How well do knowledge-silos in the work world map onto the knowledge-silos in the academy? The problem of complementarity between situated learning and academic learning is not so much the *degree* of classification (it varies in both settings) as the *content*. On that score, the substantive categories around which knowledge is organized (and protected) in the two domains appear to be significantly different.

Modes of Thought

The comparison of curricula in colleges and in nonclassroom settings also raises questions about the modes of thought they entail. From Bruner's (1996b) general perspective, for example, that comparison draws attention to the issue of the generalizability of experience. To what extent can we accept or assert the authority of experience, particularly limited experience, in learning about a general concept (Scott, 1991)? Consider the case of a member of the PAR class doing research on gentrification in an urban community. Imagine that she interviews five residents and a few shopkeepers, sits in on two community meetings, and gets a tour of the neighborhood from a local organizer. Independent of the related academic readings and discussions in the classroom, does that experience give us warrant to claim that she has "learned" the concept of gentrification? Set beside the scholarly treatises, the extensive data, and the professor-guided analysis of the concept, that experience seems limited, what academics sometimes dismiss as anecdotal. The academy, since Plato and especially Bacon and Descartes, has constructed procedures and standards (for example, the experiment) for asserting and supporting generalized conceptual claims. Those procedures and standards are rarely duplicated through experiential learning: There is no random assignment, little or no control over conditions—and, most telling, there are usually too few instances of the phenomenon of interest to justify extrapolation. That is, in terms of modes of thought, the experience lends itself more to narrative than to propositional inquiry. For those academics committed to the logic of the scientific method, that comparison undermines the utility of experience as a source of knowledge.

Of course, there are other modes of thought in the university: the interpretive, the hermeneutic, the approaches that would say one can "read" a community-based experience like a text, like a novel, like a painting

(Foucault, 2010; Hall, 1997). Even if that is true, however—and I believe it is—the question of sufficiency arises: How many instances of gentrification, or poverty, or organizational decision making must one experience and read in order to "get" the concept? Generalizing from a single instance, or even a few, may be like reading only one French nineteenth-century novel and imagining that one grasps the range and nuances of that genre. The epistemological question posed in the second chapter returns here: Are we looking for knowledge that is universal, certain, and necessary? What do we do with knowledge-use that is particular, contested, and contingent? Chapter 7 will address these questions by reviewing some of the practices of experiential educators, because on one level the answers depend on pedagogy. But they come up here in the chapter on the relationship between academic learning and experiential learning because they raise crucial issues about the nature of knowledge in the two domains.

From a more focused perspective, those issues can be examined in terms of several concepts introduced earlier: forms of problem-solving and critical thinking; the promotion of forms of judgment, especially *phronesis*.

Problem-Solving and Critical Thinking

One of the claims sometimes made by advocates of experiential learning is that student-interns have greater opportunities for new kinds of problem-solving (and even problem-formation; cf. Scribner, 1986) and engage in serious critical thinking (Roberts, 2012; Sweitzer & King, 2004). That claim, of course, needs empirical support, and some research suggests that such support is spotty at best (Bailey et al., 2004). In any case, the issue falls squarely into the purview of this chapter, as it implies the question of whether direct experience in a work or service setting enhances the likelihood that students will participate in practices that demand that form of thinking.

The term critical thinking gets bandied about so loosely that locating it in the real world poses a challenge. It implies something more than mere thinking, certainly more than rote memorization, and is said to entail such mental procedures as identifying and clarifying goals or ends, analyzing factors influencing situations, gathering and utilizing evidence that speaks to the problem at hand, employing appropriate and effective logical methods for reasoning from the problem to the evidence to the solution or argument. More, it means going beneath the surface of the problem to understand its context and components, to place it in relation to other, larger issues and concepts, to identify and examine one's underlying assumptions and frameworks, and to monitor and adjust one's thought processes so as to eliminate or at least minimize distorting elements (cf. Facione, 2011; Mezirow, 1990, 2000).

Another conception of critical thinking stems from the Frankfurt School and is connected to the practice of critical theory (cf. Brookfield, 2004; Jay, 1996; Rush, 2004): the analysis of social issues in such a way as to tease out the ideological dimensions of phenomena and trends, and to produce a critique of society in such a way as to contribute to changing it. This version of the process places it in a more political and contentious context, an arena where people do things and think things because of vested interests and power dynamics.

The question here is whether critical thinking of either variety happens either in university classrooms or in experiential settings. Certainly university faculty ask students to do what they regard as critical thinking: closely analyzing texts, examining complex theory, ferreting out underlying assumptions. Assignments in college go well beyond the standard uncritical book report produced in high school. Papers invoke concepts from Plato's theory of the forms to Heidegger's discussion of *Dasein*, not to mention difficult ideas in the natural sciences like chaos theory and stochastic calculus. So college-level thinking is often critical in the sense of entailing complex information and higher-level reasoning. Less often, though not never, does it require the examination and challenge of underlying assumptions, the practice of self-monitoring, or the transformation of fundamental modes of thought. Some critics of higher learning argue that too many college students do not in fact engage much in critical thinking of any sort, that courses often demand little in the way of complex thought or self-monitoring, preferring mastery of algorithmic procedures and memorization of facts (cf. Arum & Roksa, 2011).

In experience-based education, on the other hand, the practice of critical thinking assumes a different form, when it appears at all. People in the real world rarely operate on the basis of explicit, articulate explanatory theories, critical or otherwise. Instead, what practitioners tend to regard as theory are reasonably well-formulated ideas about what will happen if they do certain things. Certain management scholars like Chris Argyris and Donald Schön (1974) argue that organizational leaders do in fact operate from the basis of theories-in-practice, complex sets of principles and observations that constitute a framework for understanding and action; they advocate the practice of action science, a systematic method by which managers can generate knowledge useful for practice (cf. O'Neil & Marsick, 2007). But those methods are very different from what postmodernist academics call theory: Foucault, Lacan, Žižek, and the like.

Clearly, some people think hard—complexly, intelligently, even critically—in work contexts. The long and contentious history of debate on deskilling (Braverman, 1974), Fordism (Appelbaum & Batt, 1994), and the growth of the information economy (Reich, 1991) suggests, however, that there has been a bifurcation in the distribution of high-level knowledge-use in the workforce. As opportunities open up for creative, complex thinking among designers, consultants, and other knowledge workers, some observers maintain, the jobs of the less educated are dumbed down, automated, and stripped of cognitive challenge. That is not to say that lower-level workers have no skill or knowledge—commentators from Ken Kusterer (1978) to Mike Rose (2004) have documented the hidden and underappreciated demands of front-line labor—but that they often enjoy relatively little leeway in their exercise of intelligence, and certainly find few opportunities for critical thinking. Matthew Crawford argues in *Shop Class as Soulcraft* (2009) that much modern work, especially in bureaucratic organizations, deadens the spirit and smothers the mind—though independent crafts (for him, motorcycle repair) provide deep meaning for the worker. The literature that critiques the quality of modern industrial and bureaucratic work is too large to review here, but it supports the claim that a substantial portion of the workforce rarely engages in complex, creative, or critical thinking.

The immediate issue is whether college interns have the opportunity to use their minds in ways that develop their capacity for critical thinking, in whatever form. Of course, the answer is that some do and some don't. But our studies in dozens of internship sites suggest that more lower level (high school, community college, lower-division) don't than do (Bailey et al., 2004; Moore, 1999). In those cases, interns occupy relatively low-level positions in their organizations—they are, after all, not only neophytes but short-timers—and therefore take on fairly simple tasks, with fairly limited possibilities for decision making or problem-solving. What problems there are tend to be mechanical, or simple snags in the production process, not substantial challenges requiring deep reflection or complex strategizing.

Of course, there are other interns whose work is substantive and demanding, who exercise considerable intelligence and skill in the performance of their work. Heather, for example, developed subtle and extensive knowledge about state history, about school children, about public speaking. In the conduct of a typical tour, her cognitive and social tasks fell into a relatively routine format, which meant that she faced few "problems" that needed "solving." That is not to say that she was not learning—she continually encountered new tidbits of history, was asked new questions by the children, and found new resources in the department library—but that she rarely had to adjust the plan, improvise in the face of unexpected snags, or mop up after serious mishaps. Still, she did have occasion, especially in weekly meetings with the director and casual conversations with her colleagues, to reflect on and even critique her own practice.

Sunil, a college junior who worked in a small investment bank, was charged with collecting data on start-ups and other small firms that the company might want to put money into. Taken as a whole, the decision about whether to invest in a specific outfit demanded both a great deal of data and a considerable exercise of judgment, not all of which could be subjected to algorithms. Sunil did hear about the larger process from his supervisor, who took the intern's data further up the decision-line, but he essentially let go of the information when he turned it over. This feature of the process speaks as much to the pedagogy of experience as to the curriculum, but it shapes the latter in terms of the elements of the social stock of knowledge in the bank to which the student had access: He learned a lot about the kinds of information used by investment bankers in their decisions about allocating funds; he learned less deeply and more schematically about the subtle factors that informed the final choices. At base, his work demanded less than one might expect in the form of critical thinking or complex reasoning: In essence, he mined data and inserted it into spreadsheets. He had no occasion at work to engage in a Frankfurtian form of critical analysis; his supervisor was not likely to entertain larger political questions about the depradations of late capitalism.

On the other hand, there are college-level interns who perform highly complex, demanding cognitive and social tasks; who exercise enormous skill and nuanced knowledge as they teach children, plan corporate events, research community conditions, and organize political campaigns; who grapple with nagging social issues and delicate organizational dynamics, and identify and solve difficult problems in production, service, and analysis. They sit in on meetings where strategies are devised by corporate officers or community members, observe complex tasks being performed by experts, and run into colossal disasters in their workplaces. The PAR class involved in community-based research on gentrification certainly performed complex mental (as well as social) operations. I am by no means arguing, in other words, that no college-level interns experience higher cognitive and social challenges in their placement activities. I *am* arguing, however, given my own experience both as a researcher and as an internship instructor, that advocates' claims for these challenges—and the consequent learning—may be overstated.

Judgment and Phronesis

Another layer of the modes of thought promoted by curricula inside or outside of school draws on Aristotle's analysis of the intellectual virtues in *The Nichomachean Ethics* (2009). In this treatise, Aristotle proposes three cardinal forms of knowing: *epistemé* (analytical, scientific, universal knowledge); *techné* (technical know-how, knowledge of how to do certain things); and *phronesis* (practical judgment mixed with values, reason capable of action informed by ethical conceptions of the good) (cf. Flyvbjerg, 2001).

The question here is whether internships and civic engagement produce *phronesis* in ways that transcend the learning done in school. Typically, we think of the knowledge encountered in college as basically either *epistemé* or *techné*, or sometimes both. The liberal arts curriculum aims at rigorous analysis yielding universal, decontextualized claims about the world (nature, society, literature, and the arts), while the preprofessional curriculum develops practical skills, how-to-do-it knowledge that will inform professional practice. Of course, the two are not distinct or mutually exclusive: Professional practice is shaped by theory (cf. Argyris & Schön, 1974). In general, the university as an institution tends to privilege *epistemé*, making it foundational or prior to practice; practice is thought to be enhanced by objective, scientific knowledge based on careful, dispassionate, disinterested inquiry and epistemic knowledge. To be sure, professional schools also attend to matters of value and ethics. But for present purposes, I focus on the liberal arts college, where *techné* tends to attract disdain and to occupy a second-class status. In the liberal arts, pure knowledge "for its own sake" carries greater prestige than "applied." Even in the social sciences, where *phronesis* could play a greater role (Flyvbjerg, 2001), a misguided desire to emulate the natural sciences—to achieve objectivity, to use the scientific method—tends to promote value-neutral forms of inquiry (if there are such things).

Flyvbjerg's (2001) cogent argument is that the traditional epistemic form of knowledge misconstrues the proper role of the social sciences—and more broadly, I would argue, of the liberal arts—as conceived by Aristotle in the notion of *phronesis*. Knowledge of the social world must, he maintains, account for context; it must engage judgments about what is good and what is not, about the interests of the actors in a social process. He also argues that Aristotle omits another feature of social process that needs to be analyzed if practical wisdom is to be enhanced: power (cf. Dunne, 1993). So *phronesis* tends not to be promoted in college classrooms.

But is it promoted more frequently in experiential settings? Our observations in more than 60 internship sites suggest that the only ones that tend to enhance *phronesis* are those in service-learning programs, where the work clearly falls into the realm of values-based, ethics-related activities. In the for-profit and even in the government sectors, students rarely enjoy the opportunity of examining ethics and politics in their communities of practice. Instead, they generally take for granted on the job the matter of whose interests are being served: the company's, the agency's. Questioning the rightness—or at least the desirability—of working to improve the organization's efficiency, productivity and, above all, profit puts one beyond the pale and risks censure: That's the "bottom line."

Lisa, in her work at the fashion magazine, thus could not challenge the assumption that glorifying movie stars and encouraging the sale of obscenely expensive handbags was a necessary and good thing to do. Sunil, in the investment bank, could not question the morality of funding a video-game company that produced violent, sexist products for children; if the return on investment was high enough, and the product was legal, the issue remained unspoken. As it happened, Lisa and Sunil were not inclined to question the basic ethical premises of their companies' work anyway—but that fact meant that their experience was unlikely to build their capacity for *phronesis*. They could make rational and instrumental means-ends decisions: "This will pay off." But they missed the opportunity to analyze the values-rationality, the ethical dimensions of the organization's work, the question of whose interests were being served and whose were not, and the issue of who wielded power over whom.

On the other hand, the students in the PAR class did engage matters of judgment. They aligned with the interests of their community partners, and thus against the interests of the chain stores and real estate developers. They both analyzed and experienced the power relations between the neighborhood residents and the larger economic players. They rejected the assumption that "creative destruction" of that working-class community was a natural and productive feature of capitalism (cf. Schumpeter, 1994). They witnessed firsthand the consequences of one instance of the gentrification process. Moreover, their instructor pushed on those issues, not leaving them to chance. This kind of learning occurs far more often in community engagement projects than in work-related internships (cf. Butin, 2005; Jacoby, 1996), both by design and by circumstance.

Here is another domain in which the curricula of school and of experience seem potentially complementary: Real ethical and political issues arise in the latter, and might be examined in the former. But that option is typically rejected by academics who insist on dispassion and objectivity, who find political commitments anathema to academic quality (cf. Schram & Caterino, 2006). Service-learning practitioners work to overcome that objection—but they are still in the minority in the university. As an intellectual virtue, phronesis *could* bridge the chasm between the academy and the world of action. In both arenas, however, certain forces and customs limit its use.

Conclusions

On the whole, one must conclude that the forms of knowledge and ways of knowing found in school and in the rest of the world are substantially different. While knowledge-items may occasionally be *about* the "same thing"— facts about colonial life in Heather's case, the content of employment law in Roberto's—they are not experienced, used, or processed in the same way. And more often, knowledge in the world and in the classroom are in fact about different things: about celebrity yachts or gala dresses, not about analyzing a poem; about assigning an employment case to an investigator, not about the principle of due process; about controlling one's anger while being reamed out by the boss, not about theories of child development. Whereas knowledge in the college classroom tends to be propositional and abstract, stripped of context (other than the context of the classroom itself, or of scholarly inquiry), knowledge in the work or service setting is normally instrumental, designed to support the performance of situated activities and the accomplishment of consensual purposes (cf. Flyvbjerg, 2001; Resnick, 1987; Scribner,1986). The meaning of the display of knowledge in the different settings varies, as well. In school, if one answers a professor's question well, one is judged as having intelligence (except perhaps by those who regard one as a wonk and a suck-up); at work, a display of knowledge bolsters an identity as a competent worker and a team player (or perhaps as a quota-pusher and a suck-up!).

Facile claims about the "application" of school-derived knowledge and skill overstate their isomorphism with workplace knowledge. Even in technical domains like accounting and engineering, where students learn specific procedures for performing specific tasks—double-entry bookkeeping, for example—the transfer of the textbook version of the process to the real world is rarely seamless. School-like forms of knowledge generally overlap with practical knowledge at work less than educators assert.

Moreover, as we have seen, the sequence and coverage of situated curricula vary considerably from the curricula and syllabi students encounter in their classes. In school, they are exposed to well-formulated knowledge in a logical sequence dependent on factors like degree of difficulty or the principles of conceptual order. At work, they encounter and engage knowledge on a need-to-know basis: They get access to that portion of the overall stock of knowledge that they need in order to perform their jobs, not to the whole array in the setting. Unlike operations in the school classroom, where all students confront the same knowledge base, work in the real world is usually divided, meaning each role carries its own set of socio-cognitive demands. No one person in an automobile factory knows everything about building a car. Even in companies committed to progressive forms of organization like socio-technical systems design or participatory management, where the workers handle a wider range of tasks than in the Fordist factory, much labor is still divided, distributed over a complex workforce with different skill sets (cf. Appelbaum & Batt, 1994).

Even the generic skills that employers want new entrants into the work-force to possess—critical thinking and problem-solving, oral and written communications, teamwork and collaboration, and so on (cf. Casner-Lotto & Benner, 2006)—differ between the workplace and the school. We rarely saw college interns (or especially high school interns) writing the kinds of com-plex prose that they were supposed to be learning in their classes, or using sophisticated mathematical skills (Bailey et al., 2004). Moreover, the kinds of critical thinking taught in school are not the same as those performed at work, and interns tend not to confront as much high-level problem-solving as experiential learning advocates claim. Ironically, recent research chal-lenges the claim that students learn those skills even in college as much as they should (cf. Arum & Roksa, 2011).

So I argue that the kinds of things learned in college classes differ rather substantially from the kinds of things learned in experiential sites: School knowledge really is different from practical knowledge. On the other hand, I will also argue that—*under the right conditions*—the two forms of knowl-edge can be compatible, complementary, and mutually expansive.

Much of the content of experience lends itself to academic inquiry, even though that might not happen now. In the introduction, I mentioned the case of a student reading Max Weber on bureaucracy in a course on organi-zational sociology while at the same time doing an internship in the educa-tion department of a large city, and raised the question of how the two forms of knowledge intersected, coincided, or enhanced each other. Similarly, Roberto had taken a course in constitutional law before enrolling in the fair-employment internship; one can ask whether the first informed the lat-ter, and whether in retrospect he deepened his understanding of the law by working in the agency. On one level, those questions are empirical: One could check to see whether and how these two types of experiences enrich each other—although no one, to my knowledge, has done that yet. In the abstract, at least, one could imagine ways in which those two sets of knowl-edge could be seen to intersect in productive ways.

On another level, however, the questions raise issues that will be addressed in the next chapter: pedagogical questions about what can and should hap-pen back at school to make experiential learning meaningful as a part of the college curriculum. That is what I meant by saying the two forms of know-ing could enhance one another *under certain conditions*: I will argue that the potential for the school's adding value to the experience is a matter of pedagogy, of teaching practices and, more largely, of institutional mission. The practical experience, I will argue, cannot be left alone by the school. If it warrants credit, if we are to be ethical in charging tuition for an internship, we have to *do* something to enlarge the student's learning beyond what she would do simply by virtue of having the experience. The next section will explore that possibility—and the challenges embedded in it.

CHAPTER 5

Discovering the Pedagogy
of Experience

The previous two chapters proposed a framework for analyzing the curriculum of experience, the *stuff* students learn when they engage in activities at work sites and service settings, and compared that content to the kinds of things they learn in college. In this chapter and the next, we will shift focus to the *way* that happens, to the pedagogy of experience, defined as the social organization of the processes and resources by which people learn—whether in a museum or an investment bank, in a classroom, or around a family dinner table. The structure of this exploration echoes that of the discussion of curriculum: Chapter 5 lays out and illustrates the elements of situated pedagogy, its general features, and the factors shaping it. It implies a judgment about the claim that "experience is the best teacher," namely, "Well, it depends." Chapter 6 shows how that natural process compares to what happens in college classrooms. Chapter 7, the last section of this part, analyzes and critiques some of the ways experiential educators in universities try to enhance, direct, and assess their interns' learning.

Like the curriculum analysis, this section rests on the theoretical traditions laid out in the second chapter: Dewey's (1938) notion of learning from experience, particularly his focus on the importance of the interaction between the learner and the socially-constructed environment; Lave and Wenger's (1991) insistence on learning as a function of participation in communities of practice; and the studies of workplace learning centered on the affordances and constraints inherent in work organizations (Billett, 2001; Fenwick, 2003; Raelin, 2008). The basic phenomenon of interest remains the same—the ways activity systems and their members learn in the course of practical experience—but we are changing lenses, from the curricular to the pedagogical, from the content to the process, and in particular to the social means by which participants come to encounter and use various forms of knowledge. The basic aim of this section is to provide the reader—whether a researcher, a teacher-advisor, or an administrator—some conceptual tools for making sense of the educational dynamics of firsthand experience.

Task Analysis

Building on the premise that people (and systems) learn things when they engage in activities that entail the use of (attention to, apprehension of, application and transformation of) knowledge about those things, this framework for analyzing the pedagogy of experience begins with a detailed examination of the situated tasks students and their organizations perform, then moves on to more and more expansive perspectives on the learning process. We begin with the *task episode*—the start-to-finish performance of a meaningful piece of production—as a unit of analysis because participants in a work activity or service project orient themselves to that chunk of experience; it is often the focus of their attention and conversation, and is a device by which they hold each other accountable for competent performance. As we have already discovered, the task carries with it the socio-cognitive demands and pragmatic features that underlie the curriculum of experience. As we will see in this chapter, it is socially organized in ways that constitute at least the first layer of the pedagogy of experience. The framework will expand to include broader levels of the process—task sets, roles, entire organizations and their environments—but the task is a good place to begin.

In what follows, I will once again invoke scenes from real cases studied in our research to illustrate important concepts and issues: Heather in the history museum, Roberto in the fair-employment office, and Lisa in the fashion magazine, but also a range of others, from an intern in a veterinary clinic to an editorial assistant in a curriculum development firm, from a complaint-handler in a consumer protection bureau to a cub reporter in a community newspaper, as well as others. This section will *not* examine the experiences of students in the Participatory Action Research (PAR) class, or other community service projects, because those enterprises are best regarded as school-based, driven as much by an instructor's pedagogical strategies as by the exigencies of a production organization. We will come back to these hybrid pedagogies later.

So when we examine tasks, we will be considering the social organization of such activities as Heather's doing the artifacts cart during a tour; Roberto's interviewing a complainant; Fred's preparing the materials for a spaying operation in the clinic, and Latoya's writing an article on department-store Santas. The granularity of the definition of a particular task can vary according to the purpose of the analysis. If one wants to understand the fine-grained details of the discursive practices of museum docents, for instance, one can examine a videotape of an event as narrow as Heather's exchange with a specific student about a bed warmer. On the other end of the spectrum, one might want to look at the entire intake process in the fair-labor office, from the greeting to the elicitation of information to the referral. Almost all work-related activities can be decomposed into smaller and smaller units, or aggregated into larger ones, for a variety of analytical purposes. Moreover, we will look at the ways tasks get combined into large-scale processes, into roles, and into organizations. But we will begin with discrete tasks.

The process by which a student engages in performing a particular task may profitably be analyzed as encompassing three phases: *establishing, accomplishing,* and *processing* (cf. Moore, 1981a; Bailey et al., 2004). Members of a work group employ a variety of interactional procedures to get each one of them done; that is what we will call the *social means.* They organize and utilize the human, informational, and material resources in the environment in such a way as to make it (more or less) possible for the student to handle the work as it is defined in practice—that is, for the student to encounter, engage, and own that element of situated knowledge.

The term *phases,* by the way, is not meant to suggest a strict chronological sequence: first establishing, then accomplishing, finally processing. In some cases, to be sure, these elements of the process do unfold in a clear order, but in some the stages occur simultaneously; in yet others, the activity moves back and forth. In essence, these segments represent functions that in one way or another and to a greater or lesser extent get done during the task episode. What is interesting and instructive is to identify the varieties of social means available within each phase, the very different ways each of them can be performed. In this section, therefore, we will examine each of the phases, suggest the functions that constitute each one, and review some of our empirical data on the varieties we saw utilized in internship sites.

Establishing

In this segment of the task episode, the student encounters the task and gets information (in varying forms and to varying degrees) from someone or something in the environment about its nature, about what it takes to perform it, and about the criteria by which that performance will be judged.

In advance of undertaking certain aspects of the work, that is, the student needs certain kinds of information, and the term establishing refers to the social means by which participants in that scene organize that information and make it accessible to the newcomer—or don't.

The first category of necessary information concerns the definition of the task: "This is what needs to get done." This material may be expressed in fairly broad or rather specific terms: "We need you to handle the phones," or "We need you to answer phone calls, take messages, refer callers to appropriate offices, and keep a log." It may or may not include information about the function of the task, about its purpose or rationale in the larger scheme of things. Second, the intern needs information about the procedures for completing the task: knowledge, skills, methods. In this component of the establishing phase, the student may receive instruction, information about the requisite knowledge and skills, and perhaps an opportunity to rehearse the work. If particular procedures are customarily used to do this work, this is the phase in which the student finds out about them. In the third element of establishing, the student gets information about the standards by which the performance will be assessed by relevant participants in the situation: supervisor, colleagues, clients.

The information provided through establishing may be more or less complete, and more or less familiar to the student, depending on the situation and the task itself, as well as on the intern's prior experience and knowledge. Somehow, though, these terms of the task are communicated to the student to one degree or another. By the way, that degree may in fact be next to nothing: We have seen situations in which students were provided only the barest of orientations to the work, leaving them to sink or swim.

The issues of legitimacy and motivation also arise in this phase: How is the student convinced that the task is warranted, valued, and worth her effort? There are several ways a supervisor (or other worker) might establish task legitimacy. First, she might invoke her authority, saying in effect, "Do this because I told you to." This procedure works when the intern has reason to accept the authority figure, whether that reason be naked power, respect, or fear. She might invoke the natural function of the task, saying something like, "Do this because we need it done for these reasons..." This strategy requires that the student either know and believe in the function of the activity complex within which the specific task appears, or have faith that the supervisor speaks the truth in saying that the task is important. This second reason may depend more on trust and affect than on power or authority. Finally, the instructor might claim benefits to the student, saying something like, "Do this and you'll learn something interesting, or you'll get skills you can use in a future job, or I'll give you a good recommendation…" The motivations might be intrinsic or extrinsic, or some combination.

The dimensions along which the establishing phase might vary can best be represented in a set of questions that can be posed by an analyst or practitioner. First, who initiates the task as something the student will do? In some cases, the intern's direct supervisor sets a task episode in motion. In others, the task exists as a regular function, and begins when a client or customer or colleague shows up and asks for something. In still others, where the task is routine, it may be available for working on whenever there is a lull in other activity: "Well, I'm done with A, B, and C; now I can pick up D…" Finally, the student may initiate the task herself.

A student interning with a professional photographer once sat talking with our researcher when the paid assistant walked over and asked him to help set up a shot. Throughout the session, the assistant gave the intern orders, specific instructions to do one or another thing: "Put that light here, and point it there." That kind of order was, of course, common in many sites. But we also saw particular task episodes set in motion by a client or visitor. Several interns at a major science museum were once helping the staff reconstruct a dinosaur skeleton in one of the public exhibit halls. Passersby occasionally asked them questions about the process and about the animal itself, unexpectedly initiating an ancillary form of work. And on occasion an intern actually invented a task: After working for a few weeks in a city councilmember's office, Conrad suggested to his supervisor that he organize a database system to keep track of current bills as they moved through the legislative process. He had noticed that aides to the councillor sometimes struggled to locate information about what votes were coming up, about what bills were in committee, and about which issues might attract public attention. He had some experience designing databases, and wrote up a proposal, which the supervisor gratefully approved.

Another variable in the establishing phase is the form and channel in which information provided about the task: oral or written language, gestures or demonstrations, material objects. Descriptions of the task might be displayed in an instruction booklet read early in the internship term, or announced verbally as the supervisor rushes to contend with an emergency. Methods and procedures might be available in an online tutorial, or simply through repeated on-the-job performances by senior workers.

The consumer protection bureau, for example, provided all new volunteers with online manuals detailing consumer regulations and procedures; then they were tested on their formal knowledge, and could not answer the phones until they had passed. Before they actually spoke with consumers, they listened in on extension phones as a veteran demonstrated the proper methods for handling calls. This redundancy of channels for instruction was unusual, but symptomatic of an activity system with official, law-based rules and procedures. Many other sites provided nothing in writing or online for new interns; supervisors simply and briefly told them what to do—often just once, unless there was a problem.

A third establishing variable is the extent of information given to the newcomer about the basic nature of the task, about the knowledge and skills needed, and about the criteria for judging the performance. The settings we observed varied enormously on this dimension. Some, like the consumer protection bureau, supplied massive amounts of information, in several forms, at different stages of the experience. Others gave the barest of descriptions of the work, then set the student to getting it done. Sometimes the supervisor assumed nothing about the newcomer's preexisting knowledge, and sometimes she took for granted that the intern could handle the job.

Linda, a student working in a curriculum development firm, a for-profit company that designed and produced educational materials for urban school districts, among other things had to proofread new lesson plans before they were approved for printing. To set up this work, her supervisor gave her an extensive verbal description of the project (a set of lesson plans for a course on life skills); she then gave Linda a printed sheet on proofreading that displayed the appropriate markings for each kind of problem (errors in spelling or punctuation, format issues, etc.); finally, she sat with the intern as she worked through a sample page marking the errors, and gave her feedback and hints. On the other hand, when Latoya got the assignment to write an article on department-store Santas, her editor gave her next to nothing in terms of up-front instructions; he simply said, "Go to these stores, interview the Santas, and watch what they do. Then write it up." (To be fair, he gave her extensive feedback on her first draft, and made after-the-fact suggestions about interviewing strategies.)

Another question about establishing is the extent to which the student can negotiate the terms of the task, effecting changes in the nature of the demands or expectations. At some sites and in some situations, the intern was told in no uncertain terms, "Here is what you have to do . . ." In others, she could say, "Well, how about if I . . . ?" For example, a second student at the community newspaper felt uncomfortable about interviewing people for articles. When her editor asked her to call several people for a story about graffiti, she resisted and delayed, and finally asked if she could work instead on organizing back issues of the paper. In a corporation's legal affairs office, a student bored with extensive filing assignments spoke with her supervisor and negotiated a switch to a task involving summarizing case reports for the lawyers.

Fifth, how much discretion is left to the student in the choice of means for doing the task? Sometimes procedures are algorithmic, prescribed to an extent that leaves little room for variation, invention, or choice. In other situations, even lowly interns have room for creativity and improvisation. Janet, who worked for a Jewish website, blogged about a number of issues of her own choosing. On the other hand, exercising that kind of discretion could sometimes get an intern in trouble. One of the students at the consumer protection bureau encountered a question from a caller; although he was not familiar with the specific regulations governing the case, he had personal experience—and thus some opinions—on the issue, and so he hazarded a suggestion. In the process, according to his supervisor (who was listening in for training purposes), he had violated agency procedures. He was reprimanded for this ad-lib by his supervisor, and told to be more cautious and to stick to the official procedures.

In our research, we witnessed a number of general types of establishing procedures, categories of social means that differed on the dimensions discussed above. These types are not mutually exclusive—they can be mixed and matched—but they provide a sense of the options available to participants in a setting. In some instances, the supervisor or a more experienced worker did what we called show and tell: She performed the task herself while the student watched, sometimes providing a running commentary ("See what I'm doing here?"), sometimes not. Toward the beginning of her internship at the history museum, Heather followed veteran guides around as they led several school tours. In that situation, she did not have the opportunity to ask questions as the events unfolded, nor did the docent make asides for her benefit, but Heather and the veteran guide did have a chance to debrief on the tour after they had seen off the class. That sequence represents a temporally different form of establishing: show and *then* tell. In a different model, a student working in the accounts payable office of a large university sat and watched her supervisor enter figures into a template; the supervisor explained step-by-step what he was doing, and answered the student's questions: show and tell *now*.

Another type of establishing can be called sink or swim: The supervisor assigns the student to perform a task with minimal or no instruction or explanation—"Go do such and such…" Those tasks tend to have minimal logical-technical demands and not much pragmatic weight. At the veterinary clinic, Fred needed little direction in how to walk dogs or clean cages; Anya got only the barest of instruction in how to file documents in a PR firm's legal office. But sometimes we were surprised by the lack of prior direction for tasks that were relatively important: Some interns at a neighborhood council were charged with posting flyers for a public meeting, but were not told in clear terms that the posters were a legal requirement; they ditched most of the flyers and blew off the task. And sometimes sink or swim could be an intentional and beneficial teaching strategy, as in the case of Latoya at the community newspaper.

On other occasions, the supervisor opts to give front-loaded instructions, verbal descriptions of the task without explicit demonstrations: "I need you to do this, that, and the other thing." The boss typically provides the information and tools necessary for performing the task. When the curriculum firm intern was assigned to calculate the reading level of some of the texts being produced, her editor explained how to do it—"Find the harder words in this manual, and see what grade level they fall into..."—and provided a calculator, but did not demonstrate the process.

At the other end of the spectrum is self-starting: An episode is initiated by the student, and he defines the task, locates the necessary resources, and figures out how to do it himself. Conrad, the city council intern who designed a legislative tracking system, was perhaps the best example of that strategy.

Accomplishing

In this second element of the task episode, the student-worker uses information, material objects, and skills to get the task done, perhaps in collaboration with other people. The social organization of this performance can be described in terms of a number of general dimensions. The first is how many and what other persons take part in the performance of the task. Who provides support, assistance, or guidance? How are those people configured in terms of role structures, power relationships, and social dynamics? It makes a big difference whether you are the solo practitioner on a job at the moment it is being performed (think of a toll collector, isolated in a booth before she goes back to the office for a break or a staff meeting) or you are a member of a large and complex team. And it makes a difference in the latter case whether you are solely responsible for carrying out one crucial element of the overall activity (imagine being the person on an auto assembly line who inserts the engine into the chassis: The whole line depends on your doing your work) or, on the other hand, are just one of many people contributing to the same task.

José, a student-intern working in the facilities office of an airport motel, was assigned to track the housekeepers' completion of room-cleaning chores. He used a customized database system for the work: As housekeepers finished a room, they called down to him and he checked them off on the spreadsheet; then he assigned them to new rooms. His work, in other words, did entail interactions with the housekeepers, but only on the most superficial level: "I've finished 2304"; "OK, do 2308 next." If there were problems—a housekeeper took longer than expected to finish a room, or there were unusual messes in a room—the student passed the issue along to his boss. So he was part of a larger activity system, in the terms described earlier, but most of his work was actually solo.

Leading a specific tour in the history museum was also a solo performance—not counting the audience—but Heather did have occasion to interact with other members of her community of practice: getting advice from the department director, exchanging war stories with other tour guides in the department office. Moreover, on some level, she had to treat the class teachers as her colleagues as well as her clients. Lisa, the intern at the fashion magazine, sometimes did work on her own—Googling for information on particular celebrities, then emailing it to the writers—but she also took part in work-related conversations in the office, discussions of story lines, gossip about movie stars and designers, reports on stories that appeared in other popular magazines.

A second dimension of accomplishing is the number and kinds of material and informational resources the intern uses in performing the task. At the consumer protection bureau, for example, a student (like all volunteers and staff) had access to an online help manual, where she could look up referral numbers, agency regulations, and other useful information. For the data she had not yet memorized, the manual was an invaluable and handy resource. On the other end of the spectrum, the community newspaper intern who prepared an article on graffiti did not need much in the way of materials (a steno pad and a pen, at least during the data-gathering phase of the process), but did need a good deal of information that was challenging to find: examples of graffiti in the newspaper's neighborhood, reactions to it among various people in the community, the legal responses by city officials and police, and so on. Moreover, once the reporter had that information in hand, she had to organize it effectively for presentation in the article. Guidance on how to get and how to organize that other information was, however, available in the person of the editor.

Third, what does the student-intern have to do to get access to these varied resources during performance of the task? Here is a crucial element of the social means issue; we will consider it further when we examine the factors shaping the pedagogy of experience. But in doing task analysis at the first level, one must acknowledge the access problem. Some resources are readily available, some take considerable effort to locate and secure, and others are simply not accessible to low-level members (cf. Perkins, 1993, on the "access characteristics" of a learning environment).

In the accounting department of a public relations firm, for instance, an intern processing expense account statements could quickly pull up on her computer both historical data—records of past transactions—and current guidelines and standards for executives' claims. Not just anyone could access these materials: She needed a password revealed only to members of the accounting group, but that was all. The calculations that she had to perform on the statements were actually built into the spreadsheet, so she didn't have to recall or even perform them. Nor did she have to track down the executives and coerce them into submitting their expenses; the statements simply showed up in her in-box. Similarly, a student interning in the physical therapy facility of a large urban hospital could find any equipment he needed readily at hand: walkers, parallel bars, weights. Since his supervisor controlled the flow of patients in the gym, he did not run into situations where another aide had claimed the devices when he wanted them.

On the other hand, some sites posed challenges for workers looking for particular materials or information. In a community-based food cooperative, for example, a student frequently needed information about the particular vegetables stocked in a given week—where they came from, how much they should cost, how to prepare them—but she often had trouble finding answers. She had to ask several coworkers or, if she could find him, the supervisor; or she had to track down the receipts for the week's supplies and pore over them to discover costs. The organization ran on a shoestring, with a largely volunteer staff, and lacked some of the organizational resources that would streamline the process of purchasing, displaying, and selling the food.

The question of access does not determine the educational quality of an internship. The fact that materials and information are easily available can on the one hand intensify the volume and efficiency of the learning process. On the other hand, in a situation like the accounting office, the standard use of the built-in algorithms and computer tools for processing expense accounts may in fact have *reduced* the intern's opportunity to figure things out on her own; much of the cognitive work was off-loaded onto the technology. Conversely, the food co-op's very lack of organization may have given that student more challenges and problems to solve, and therefore provided a richer environment for building cognitive and social skills.

A fourth dimension of accomplishing is the extent to which the worker follows mandated procedures or, conversely, creates new solutions. Some work sites enforce very specific procedures for doing certain kinds of work; the methods and procedures manual in the consumer complaint division provides a good example. Others allow considerable leeway, even opportunities for invention. Again, the educational quality of those respective systems is not consistent in either direction: Algorithmic procedures can sometimes move a legitimate peripheral participant further into the heart of the community of practice, making more learning possible; on the other hand, they can reduce the cognitive load of the work, making it routine and, in the end, boring.

Like the establishing phase, accomplishing tends to fall into one of several basic types. There are, of course, multiple forms of getting the work done, varying on dimensions like who was involved, what resources and tools were needed, and spatial and temporal constraints. One of the more important dimensions is the degree to which the work is carried out according to algorithms or strict methods and procedures. The phrase "following the script" describes a task in which the intern effectively follows detailed instructions from the supervisor or a veteran worker. The accounts payable student applied lockstep procedures to the materials she was given; in fact, the relevant steps were given by the structure of the spreadsheets and forms she worked with, and most of the calculations were actually performed by the Excel program—she didn't need to do them herself.

Some tasks, on the other hand, give the student an opportunity for improvising the performance of the work, even if within broad guidelines. Heather's approach to doing the artifacts cart worked with a basic grammar: Wheel out the cart, make some introductory remarks about household life in the colonial period, pick up each item in succession and either ask the kids whether they know what it is or say something about it yourself. But that procedural syntax left a lot of room for varied realizations: Heather could tell different stories, emphasize different points, switch up the order, answer questions or ask them, and so on. Like actors or comedians who improvise on stage, she always worked from certain prestructured elements, mixing and matching as she proceeded. Any teacher (other than one reading from lecture notes all the time) knows about this process, as well.

Some other task episodes entail taking plays from the sideline: The student carries out the task, but with continual coaching from the supervisor or a more experienced worker. The student painting dinosaur bones did that, at least during his first day at the job. But that method rarely continues throughout the term—no supervisor could spare that much time away from her own work.

Another, more complex version of accomplishing takes the form of teamwork: One or more interns collaborate (sometimes just with other students, sometimes with other workers) in the execution of an organizational task. Kevin McEvoy (2010) describes a special case: an internship program at a major American corporation in which a small group of marketing graduate students worked on a project calling for a mix of research, presentations, and recommendations. The interns had to devise a collective strategy, distribute the labor, do their own parts, and then put the pieces together in a coherent and effective solution. Other instances of teamwork afford the students more limited roles. For instance, an intern in an operating room of a large urban hospital worked in the presence of surgeons, anesthesiologists, nurses, and orderlies; her role was to set up the anesthesia cart and ensure that it kept functioning properly during an operation. She was in the presence of people doing far more advanced work, but carrying out her own job did not mean that she needed to understand the others'. In other situations, teams provide considerable learning support.

The last example of a form of accomplishing might be called punting (to continue the sports metaphors): In some situations the intern somehow managed not to do a task at all. The students ditching the flyers at the neighborhood council represent a case of punting; so does the community newspaper reporter who put off calling local merchants for interviews until the impatient editor assigned the job to someone else. Punting might happen for several reasons: mere laziness, not understanding the task (and probably being unwilling to ask questions), being uncomfortable with a particular type of activity. And it can have different kinds of consequences: none at all (as in the poster example), redoubled instruction, reassignment to other work, or in the most extreme case dismissal.

Processing

In this third phase of the task episode, the student engages in a complex set of activities and interactions that provide information through which she may (a) judge the quality of her performance on the task, and (b) reconstrue the terms of the problem and the strategies for solution. Processing may take the form of monitoring and feedback, in which the supervisor or a senior member of the group watches the intern do the work and says something about how well she did. The feedback may come from other sources, as well, including customers or clients. It may also take the form of opportunities for reflecting on the problem and rethinking (even relearning) ways of handling it. This phase is particularly important in the analysis of experiential education: This is a moment when much of the learning happens, or at least is extended, deepened, and consolidated. Moreover, much of the earliest literature on college-level internships (cf. Keeton, 1976) focused on the issue of assessment, asking how one can determine what and how well a student has learned through prior experience, and decide whether that learning qualifies for academic credit.

Mainstream college professors often worry about this element of nonclassroom education; it is at the heart of much of the skepticism about experiential learning. Teachers are generally in a position to check whether a student has learned the desired materials: They can ask questions in class (even questions to which they know the answers; cf. Mehan, 1979), require papers, give tests. My hunch is that much of the research on experiential learning focuses on assessment precisely because that phase of the educational episode is most likely to drop out in the absence of a teacher in out-of-classroom encounters. If someone performing a task gets no feedback on the quality of her work, they wonder, how can she be learning?

This evaluation function may in fact appear in natural settings, but in forms unfamiliar to classroom teachers. Indeed, the interactionist conception of social encounters suggests that participants continually provide information for each other concerning situated definitions of competence, that is, criteria by which members will assess each other's performance. The socially organized environment constantly provides information to people by which they may fine-tune their behaviors and displays, interpret others' actions, and read the situation. The problem here is to discover the various forms and processes by which the social environment organizes and provides both feedback information and opportunities for rethinking problems and strategies, both for newcomers and for other workers.

Part of feedback entails judgments about competence. The criteria by which situated competence (whether linguistic, behavioral, or interactional) is defined fall into at least two categories: correctness and appropriateness. Applications of those terms may be more or less predetermined, more or less fixed. If a teacher in a classroom asks, "Sally, what is the formula for water?," Sally may respond *correctly* in only one way: "H$_2$O." Standards for a correct answer—one the teacher wants and expects—are narrow here: Sally has little choice. She may respond *appropriately* in a few more ways: "I don't know"; "Let me look that up"; "You didn't assign that chapter." Saying "None of your damn business!" would probably cross the line into inappropriateness; the form is not considered suitable to the situation. The question "What do you think of Coldplay?," on the other hand, may evoke a wider range of appropriate responses, none of which is more "correct" than another: "I love 'em"; "I think they represent a major force in the history of alternative rock"; "Good beat, I'll give it an 85." Standards for appropriateness are probably similarly broad in that case: The student may speak briefly or at length, may ask questions of the questioner ("Why, do you like the band?"), or may even pass the question along to the rest of the class. Internship sites manifest a huge variety of standards by which student performances are deemed correct and/or appropriate. Some are quite specific and inflexible ("Type this

letter exactly like this other one") or vague and open ("See if you can figure
out a better plan for this brochure; it doesn't grab me"). The sharing and
enforcement of these standards represent an important element of the processing component of situated pedagogy.

In all of our observations, we witnessed types of processing that cor-
responded to the conventional distinction made in educational research
literature between formative and summative evaluation. In the terms I am
proposing here, formative feedback serves an instructional function: It is
meant to help the student improve performance—to *learn*—relative to
certain criteria. Summative feedback, on the other hand, stands more as
a judgment, a comment on the ability, personality, and/or general performance of the student, a summary assessment. Its purpose is not so much
to help the student improve—in fact, the student might not get to under-
take the same task again—but to communicate that judgment, and perhaps to contribute to a formal decision about whether or not to retain or
reward the worker. This distinction bears on the social relations between
the supervisor and the intern (as between the teacher and the student in
a classroom), on the degree of power and authority wielded by the boss,
and on the extent of hierarchy among the actors. Summative feedback is
more likely to occur, it appears, when the supervisor knows in advance
what constitutes a competent performance; this is the equivalent of her
knowing when the Erie Canal opened, and asking a student to see if he
or she knows. If the premise of the interaction is that the boss knows
and the intern doesn't, then the student's job is to find out what the boss
knows and to display mastery of that knowledge. That relation—whether
in the workplace or in the classroom—puts the supervisor in a position
of power: She has the authority (1) to determine what constitutes a correct and appropriate performance, (2) to judge the student-intern's performance according to that standard, and (3) to wield sanctions of one form
or another to reward or punish the student's performance and to get the
student to do what she deems necessary to achieve and display mastery
and, more important, to serve the needs of the organization. The student,
of course, stands then in a subservient position—although, as Foucault
(1980) rightly argues, that does not mean that the student has *no* power in
the working relationship.

There are many situations, in and out of classrooms, where the conditions underlying summative evaluation—tasks with known procedures and
solutions, hierarchical power relations—do not obtain. At times, a fuzzy
and unexpected problem admits of many solutions and no one knows in
advance which solutions will work better than any others. In this instance,
the nature of knowledge-use is altered: It is not predefined, mastered, and

authorized by the power-figure, but is a matter for search, speculation, and invention: "Let's see what we can do with this wicked problem." Social relations are similarly altered in such situations. Instead of there being one person who "knows" controlling many who "don't know," all parties engage as peers or colleagues in the solution of the task. In between those poles lie many gradations in the distribution of knowledge and power.

Evaluation and judgment are not the only components of processing, however. We are also concerned with the extent to which the student-worker is afforded an opportunity to reflect on the task-problem, to reconstrue the terms of the task and consider alternative strategies toward solution. In *How We Think*, John Dewey (1910) suggests that this kind of reflection is an essential part of learning through experience. In fact, the concept provides either tacit or explicit justification for the concurrent seminars in which many students in experiential education programs gather regularly to discuss and analyze their field experiences. I will examine those school-based pedagogical devices in chapter 7; at this stage, my point is that the extent to which these off-task reflection exercises are necessary depends in some respects on the degree to which reflection is somehow built into the naturally occurring interactions in a work site. We witnessed a wide range of possibilities in this regard. In some settings, intensive reflection on the work happens as a feature of the normal activity. Think of the newspaper editor reviewing a draft of an article with the cub reporter, giving her detailed suggestions about how to approach a story. In others, there is little opportunity for the student-worker to rethink her performance: Picture a student at a small music label making calls to retailers asking them how many copies they had sold of various recordings—this was in the days before iTunes—and submitting those numbers to her supervisor, who never said a word to her about how she was handling the task.

Another feature of the processing phase deserves mention here. The notions of both evaluation and reflection highlight the connectedness of one task episode to others. We cannot look at *a* task episode as if it were separate from the ongoing stream of activity in the work environment. The task episode is not a molecule mechanically entrained with other molecules to produce a "situation." Rather, the concept of processing reminds us to see the ongoing task work as evolving, checking back and looking ahead, using emergent information to reconstrue (redefine, reconceive, reevaluate, transform) the problem and its solution. Processing involves coming to terms with the task in its broader context, comprehending and dealing with its connection to other tasks and to various aspects of the environment. I will discuss this feature more fully when I show how task analysis moves to broader and broader perspectives.

Finally, the notion of processing draws attention to the intellectual, cognitive, and interpretive work the intern must do in the course of performing a task, that is, to her curriculum. She does not simply take in information and respond to it in predictable, algorithmic, hard-wired ways. Rather, she *uses* information of many sorts, interprets it, relates it to other information, selects it, transforms it—*processes* it. The opportunity to do this kind of reflecting, interpreting, and processing is socially organized, not simply a matter of individual choice. Therefore, part of our challenge in understanding situated pedagogy is to understand that phenomenon: how the activity system organizes the social, material, and informational resources the worker needs to process her own performance.

As in the case of establishing and accomplishing, the processing phase of the task episode raises several issues. First, who provides the processing: the supervisor, other workers, the intern herself, clients or patrons, computer programs, material objects? Feedback might come from any number of sources. In the consumer protection bureau, for instance, an experienced senior volunteer listened in while the student first answered complaint calls. Following each call, the coach commented on the procedures and regulations governing the specific case, suggested alternative strategies, and pointed out strengths and weaknesses in the intern's performance. In the (rare) cases where the veteran volunteer didn't know something about a particular complaint, the two could refer to the online manual available or call on the phone-room supervisor for guidance. That is, this setting provided several sources of feedback and reflection for the intern: printed materials and two layers of more-experienced colleagues. Here was a perfect example of Vygotsky's (1978) concept of the Zone of Proximal Development: The intern could do more—and learn more—with the support of others at a higher level of skilled knowledge-use.

Sometimes the people for whom the intern provided a service gave her direct feedback. When Heather led an elementary class in a discussion of colonial household artifacts, for example, the kids in the class did things that she could read as information about her performance: They listened raptly and asked interesting questions, or they looked bored and chatted among themselves. Heather could correlate features of her performance—the way she explained how a bed warmer worked, for instance—with features of their reactions, and learn something about what worked and what didn't. After the tour and back in the department office, she could also ask for tips from veteran guides: "One of my classes was really noisy today. What would you do if...?" Or, stumped by a specific question from a child, she might use the library to search for related information: "Oh, the last Dutch-speaking governor of New York was Rip Van Dam." That is, the museum provided multiple sources of information, and multiple opportunities for reflection.

Some sites, on the other hand, effectively provided *no* processing opportunities: The intern was basically left to her own devices in figuring out how she was doing and what she might do differently. This was especially true of back-office operations like the general counsel's office of a public relations firm, where the student was assigned to file documents. Once she had been instructed on the filing methods, she simply did the work, and nobody checked up on her regularly or gave her feedback. We can assume that if the lawyers had discovered that files were often misplaced or lost, someone would have let her know, but short of egregious errors or gross incompetence no one was likely to say anything. To be sure, she could think about her work on her own—nothing prevented her from processing her own performance—but she didn't have much information to reflect on. Completing a task was for this intern akin to tossing a message-in-a-bottle into the ocean from the beach of a deserted island: She was not likely to get anything back.

A second dimension of the processing phase is the form it takes: verbal comments, written evaluations, observable behaviors, changes in material conditions, and the like. Interns, like workers in general, garner useful information about their performance on tasks through a number of channels. In the reproductions department of the natural science museum, we once saw the supervisor look over an intern's shoulder as he was painting plastic dinosaur bones and say, "That's a little dark." That kind of immediate verbal feedback was common in situations where the boss was present and the work was visible. The veterinary technician supervising Fred in the animal clinic could see what he was doing, and comment on it ("Put the spaying kit on this side of the table, not over there"); the community newspaper editor could sit down with the intern and go over the draft of an article ("Try to draw the reader in with a catchy opening line"). Verbal feedback also appeared in weekly supervisory sessions, in water-cooler conversations, and in spontaneous moments of anger and tumult, when the intern might either overhear or be the target of the supervisor's yelling about some mishandled process.

Workers also get feedback from the emergent product itself. In the city councilmember's office, Conrad could try out his bill-tracking system to see if it did what he hoped it would, and tweak it if it didn't. Of course, in that situation the worker himself had to know the criteria by which he would assess his own work: Could he find bills by topic, by sponsor, by stage of consideration? Without those benchmarks, the successive approximations would have been random and ineffective.

In some settings, student-interns received written evaluations of their work. That kind of formal feedback was relatively rare, perhaps because of the short duration of the placements, and tended to be summative rather than formative. Being told how you did as you walk out the door does not give you an opportunity to reconstrue and improve your performance, although it might contribute to a kind of after-the-fact learning. Another example of written feedback could be found in emails between the supervisor and the student-workers. In the curriculum development firm, the intern proofread a draft of a life-skills package and turned it in by email; her supervisor sent it back, asking her to fix certain mistakes. That event, by the way, reinforces my earlier point that the elements of the task episode—establishing, accomplishing, and processing—do not constitute a clear-cut sequence of formally distinct activities. In this case, the task (proofreading a lesson plan) had been established and then accomplished, but the processing ("this is an error") also constituted a new phase of establishing ("do this over again, and be sure to…"), leading to a new round of accomplishing. The three terms refer to *aspects* of the task activity rather than strict *phases* in a lockstep sequence.

A third question about processing is *when* in the course of the task episode it happens: during the accomplishing phase, as the work is being done? Right after it is completed? At periodic intervals, such as weekly supervision sessions? In the museum reproductions studio, the verbal feedback happened as the work was done: "Oh, look, that's too dark." In other settings, the verbal feedback was more time-delayed. Heather heard constructive comments from her supervisor in a private conversation at the end of the tour during which she first did the artifacts cart. Conrad's boss couldn't quite see what he was doing from moment to moment as he designed the bill-tracking system—it was embedded in databases and other online documents—but she met with him every Friday for an update. Another student working in a municipal housing agency got verbal commentary from her supervisor not as she was doing the work but in weekly sessions. Then, twice during the semester, her boss wrote formal evaluations that were inserted into her file; had she been a permanent employee, those documents would have been used in determining merit raises, promotions, and other employment conditions.

One important implication of the timing of the processing was the extent to which the feedback was formative or summative. Millie, one of the student-interns at the consumer protection bureau, appeared to her supervisor to lack the social-relational skills necessary for handling complaint calls; she did not "sound confident." The supervisor informed her of this problem verbally in a series of several private conversations, and tried to get her to improve her performance. That part of the processing was formative, though not effective. Midway through the semester, the supervisor gave Millie a formal evaluation critiquing her call skills—and reassigned her to a more clerical role that did not include speaking with consumers on the phone. That part of the feedback was summative, a final judgment before taking Millie off the complaint-handler job. On the other hand, the intern-reporter got frequent feedback from her editor about successive drafts of the story on department store Santas. That helped Latoya to rethink her approach to the article and to organize information more effectively. She used what she had learned in this first story as she was sketching out a strategy for the next piece, on graffiti in the neighborhood.

Fourth, to what extent is the student held accountable after the fact for the performance of the task? Processing carries different weights in different circumstances, depending partly on the pragmatics of the specific work being done. The consequences of the feedback and judgment vary from the negligible to the serious. The two students working for a neighborhood council who punted on posting legally required flyers were never found out by their supervisor, who got no direct information about whether or how well the task had been completed—and thus never held the students accountable. On the other hand, a young man who spent a short time in a progressive elementary school working with kids in a class for the emotionally disturbed was removed from his position when the teacher determined that he was not sensitive enough to their needs and feelings.

One of the pragmatic features of tasks mentioned earlier was demandedness: the degree to which the work is central or necessary to the organization's mission and core technology. The dimension of social means discussed here—accountability—would seem to follow naturally from that task feature: One would expect that students performing important tasks would inevitably be held accountable for the quality of their work. Curiously, that assumption did not always pan out, as the neighborhood council story suggests. Despite the fact that the work of posting the meeting notices, though mundane, was legally required, the students were not held responsible for not doing it carefully; perhaps if a community resident had complained about the lack of notice for the meeting, the supervisor would have chastised the workers. In any case, the relation between the task and the social means for setting it up varies substantially across settings and across incidents.

Processing might be described as falling into several main types. One, as suggested above in the discussion of accomplishing, could be called coaching: The supervisor (or a veteran worker) is present during the performance of the task and gives the intern regular guidance, instruction, and feedback. Several high school students in the early study interned in a woodworking shop where the owner fancied himself a master craftsman akin to a medieval guild member, and treated the students like apprentices. In his small and noisy workspace, the master could always see what the student was doing, and frequently called out detailed instructions, along with pointed commentaries: "OK, now measure the drawer twice, and call out the length...A craftsman is always precise and careful when he's assembling the pieces of a cabinet." The master-craftsman not only oversees but also participates in the work; he is a sort of player-coach.

Much of the more intensive processing happens in formal supervision, when the boss schedules regular meetings to get caught up on the intern's work and progress, and to comment on both. More often than not, the student and the supervisor are in the same space at the same time during other occasions, but the formal supervision scene takes a more intentionally instructional shape. The city councilmember's staff director met periodically with Conrad, and commented on what he was doing with the new bill-tracking system, gave him feedback on his constituent-complaint work, and suggested areas where he might improve. But she was also present every day making assignments, providing resources, and organizing team efforts. That aspect of processing might be called informal supervision.

A third form of processing occurs during the accomplishing phase: testing the product. The research team first identified this category in examining the field notes on the science museum reproductions department, where an intern worked on making plastic dinosaur bones from molds. As it happened, one step in the process entailed using a razor blade to shave off the raised seam where the two halves of the mold joined. The student ran his finger along the edge where the shaving had been done, checking to see if it was smooth, and sanding it down if it was not. We used this moment as an example of processing, of the intern's looking at (or touching) the product of the work to generate an assessment and fix the job if necessary.

Extending the Framework: Vertical Elements

The task analysis framework needs to be extended, both vertically and horizontally, or it runs the risk of oversimplifying the experience of students in internship sites. The intern does not simply perform isolated tasks unrelated to each other; nor does she think about her experience only in terms of these discrete tasks. So by vertical extensions, I mean increasingly inclusive perspectives on the ways the learner is embedded in systems of relationships and activities. By horizontal extensions, I mean attention to changes in the experience over time, in the ways participants organize their work and their resources. This section lays out the terms of these more encompassing elements of the pedagogy framework.

We have already discussed the first layer of the vertical dimension, analysis at the level of what we call the *task item*: a single piece of work, an action accomplishing some discrete segment of the mission of the organization; for example, "doing the artifacts cart" in the museum. The questions described earlier provide a method for interrogating the use of knowledge at that highly granular level. But tasks do not generally get performed in perfect isolation from each other; more often members imagine them as enchained or related in a meaningful and productive way. We call that grouping the *task set*: a connected series of task items that together constitute a coherent, emically identifiable segment of the mission of the organization—for example, "the tour."

At a higher level of generality, we can examine the way the student-intern comes to occupy a *role*: a set of expectations, rights, and obligations attached to a position in which the student is placed relative to other actors in the organization—for example, "tour guide." That device gives us a more comprehensive handle on the learner's engagement with the setting. Finally, and most inclusively, we can analyze the *environment* (or institutional setting): that broad combination of roles and statuses, relations, activities, events, beliefs, values, and ideology that constitutes the social system in which the student works—for instance, the "museum." Together, these four nested terms provide a device for adjusting our perspective—changing our lenses, or stopping the microscope up or down—depending on our analytic or educational purposes.

Some of these concepts, to be sure, leave ambiguity and overlap in certain situations. The distinctions between and the relations among them are not clear-cut or stable; they are often a matter of perception, local language, and even power. First, the boundaries of each one are more or less arbitrary, and depend on the granularity of the analysis. For instance, where does the task item end and the task set begin? At the city councilmember's office, handling a constituent-complaint call was regarded as a discrete task item, something the supervisor could assign to Conrad: "Get that call, will you?" The chore had a beginning (answering the phone), a middle (speaking with the caller, taking notes, filling out forms), and an end (filing the record of the call); but it also had related sequellae (researching the problem, negotiating a resolution, calling the person back, and so on). Each of these components could be decomposed or aggregated. Settling on a unit of analysis might depend on the terms members use, on their emic conceptions of the boundaries; or it might depend on the purposes of the immediate investigation, on what one wants to explain. If one is trying to analyze the evolution of the student's role in the office, then perhaps the task set of "handling constituent problems" is more important than the task item of "eliciting information about a tenant-landlord dispute." If, on the other hand, one wants to understand how the student learns to ask effective elicitation questions, then the task item might be the preferred unit of analysis.

The concept of role is even trickier than task item and task set. For one thing, the intern is always in the curious position of being a student-worker, that is, a learner in a putatively productive role. That paradox generates tensions that can be resolved in either direction—student or worker—or in some kind of equal balance. Since the intern—as distinct from a new worker or apprentice—is generally in fact a transient in the role, and not a highly skilled one at that, some work groups may regard her as a peripheral member; others may rely on her productive capacities, and play down the learning piece. Moreover, the particular role(s) the student occupies are likely to shift across situations within the organization, and even within a situation. The definition of the student's role may shift mercilessly—as, indeed, may anyone's, as ethnomethodologists (Garfinkel, 1967; Mehan & Wood, 1975) and postmodernist social theorists (Foucault, 1980; Hatch, 1997) demonstrate convincingly. The traditional structural-functionalist conception of role (Merton, 1949; Parsons, 1964) simply reifies status and role too much. Some students whom we observed in the several studies, in fact, occupied nothing like a stable role, but rather acted as a filler, a person available to assist on whatever work someone wanted done. This is not even so regular or skilled a position as Claude Levi-Strauss's (1968) *bricoleur*. The extent to which student-interns' roles developed stable characteristics varied enormously across sites.

The third conceptual difficulty in locating the student's role lies in the difference between people's plans and claims on the one hand—that is, what they said and expected the intern would do as a member of the organization—and their actions on the other. As the interactionists and situationists reviewed in chapter 2 suggest, a role is more an interactional accomplishment than a structure into which someone is inducted. The relationship between the claims and the actions has to be regarded as an empirical question, not as taken for granted. These caveats notwithstanding, analysts and practitioners of experiential education need to examine the nature of the roles students are expected to inhabit and actually do enact.

The highest level concept in this integrative framework, the environment, is the hardest of all to nail down. Moreover, it may not fit entirely into the logical argument I will propose here: that both roles and environments, like task items and task sets, are in varying ways established, accomplished, and processed. Nevertheless, there is some utility to suggesting that the student-intern is integrated to some extent into and expected and enabled to learn something about the organization as a whole: structures (and, after Mehan, 1979, structurings), processes, beliefs, values, narratives, histories, myths, other roles and skills, and so on. To say that the student will learn "everything about city government" by means of working as an intern in a city council office, as some experiential educators do, is clearly going too far. But it may, in fact, be possible to locate those aspects of the broader environment about which the student learns, and how she learns them.

Finally, there is an element of the student-intern's experience not addressed by these work-related terms: what we call being there, or what would in school be called off-task activities. We observed students engaged in many encounters where, although they were not performing work, they probably learned something: taking part in lunchtime conversations where ideologies and explanatory systems were displayed by their coworkers; observing arguments in public spaces, where issues were defined and power relations displayed; reading brochures and newsletters during downtime. The straightforward task analysis framework put the being-there phenomenon on the proverbial back burner, and diverted our attention to this more narrowly defined class of action. But it may be a site with considerable educational significance.

In any case, these nested concepts—task item, task set, role, and environment—can all be analyzed in pedagogical terms: the social organization of the process by which the newcomer learns about each level of engagement. Task items and task sets may be established, accomplished, and processed in similar ways—but so may roles and environments as a whole. In an orientation session, the supervisor might verbally describe the intern's role: "You'll be a tour guide, which means…" Or she might simply assign a number of tasks until the student intuits the features of her role. Processing a role might be explicit ("You're just not working out as a complaint handler") or implicit. The extent to which the intern builds a knowledge base about the organization as a whole will depend on the extent to which she has access to a full range of activities. A student assigned to a peripheral task in a back room, with no chance to observe (much less participate in) the complex interactions constituting the environment will learn less at that level than, say, Lisa, who played a marginal role in the magazine but witnessed a great deal of what went on there. All these levels, then, as well as being there, need to be regarded as important perspectives on the student's learning.

Extending the Framework: Horizontal Elements

On the horizontal dimension, we need to add historicality to the analysis of interns' experience, looking not just at their individual tasks, but at changes over time in the social organization of their involvement in tasks, roles, and organizational activities. Student-interns—at least some of them—not only encounter different kinds of knowledge as they move through the placement period (the curriculum side), but they display different modes of participation, drawing on different kinds of material, informational, and social resources (the pedagogy side). Those changes speak profoundly to the nature of the educational experience. Indeed, one could argue that those changes *constitute* the educational experience.

The task analysis framework described above gives us the terms by which those changes can be described. In chapter 3, we saw that the student's curricular trajectory can be described in terms of changes in the types of tasks the student encounters, the types of knowledge she is asked to use. Now I will suggest that the student's learning can also be analyzed in terms of her pedagogical trajectory, that is, changes in the types of social means by which her tasks, roles, and environments are established, accomplished, and processed. These questions are problematic, in the sense that we cannot assume that any given student will experience changes on any or all of these dimensions, or that all students will experience the same kinds of changes. But asking the questions moves us toward a richer understanding of the processes of situated learning.

Changes in pedagogy might take different forms. Does the student initiate more of her own work as time goes on? Does she have the opportunity to work independently more often, or perhaps to collaborate with regular members of the group? Does the supervisor intervene less frequently—do less coaching, less directing—as she grows in knowledge and skill? Do her role and status in the organization change? Are new resources made available to support the work, and do they demand new knowledge and skill?

One scheme for describing changes in the student's role distinguishes three broad levels of responsibility: observing, helping, and performing. The educational significance of this hierarchy stems from the claim made by constructivist theorists (as well as Dewey) that people learn what they do, and these terms indicate increasing intensities of the doing. In her first days at the history museum, for example, Heather merely observed as veteran docents led tour groups around the facility. After a couple of sessions, she began helping out with a drawing exercise in one of the exhibit halls: She sat with a small group of children as they tried to draw examples of the carriages and carts used in colonial days, giving them pointers and feedback. On her fourth tour, she was suddenly and unexpectedly thrust into the position of doing the artifacts cart when the regular guide was called away; after that episode, she returned to her support role. Gradually, over the course of the next few weeks, Heather was inserted into each of the slots constituting the full tour: She gave the opening talk, showed the film about domestic life, set up the drawing exercise, commented on the exhibits, and saw the group off at the door. At first, she did those things as a fill-in for the regular guide, who would stand aside as she took the reins temporarily. Eventually, when she had done each of the elements a couple of times, Heather was given responsibility for leading an entire tour—but her supervisor followed her around the first two times, and met with her afterward in the office to debrief. Finally, about halfway into the semester, Heather soloed as a tour guide, with no immediate supervision.

Jerome Bruner (1996b) coined a useful term for describing this sequence: *scaffolding*. He was examining the process by which a toddler learns to participate effectively in a conversation. Reading to her child while he sits on her lap, a mother starts by carrying on both parts: "What's that, Billy? Right, a horsey!" Over many of these events, Billy learns to fill in the answers and to take appropriate conversational turns. That is, his mother initially provides support and guidance, but removes it as his competence grows. In the same way, Heather moved through phases of participation in the tour, progressing from observer to helper to fill-in to full-scale guide. The activity system provided useful supports (material resources, immediate supervisory guidance) at each step, then removed them and enabled her to perform the work on her own. At each stage, her participation deepened and her knowledge grew: She *learned*, both in the sense that we normally use that term and in the "legitimate peripheral participation" sense proposed by Lave and Wenger (1991). The trajectory of her career in the museum climbed steadily upward as she mastered more and more of the role of a full participant.

Students' experiences do not always change over the course of a semester in such dramatic ways. Some interns perform the same tasks on the last day that they did on the first. For instance, on his first day at County Hospital, Charles was shown how to prepare blood samples for endocrine tests. Throughout the entire semester, he performed the same task over and over again—and only that procedure. When there were no samples to be prepared, he and another student chatted, read science texts provided by the supervisor, and went to lunch. To our knowledge, he never encountered any other aspects of the lab operation. His trajectory was flat.

Another example of a trajectory might be called "low-steady with flashes." In this case, the student performs essentially menial, simple work repeatedly over the whole term, but occasionally takes part in some special event. Beverly, a student placed at the Community Video Center (CVC), was primarily an office worker: She kept track of petty cash, answered phones, gave out information about the center's programs, and made calls to remind people about classes. She did learn to handle these tasks more efficiently and effectively, but they remained fairly constant during her time there, and were not particularly demanding. But there were moments when special things happened. She helped a staff member set up a video fair, an exhibition of documentaries made by professionals; in the process, she got a chance to view a number of excellent works in the field, some of which raised her consciousness about specific political issues. Twice she was given the responsibility to do a shoot: to videotape an event for someone outside the CVC. These flashes were basically apart from and interspersed with the common clerical work that occupied most of her time. So her trajectory sloped only slightly upward, but had periodic spikes.

Unfortunately, there is no easy method for determining the relative importance of these distinct categories of tasks: the menial clerical work and the special opportunities. We cannot say how decisive the one-off events were in Beverly's overall experience, although our impression is that they certainly produced learning out of proportion to their frequency and duration. They definitely gave Beverly access to segments of the CVC operation that she would not have experienced otherwise. How effective that exposure was in an educational sense would be difficult to calculate in the absence of clear consequences or displays. But the fact that her organization made these episodes available represents a key feature of the situated pedagogy.

These three examples of career trajectories hardly scratch the surface of possibilities in other internship sites. Nonetheless, they illustrate the power of the longitudinal, developmental, historical use of the task analysis framework, and provide the terms of a comparative approach to different educational environments. If we can locate changes over time along the dimensions of social means, we can speak more systematically about the nature of the interns' learning experiences in these settings. Where there appears to be little change, where the student essentially performs the same tasks from Day 1 to Day N, and where those tasks can be mastered quickly and then simply repeated, education is likely to be minimal, at least in Dewey's (1916, 1938) sense. Where the social organization of knowledge-use does change, learning happens.

Repetition constitutes another pedagogical device, but may or may not promote learning. Practice, in the sense of doing something over and over again and tweaking one's work at each iteration, may enable a person to hone skills, to improve in the quality and speed of performance, and to move toward a form of expertise. But, as the task analysis framework can show, repetition may simply lead toward mindless habit. If the work organization requires the intern to perform over and over a task that demands little in the way of knowledge or thought, practice becomes miseducative if and when it makes the intern less likely to learn in the future (Dewey, 1938). Among both my research subjects and my own students, I have seen that happen repeatedly: An intern performs the same basic task over and over, becomes bored and disaffected, and learns very little.

On the other hand, where the student (a) encounters new tasks that are progressively more interesting, more demanding, more prestigious, and more important, and (b) interacts with supervisors and other workers in ways that are progressively more responsible, autonomous, and competent, then we can confidently say that education is taking place. In fact, documenting and analyzing the social organization of these phenomena provides a key to the understanding of this kind of work-related education.

Features of Situated Pedagogy

Several features of situated pedagogy stand out as especially important; they can be regarded as affordances and constraints provided by the activity system (Billett, 2001; Erickson, 2004). One is the organizational structure of the setting where the student works. From the perspective of learning, one issue is the degree of structural rigidity and persistence in the organization, the extent to which practices and social relations vary over time. A highly segmented setting with a strict division of labor—something Taylorist or Fordist—presents opportunities very different from a flat, open structure (Appelbaum & Batt, 1994). Bernstein's (1975) notions of classification and frame deepen this analysis, as does Perkins's (1993) focus on access features of the setting, the things one needs to do to participate in various kinds of knowledge-use.

Another issue is the question of whether the organization has developed regular practices and institutional structures for enhancing interns' experiences. Some companies have created regular internship programs, with a paid employee in charge, that offer orientations, workshops, regular supervision, and serious formative evaluation procedures in place. In a sense, they have produced an in-house pedagogy of experience, modeled to some extent on college programs. Others, especially small outfits, tend to improvise their work with interns—and that sometimes works, but sometimes doesn't.

Theories of distributed cognition (cf. Resnick et al., 1991; Salomon, 1993) point to another crucial feature of situated pedagogy: the extent to which cognitive work is spread across participants, units, and technologies. If a task set is organized in such a way as to assign different elements to different actors, then the problem of partial knowledge-use arises for the intern. Just as no single member of an automobile assembly line knows how to build a car, Lisa was not in a position at the fashion magazine to carry out the full array of processes leading to a finished article. She performed pieces of that work—Google searches, especially—but at best observed some others. The community newspaper reporter, on the other hand, saw the work through from generating a story idea through collecting information to writing it. Those are educationally distinct experiences.

Finally, educators and analysts need to pay attention to power as a feature of situated pedagogy. Kolb (1984) overlooked this element, but more recent scholars (Butin, 2010; Rhoads, 1997) have drawn on Foucault, Bourdieu, and other postmodernists to understand the way power differentials—between teachers and students, between academics and community residents, and so on—shape the pedagogical process. Relations of race, gender, class, sexual orientation, and other factors play a role in solutions to the access question, to who gets to know and do what. These investigations have appeared in studies of civic engagement programs far more than in work on internships or cooperative education (cf. Jacoby, 1996; Stewart & Webster, 2011).

Conclusions

Taken together, these questions about situated pedagogy—about the social means by which participants come to engage various kinds of knowledge—provide the basis for a detailed description of work-related activities: How did this or that get done in this particular instance? Who takes part, and what are their social relations? What do they need to know and be able to do in order to complete the task effectively? What is the meaning of the work in the larger context of the organization? These dimensions do not lend themselves, of course, to easy quantification or coding schemes; they are not meant to be used as a mechanical checklist against which features of specific situations may be described. Rather, they function as a framework for a rigorous interpretive process carried out by either an observer-scholar or a participant-practitioner—or even by a student. In using the tool, the analyst needs to exercise creativity and discretion to answer questions and understand their relative importance. Every question can be answered in every situation—these are parameters, variables for which there is always some value—but in some cases the answer may be "not at all" or "it doesn't matter." Still, the framework at least calls attention to a comprehensive range of issues in relation to the performance of tasks by student-interns. Again, that phenomenon does not exhaust the educational possibilities in a particular site; the student may construct knowledge not embedded in the actual task activity.

Toward the beginning of the high school study, as we discovered these dimensions of the task analysis framework, we hypothesized that we would discover a predictable relation between the kinds of tasks interns performed and the social means by which they were established, accomplished, and processed. That is, we thought that certain kinds of curriculum would require certain kinds of pedagogy. But here is one of the more surprising—and educationally perplexing—elements of these studies: We could find no such predictable relations. In different situations, people use very different methods to set up, perform, and assess work that looks fairly similar. The pedagogy of experiential learning seems enormously variable—as we will see in the next chapter, far more variable than college teaching.

One clear lesson can, however, be drawn from the framework sketched in this chapter: Simple claims about what and how student-interns learn as they engage in situated work experience—for example, that a student placed in an investment bank learns all about finance, or that one working in a fashion magazine learns all about the media—lack the rigor necessary for justifying (or, for that matter, criticizing) experiential education. Whether and what an intern actually learns depends on a raft of subtle features of the experience, not on the global features of the setting. The devil is in the details.

CHAPTER 6

Pedagogy in School and Field

The analysis of situated pedagogy in the previous chapter begs this crucial question: How do pedagogical processes in work and community settings compare to those in college classrooms? The framework laid out there provides the logic and the terms of an answer to that problem. We can investigate the pedagogical properties of classrooms using the same concepts: task analysis, socio-cognitive task demands, social means, and so on. That is the plan for this chapter: to describe the places where the two domains seem similar or different, to identify areas of compatibility and conflict between them, and to articulate the challenges and opportunities faced by experiential educators in the academy. The next chapter, then, will consider the kinds of strategies that programs based on engaged learning use to address those possibilities.

Two lessons stand out among the earlier observations about naturally occurring pedagogy in the workplace. First, the social organization of the process by which newcomers (and veterans, for that matter) encounter, engage, and construct new knowledge stems not from a rational and conscious decision about what they need to do in order to learn, but from the exigencies and dynamics of the production process. That is, except in the occasional cases where participants focus on training and development (whether in the form of specialized off-site workshops, on-the-job training, or supervisory sessions), learning must be regarded as a by-product of the work itself. Members are trying to get something done, not to learn. To the extent that they do learn, it is typically in the service of improving production: They want to do something better.

Second, the division of labor in the workplace production process often creates a very partial engagement with the social stock of knowledge for any particular participant. If we think of that social stock of knowledge as a property or resource of the activity system, then its range is often pretty considerable. In the history museum, it includes historical data and interpretations, understandings about children and their learning processes, public speaking, and so on; in the hospital operating room, it covers everything from the etiology of disease to surgical procedures to the functions of specific tools like scalpels and anesthesia machines. But as we have seen, any specific individual who participates in that activity system—especially a newcomer or intern—may engage only a small fraction of the overall body of knowledge-in-use in that system. The student interning in the hospital, for example, actually performed only the low-complexity task of hooking up and maintaining the anesthesia machine; she did not help out in other ways, and even her opportunities to observe were limited by sight lines, the pressure of the work on the doctors and nurses, and the challenge of explaining anything to her as the operation proceeded.

So the claim, made by some advocates of experiential learning, that a setting like the hospital constituted a "rich learning environment" has to be taken with a grain of salt. To be sure, a great deal of complex and important knowledge was being used by the system, but the intern had access to only a small range of that knowledge. And what exposure she had was shaped, again, not by her learning needs but by the work process. There was no rational, systematic curriculum through which she was gradually taught what one could know about the underlying medical conditions and procedures. Rather, her supervisor showed her what she needed to be able to do to perform her limited role in the activity system; he explained the rest of the system in very general terms, just enough so the student had a feel for what others in the room were doing. Similarly, Fred, the student in the veterinary clinic, got to observe specific, limited, and haphazard aspects of the vets' work: He helped out in spaying operations, and watched one of the doctors amputate a cat's tail—a highly idiosyncratic element of the full range of anatomical, physiological, and surgical knowledge-in-use in the clinic. Most of the rest of his effort went into peripheral tasks: maintaining cages, walking dogs, cleaning up after procedures.

Of course, some students did engage a full curriculum in their internship sites. Heather, for example, learned what she needed to perform the role of the tour guide in the history museum—and that role encompassed most of the stock of knowledge used in the education department, short of program development and management. Latoya, in the community newspaper, certainly took on the full-scale role of (cub) reporter: watching events, interviewing participants, writing stories. In somewhat stripped-down form, she had access to most of what a reporter needs to know, at least in a small community newspaper. In fact, her interaction with her editor around refining an article looked to us like as solid an educational encounter as any seen in school English classes.

But wherever the labor process distributed functions across participants, the curriculum-in-practice was limited.

Comparing Domains

These features of pedagogy in the internship site begin to frame the problem of how they compare to those in college classrooms. This is not the place for a lengthy analysis of actual classroom interactions, but even simple descriptions of stereotypical teaching methods make the contrasts and similarities clear. Think, for instance, of the quintessential scene in a college course: the lecture. The professor stands in front of the assembled students and delivers a monologue containing statements of fact, explanations of concepts and theories, positions on debates, and so on. As one in a series of lectures, this performance takes its form and content from the instructor's analysis of the subject matter of the course—the nineteenth-century French novel, the sociology of poverty, quantum mechanics—and his rational structuring of that material, his understanding of what comes first, what comes next, and how the pieces fit together. Meanwhile, the students sit and listen—or try to, or don't. Some of them take notes, some text their friends or check their Facebook accounts, some discreetly nap. Occasionally, one asks a question, seeks clarification of a point, or offers an observation or opinion. At the end of the session, students get up and leave; only a few linger to speak with the lecturer, sometimes about the content, sometimes about course logistics, grades, schedules, and so on.

Analyzed in terms of the situated pedagogy framework, this event has several key features. First, the participation structure is far simpler than most workplaces: a single speaker, a mass of listeners—a one-to-many, top-down speech event. The socio-cognitive task demands on the students are, at least for the moment, negligible: They may listen more or less carefully, may or may not think about the substance of the talk, may or may not take notes, may or may not speak. They may (or, again, may not) be held responsible later, in a test or a paper, for the content (echoes of every professor's nightmare question: "Will this be on the exam?"). So the social-interactional demands are simple—be quiet, don't attract attention, don't disrupt the lecture—and the cognitive demands are variable, depending on how seriously the student engages the material. The immediate demandedness of the task of "listening to a lecture" is low.

Of course, there are reformers who propose ways of turning the lecture-class into a more participatory, active affair (cf. Bain, 2004; Bligh, 2000;

Brookfield, 2006; McKeachie, 2002). Drawing on evidence about the waning attention-span and information-retention of the typical lecture-listener, they suggest techniques like breaking every 20 minutes for feedback, comments, short-answer questions, and small-group discussions. These tools certainly engage the student more actively, and change the participation structure momentarily. But the control of the knowledge-use and the social interaction still rests with the professor.

Or picture the seminar, another common format for the college course. The teacher leads a discussion of an assigned reading, a theory, or an issue: poses questions, speaks more than any single student (often more than all the students combined), manages access to the floor. Students may respond to the questions or pose queries of their own (usually after raising their hands and being recognized by the instructor), typically addressing the teacher, on occasion speaking directly to their classmates. In some seminars, individual students present their own papers, and then the professor initiates a discussion. The participation structure, again, is simple relative to, say, the editorial group at the fashion magazine or the veterinary office, and the cognitive demands are still shaped largely by the instructor. The sequence of knowledge-use is planned, predictable, and controlled.

Even the science laboratory, a school setting in which students appear to be active in their construction of knowledge, is generally structured in rigorous ways by the instructor. Except at the highest levels of graduate study, the work is not original, but rather replicates work already done by others. One web-based guide for laboratory teachers reveals the fundamental nature of the process in the rule for self-preparation: "You should know *everything* about what you are going to teach your students" (Buzzle, 2012). That is, content is totally managed and predictable; true discovery and surprise are unheard of. To be sure, the student learns by doing the experiment, but the lab session is as planful as the lecture.

The trajectory of the student's curriculum in a college classroom, presuming she does what is expected, rises steadily: The material gets more advanced, more difficult, more comprehensive. On the other hand, the pedagogical trajectory typically remains flat: The teacher retains control, and the student performs no new kinds of tasks, exercises no more discretion, and takes no more initiative at the end of the course than at the beginning. Again, of course, there are exceptions, and plenty of reformers aim to make the learning process more active, more student-driven, and more variable (cf. Bonwell & Eison, 1991; Brookfield, 2005; Meyers & Jones, 1993).

These examples point toward several dimensions of comparison between the pedagogy in school and the pedagogy in the field setting. We have seen already that, contrary to Scribner's (1986) and Resnick's (1987) dualistic analyses of learning in and out of school, the curricula of these arenas—the kinds of knowledge newcomers are asked to engage—are in some ways different but in some ways similar, not wholly distinct. The same is true of the pedagogies in use: In some respects they differ substantially, but in other respects they coincide.

On the level of social means, for example, we can compare the practices by which tasks are established, accomplished, and processed for the students and interns. In school, tasks—whether what we call assignments, or in-class exercises, or simple discussions—tend to share a common set of features. They are initiated by the instructor, who structures them in such a way as to engage the learner with the material in a variety of ways: first exposure (for instance, through readings), rehearsal and practice (through problem sets), exploration (through self-designed writing projects), and performance (through research papers and exams). Even when the student is given some choice in the content of an assignment ("choose a public policy that has an impact on poverty in the society"), the basic nature of the work is predetermined by the professor.

By contrast, according to some advocates of experiential learning (cf. Qualters, 2010), interns and civic-engagement students take more initiative in their work than classroom-based students do. Well, yes and no. We saw examples of interns inventing new tasks and even roles for themselves—recall Conrad in the city councilmember's office—but far more often, we observed them basically doing what they were told, following orders, or repeatedly taking on tasks that fit neatly into the process flow in the organization (Bailey et al., 2004).

The establishing of tasks varies more across domains in terms of the media through which learners obtain information necessary to perform them. In school, assignments tend to be made redundantly in written and verbal form: The professor includes them in the syllabus, hands out written instructions, and announces them in class. In the workplace, on the other hand, the information may be transmitted verbally in a front-loaded training session, visually in an instructional video or in a written methods-and-procedures manual; it may be demonstrated by a supervisor or veteran worker. On some occasions—what we have called sink-or-swim—the student is left to her own devices to figure out what needs to be done and how to do it.

This raises the question of how comprehensive the up-front preparation for the task is. In college classes, students sometimes complain that the instructor has failed to give them sufficient information about an assignment: content, procedures, expectations. They are no doubt correct, even though the terms of the work can often be inferred from the larger flow of the course. Here is an interesting similarity between school and work, though: Interns frequently make the same complaint about their supervisors, saying that they do not provide sufficient guidance on a task. In some respects, then, the establishing phase in the classroom is different from the one in the work or service site, but in some respects and in some cases the two look very much alike.

On the dimension of accomplishing the task (or carrying out the role), interns tend to engage in more different kinds of activities and relationships. The classroom-based student does a few kinds of things (reading, writing, taking exams, and so on) in but a few kinds of relationships (teacher-student, student-student, independent worker). Most of her work is carried out alone; on rare occasions, she will participate in a team project, and have to negotiate a division of labor. The intern, depending on the organization and the role, may have a similarly limited array of task-performance modes: for example, an accounting student whose sole function was to process expense-account payments for executives in a public relations firm, and reported to a single supervisor. More often, however, interns perform a greater variety of tasks in a greater variety of relationships. Lisa did some tasks on her own, though she had contacts with editors, writers, and artists at the inception and hand-off points: web-searches on celebrities, organizing look-books, collecting information requested by writers for their articles. Other parts of her work were collaborative and social: She took part in office chats where the editorial staff bounced ideas around; she discussed articles with authors. Even in less-than-ideal sites, interns usually had an assortment of experiences and relationships. Fred, in the veterinary clinic, walked dogs, answered phone calls, set up equipment for operations, cleaned cages; he worked directly with the doctors, with technicians, with clerical staff, and with pet owners.

Task accomplishment in the two domains, school and work, is relatively similar in terms of the degree of discretion afforded to the student. In both, that degree varies substantially. In some courses, the student is expected to carry out procedures in an algorithmic, mandated way. The same is true of some workplaces. On the other end of the spectrum, some courses (especially advanced ones) allow a great deal of invention and negotiation in choices of readings, research topics, and outputs. Similarly, some work organizations and civic-engagement projects leave a lot of room for improvisation and creativity. It is simply not true that, say, school is restrictive and work is open: Both vary a great deal on that dimension.

Finally, the processing phase takes different forms in the classroom and the field setting. Some interns get more ongoing guidance from the supervisor than the typical student gets from the professor—though some are basically left to their own devices. Because Lisa usually worked in the physical presence of the head of the features department of the magazine, she received feedback on her work as she finished it and turned it in; in fact, she could get moment-to-moment judgments: "Does this work?" "No, try it like that..." That sort of helicopter supervision rarely occurs in college classes (though it might occur for, say, a research assistant in a lab). A student hands in a paper or takes an exam; the next week, the instructor hands it back with a grade and, one hopes, with comments. Ideally, the student reviews the exam or paper to determine what she understood and did well, and what she needs to work on the next time around—if there is a next time. The feedback, in other words, varies in completeness, and there may or may not be an opportunity to rethink the knowledge and the task and to construct a new approach for the future. For the intern, processing may vary even more, to the point of being nonexistent on one end and constant on the other.

The consequences of the processing may be similar in the two settings, as well. Both may include formative as well as summative evaluations. In colleges that pay a great deal of attention to assessment practices—Alverno College in Milwaukee is a good example—virtually everything a student does contributes to an ongoing, iterative process of inquiry, investigation, and growth. But more commonly, college students get feedback that is essentially summative: "Here's how you did." They can visit the professor during office hours to find out how to improve performance, although not many do. Instead, the feedback accumulates toward a final grade. By contrast, the field supervisor may well have an incentive to provide formative feedback: Namely, if the individual worker improves, the overall production process does as well. On the other hand, if the intern has been given a set of tasks with little pragmatic value to the core mission, then the supervisor may not bother to offer substantive processing. The intensity and extent of assessment and reconstruction, then, vary more in the field than in the college classroom. Students may not get extensive feedback in their courses, but they always get something—at least a final grade. Interns, on the other hand, may get a lot or may get next to nothing.

Key Issues in the Comparison

Several issues pervade these comparisons between school-based learning and field-based learning, and will be taken up in this section: *motivation, reflection*, and *transfer of learning*. Experiential and classroom educators make varied claims about these challenges, and I propose to comment on their arguments. As before, my basic contention is that these issues are resolved sometimes similarly and sometimes differently in the two arenas. The two are not radically and persistently distinct.

Motivation

Learning theorists spend a good deal of time discussing the problem of how human beings are induced to expend the energy and effort it takes to learn something. Bransford et al. (2000, pp. 60–61) identify such drivers as the desire for competence—the feeling that one is capable of handling challenges in the world—and for usefulness, the sense that one has an impact on others. Ryan and Deci (2006) argue that people learn best when they themselves control the learning process, when they experience autonomy rather than heteronomy. These claims suggest a set of comparative questions about experiential and traditional school-based forms of pedagogy: Which forms enhance learners' sense of competence, usefulness, and control?

As situated learning theories predict, the answers are not simple, straightforward, or uniform across contexts. Certainly a student mastering calculus in a college classroom can be motivated by her emergent competence. Success in one problem set can energize her to continue even against difficult demands. For a literature student, gradually coming to understand a challenging piece of literature—say, Joyce's *Ulysses*—can be its own reward. On the other hand, a student might feel *less* motivation if the competence either proves too difficult to acquire, or is not something she feels worthwhile or desirable, either for herself or for others. In the context of an internship or civic-engagement experience, learning to do something well can be similarly motivating. Heather, the museum guide, certainly achieved competence in her role, and persisted in her efforts partly because of the resulting intrinsic motivation. Conversely, Linda, the student working in a curriculum development firm, did build competence around such tasks as proofreading, but found them agonizingly boring—despite their obvious utility for the organization—and thus lost energy and commitment. Some experiential educators make the implicit claim that situated work is inherently more motivating than academic work—but I find that argument unconvincing. Again, it depends.

One of the challenges for both classroom teachers and experiential educators centers on finding work that is on the cusp of the student's competence. This point echoes Vygotsky's (1978) notion of the Zone of Proximal Development: Learning happens most effectively at the point where the person operates at the limits of her capacity, and is in the presence of someone with greater knowledge in that domain. Bransford et al. (2000) identify that problem as a major issue for the classroom educator—but it is even more difficult for the internship coordinator or service-learning instructor: Without even being present in the site, she has to find just the right role for the student, one that will push the individual with tasks that test but do not overwhelm her capacities, and will provide just the right supports and resources at the right time. One advantage of service-learning courses over internships as a pedagogical strategy is the greater control the school-based instructor has over those features of the student's experience. The internship coordinator, by comparison, has little power to ensure that the student's role motivates her to learn, beyond making a good placement that sparks the student's interest.

On the dimension of usefulness as a motivator, experience-based learning seems to be stronger than classroom-based education. One way to frame this difference is to invoke the *authenticity* of the experiential work. Educational theorists write a good deal about the extent to which students regard a classroom experience as "real" (Carlson, 2001; Grimmett & Neufeld, 1994; Lombardi, 2007). While the notion that the classroom is somehow not real seems flawed (and, for those of us who spend much of our time in schools, insulting), the premise nonetheless is that students engage more fully and effectively with knowledge that they see as meaningful to their lives outside of school. Some books on college teaching draw on this idea. Ambrose et al. (2010), for example, suggest that one strategy to establish motivation and value is to "provide authentic, real-world tasks: assign problems and tasks that allow students to vividly and concretely see the relevance and value of otherwise abstract concepts and theories" (p. 83).

Now, that principle may be sound for the classroom teacher, but the obverse is not inevitably true for the experiential educator. The fact that a task is authentic—which, by definition, any work in the real world is—does not ipso facto motivate a student to learn from it. Several of my own internship students working in a fashion-related business—a magazine, a design house, a PR firm—have been assigned to organize the samples closet, to manage the process of lending clothing to photographers, editors, and celebrities. To a person, they have complained about the task as boring, even, in Dewey's (1938) terms, miseducative. On the other hand, of course—and in this book, there always seems to be another hand!—the authenticity of such tasks as leading a museum tour or writing a community newspaper article does seem motivating in a way that contributes to substantial learning.

So the question of how pedagogical strategies in the classroom and the field motivate students to expend effort and to persist stands as a crucial element of the comparison between the two learning environments. Once again, the answer is not clear-cut in favor of one or the other: As always, it depends on the details and nuances of each situation.

Reflection

Another major issue in the comparison of academic and experiential learning centers on the notion of reflection. The question is the extent to which and the means by which putative learners are induced to step back from the immediate activity and think more deeply about what they are doing and why. In its strong sense, reflection means more than the standard thought process that one engages in during any kind of action. Rather, it entails an examination of fundamental premises and strategies, a questioning of assumptions and habits, a form of metacognition or thinking-about-thinking. This practice has long been a focus of attention in the literature on work-based learning. At least since Argyris and Schön (1974) proposed the notions of theory-in-action and reflection-in-action, scholars and practitioners in this field have insisted that reflection is a core element of effective learning at work (cf. Billett, 2001; Fenwick, 2003; Raelin, 2008). Experiential educators, for their part, have argued at least since Kendall et al. (1986) wrote *Strengthening Experiential Education within Your Institution* that experience alone does not constitute education, that one must reflect upon it if one is to learn (cf. Eyler et al., 1996; Moon, 2004). Finally, experts in classroom teaching such as Brookfield (2006), Bain (2004), and Leamnson (1999) agree that students learn more effectively when they develop the habit of reflecting on their thinking processes, not simply taking in and processing new information and ideas.

The pedagogical issue, then, whether in or out of classrooms, is the social means by which the reflection process is structured. The next chapter will go into that problem in some depth as it pertains to school-based experiential educators; we will consider the techniques and strategies they use to enhance, guide, and monitor field-based learning once students return to school. What about in the course of naturally occurring activities in work or service sites, and in the course of planned classroom interactions? Certainly, as we have seen, interns think about things, solve problems, acquire knowledge. But do they have occasion to reflect on their work and on their thought processes? (I am setting aside for the moment the hybrid structure of civic-engagement projects like the PAR class on gentrification; we will examine that process in the next chapter.)

The evidence from the Institute on Education and the Economy (IEE) research suggests that the answer, unfortunately, is not much. We did observe interns sitting down with their supervisors to consider what had been going on, how it went, what might be done differently. In a less rigorous sense, that conversation constitutes a kind of reflection. But in the stronger sense of metacognitive, transformational reflection, we virtually never saw that happening. Nearly always, the reflection focused on "how can I do this better?" rather than on questions like "how am I thinking about this" or "what am I not taking into account?" The deeper form of reflection does occur in the work world during certain kinds of workshops or organizational practices: socio-technical systems design, action science, and so on. But no intern in our samples ever engaged in that kind of event. And the social organization of the students' participation in situated activities never entailed deep reflection (Bailey et al., 2004).

But, for the purpose of the school-field comparison, it is safe to say that deep reflection rarely occurs in the college classroom, either. Certainly, (some) professors (sometimes) demand rigorous, knowledgeable, and even critical thinking of their students. But they do not typically ask for practices involving the questioning of basic thought processes, or challenges to dominant paradigms, or investigations of tacit assumptions. They may require students to construct plans, say, for research papers, but usually they do not make them analyze the planning process itself. Scholars of teaching promote that reflective practice (cf. Bain, 2004; Brookfield, 2006), but evidence that it happens often appears relatively scarce.

So in both arenas, there is reflection of the garden-variety sort, but not usually deep reflection. As we have seen, the nature of common reflection differs between the two domains, and the social means by which those processes are organized differ, as well. In the school, for instance, framing and control usually rest exclusively with the professor, whereas knowledge-use in the field is more complexly managed and distributed. Learning resources are made more easily accessible to a greater range of participants in school than at work. Once again, the differences are in the details: It depends. In any case, the dimension of reflection is yet another element of a comparison between academic and experiential processes.

Learning Transfer

Finally, the question of transfer of learning dogs both school-based and field-based pedagogy. A great deal of the research literature on experiential education, especially in the domain of service-learning, attempts to make the case that doing an internship or a service placement generates learning that transcends the specific activity site, that can be used in college classrooms as well as in other work and community sites (cf. Kendall et al., 1986; Sweitzer & King, 2004). Much of that research suffers from common methodological challenges: identifying the forms or dimensions of learning (knowledge, skills, values, critical thinking processes, etc.), finding appropriate metrics and indicators for the learning being claimed on the chosen dimensions, generating randomized treatment and control groups to compare the impacts of various interventions. Typically, students in experiential education programs select themselves into those activities, so random sampling is nearly impossible; even in schools where all students are required to participate, systematic quasi-experimental manipulation of the program experience is unusual. Even the most rigorous studies of the impact of experiential learning, therefore, such as Eyler and Giles's (1999) widely cited *Where's the Learning in Service-Learning?*, yield only modest results, under particular circumstances, with limited generalizability (cf. Linn et al., 2004). But the claims for the transferable effects of experiential education programs persist.

Rather than review and evaluate those claims, I want to identify what I take to be the nature of the challenge faced by university educators, both traditional and experiential, in terms of facilitating learning transfer among students. Part of the analytic framework has been mentioned before: the disparate modes of thought and action engaged in school and in the real world. Several theories contribute to a deeper understanding of this issue.

Bruner's (1996b) notion of frames for thinking, mentioned earlier, identifies several substantially different modes of thought as they appear in different social contexts. One form is largely privileged by the academic institution: the linear, propositional style that depends on assumptions of universality, control, and rationality. Whether in the hard-science laboratory or in the interpretive enterprise of the humanities, thinking in this mode is expected to be based on transcendent principles of rigor, system, and generalizability. An experiment in the lab reveals not information exclusively about that particular event, but about events *of that kind*. That is, the point is to extrapolate from the specific to the general. Making those more general claims finds support in the community of inquiry only when it abides by certain rules and conventions. When a chemistry instructor teaches students a theory about, say, covalent bonding, she intends that they will learn and practice those rules and conventions, that they will recognize arguments that are adequate and persuasive given the customary logic of reasoning as practiced by professional, credentialed chemists. That reasoning manifests what is commonly called the scientific method, whose procedures and standards have developed since the early Enlightenment.

One might argue that scientific propositional reasoning appears only, or at least most clearly, in the hard sciences and, perhaps, in the social sciences, at least those with rigorous statistical methods (there is dispute about this claim; cf. Flyvbjerg, 2001; Schram & Caterino, 2006). But I will claim that even the more interpretive, hermeneutic inquiry of the humanities—say, the study of literature—exhibits a characteristically academic mode of thought, divorced as a whole from the practical activities of the world outside the seminar room and (ideally) conforming to professional, discipline-based standards of logic and modes of argument. Imagine a class discussing a famous novel—say, *Ulysses*—and the intellectual tools they employ in the conversation. Whether they draw on some form of poststructuralist critique and look for elements of textual disunity, or apply a Marxist method to relate the latent content of the work to such themes as class struggle or historical progression (cf. Barry, 2002), they are clearly engaging in a form of propositional thinking: making claims about a phenomenon (the novel) in terms designed to be applicable to other instances of such phenomena, and to generate insights—not laws in the scientific sense, but basic understandings and theories—that transcend the particular conversation. Moreover, their discussion has no bearing on any form of action other than succeeding discussions in similar situations. So the pedagogical process in the classroom—the production and warranting of particular kinds of interpretive statements and theoretical claims—operates on the basis of this shared conception of legitimate knowledge.

In a work environment, on the other hand, discussions of equivalent seriousness and subtlety *do* proceed on the expectation that they will inform action. Picture, for example, a conversation at the fashion magazine in which editors, writers, and our intern talk about a recent movie awards program that all of them watched on television. "Oh, did you see the dress Gwyneth Paltrow was wearing?!" "Yeah, it was really gorgeous. Do you know who designed it?" One can see where this is headed: toward consideration of an article in the magazine about celebrity dresses, or about the particular designer, or about the actress's fashion sense. The comments touch implicitly (and sometimes explicitly, depending on the timing of deadlines) on elements of the story that would constitute a hook for readers, without articulating explicit propositions or drawing on theory or even on much in the way of evidence. The criteria by which participants in the conversation make and evaluate assertions ("Nobody cares about Gwyneth Paltrow any more"; "Oh, yes, they do, especially since her guest shots on *Glee!*") are very different from those in a poststructuralist discussion of *Ulysses*. Even if the editors and writers actually studied Derrida in college, his name will never appear in these events, unless in the interest of beefing up some participant's reputation as a smart person (and, depending on the culture of the specific organization, that strategy could backfire, branding the name-dropper as a pretentious pedant). The social organization of this conversation—rules about who gets to speak and how, conventions about turn-taking and content shifts, the use of informational resources and implicit logics—looks very different from the classroom discourse on Joyce.

So the transfer of learning question entails this modes-of-thought distinction. If Heather picks up information about state history as she guides the tour, does that new knowledge carry over to her American history class in school? Would it help her even in another history museum? What elements of Fred's experience in the veterinary clinic might inform his work in his anatomy class, or in a job in a zoo? When the intern goes back to school and sits in her internship seminar, what challenges face the instructor attempting to help her tease out lessons not embedded in the field experience? Conversely, what is the likelihood that things she learns in class will inform her knowledge-use in the field? (Intriguing aside: Fred actually did rather poorly in his biology course, the clinic experience notwithstanding.)

At this point, a digression is warranted into some of the academic literature on the problem of transfer of learning. Scholars typically define transfer as the process by which information, knowledge, or skill that a person learns in one situation influences performance in another situation at a later time. They usually distinguish between two different forms of transfer, using various terms—near/far, specific/nonspecific, literal/figural, verbatim/gist, high-road/low-road, vertical/horizontal—to denote the poles on a spectrum of similarity between the original setting (Situation A) and the one where the knowledge reappears (Situation B) (e.g., Cree & Macaulay, 2001; Haskell, 2001; Mestre, 2005; Royer et al., 2005). Transfer may also be positive (A-learning enhances B-learning) or negative (A-learning inhibits B-learning), depending on the nature of the knowledge, the settings, and the activities.

This concept stems from a theory, formulated a over century ago by Thorndike and Woodworth (1901), that transfer happens most extensively and effectively when A and B share "identical elements"; the more the two differ, the less transfer occurs. More recent researchers argue that that theory works only for a narrow range of behavioral responses (dogs salivating at a 500 mH tone, for instance, may not respond if the tone drops to 425 mH), and not so well for a transfer based more on the learner's comprehension and schemas (cf. Bransford et al., 2000). In any case, throughout its history, the learning transfer concept has entailed an analysis of the senses in which knowledge from one situation maps onto knowledge from another. Some theories have focused on the specific features of the environments, while others have addressed the ways the learner interprets the knowledge claims (Royer et al., 2005).

According to Perkins and Salomon (1989, 1992), low-road transfer happens when Situations A and B are sufficiently similar to trigger well-developed semiautomatic responses. On the other hand, high-road transfer "depends on mindful abstraction from the context of learning or application and a deliberate search for connections" to the new situation (1992, pp. 2–5). The high road to transfer, that is, does exist but requires more time for exploration and investigation, as well as greater mental effort. This distinction has a bearing on the pedagogical comparison between field and classroom experiences.

Many of these studies observe that learning transfer does not occur to the extent that educational rhetoric often claims. A popular video on YouTube illustrates the problem: Students graduating from Harvard, some of whom had majored in astronomy, were asked why the weather is warmer in the summer and colder in the winter. In this informal, nonclassroom setting, wearing their caps and gowns and distracted by their families, nearly all of them offered an incorrect (but confident!) explanation involving orbital distance from the sun (YouTube, 2012). That is, they failed to transfer their academic learning to a different context. The research evidence on transfer generally undermines common assumptions about the portability of knowledge. This problem is particularly salient in a discussion of experiential learning, where the two performance situations—work (or community action) and school—are indeed *very* different.

But Perkins and Salomon (1992), Bransford et al. (2000), Hakel and Halpern (2005), and other theorists suggest that there are a number of conditions, processes, and situational factors that do tend to enhance the likelihood that transfer will happen:

- *Thorough and diverse practice.* When the performance is practiced repeatedly in a variety of contexts, a "flexible and relatively automatized bundle of skills" may be carried over to other situations (Perkins & Salomon, 1992, p. 4). Note the constraint on this principle: The knowledge must be rehearsed in diverse contexts, not just over and over in the same one; time-on-task alone is not a sufficient condition (cf. Bransford et al., 2000, p. 62; Hakel & Halpern, 2005, p. 365).
- *Explicit abstraction.* When learners have abstracted the critical attributes of a situation, when they have taken their understanding of the structure of the current context to a higher level, they are more likely to grasp new situations in similar terms. Bransford et al. (2000, p. 63) see the issue as one of problem representation: Transfer increases when learners produce abstract representations of the concepts in question; this suggests that transfer depends to some extent on tasks that share cognitive elements. Perkins and Salomon (1992) also suggest that using metaphors and analogies—likening the material at hand to something at a distance—enhances transfer, as well.

- *Active self-monitoring.* Learners are more likely to effect transfer when they reflect on their own thought processes, so they recognize and can repeat the kinds of cognitive strategies they used before to solve problems and construct action (Perkins & Salomon, 1992), when they actively choose and evaluate their approaches to problems, when they get useful prompts and feedback (Hakel & Halpern, 2005), and when they consciously draw on previous experience.
- *Arousing mindfulness.* The concept of mindfulness, popularized by Ellen Langer (1989), refers to "a generalized state of alertness to the activities one is engaged in and to one's surroundings, in contrast with a passive mode in which cognitions, behaviors, and other responses unfold automatically and mindlessly" (Perkins & Salomon, 1992, p. 4). A person in this mindful state will be more likely to achieve transfer, especially through explicit abstraction and active self-monitoring.
- *Cultural compatibility.* Bransford et al. (2000) suggest that transfer happens most effectively when organizational and personal cultures are aligned, when features like the nature of knowledge and social relations are similar in the two situations, and when the learner understands those cultural features. Discontinuities between the settings make transfer more challenging.

This set of conditions under which transfer more often succeeds provides a backdrop against which situated and academic pedagogies might be compared. First, the principle of practice—repeating the skill or using the knowledge over and over in a variety of situations—sometimes manifests in both kinds of settings. The problem is that the criterion of diverse contexts often fails to materialize—in both environments. The accounting student interning at a PR firm engaged in frequent practice both in her classes (doing problem sets in double-entry bookkeeping) and at work (calculating expense account reimbursements for executives). But in each arena, the situational variation was minimal: Problem sets are problem sets, and expense-account calculations quickly become routine, especially when the spreadsheet program does them itself.

Sometimes task-and-knowledge rehearsal does vary over time in the field. Heather's work with school groups was structurally repetitive once she assumed the complete role of tour guide, but the details changed: Each class had a different content agenda (household implements, transportation, and family rituals, for instance), the artifacts cart conversation went in different directions, the visiting teachers' classroom management styles swung from strict to permissive. So Heather's experience probably met this criterion. The same might be said of Lisa's repeated use of Google and other search engines to find information for writers at the magazine: The technology remained constant, but the content variations forced her to explore different strategies, different interpretations, and different applications.

College teachers often structure practice into their pedagogy: the problem sets in accounting class (and economics, physics, engineering, etc.), successive assignments requiring the use of library resources in history class, language lab sessions in French. The major difference between field-based and classroom-based learning on this dimension of the transfer problem is that the practice in the latter changes in content over time: Students work on a given skill for only as long as it takes to master it, then move on to the next one. In some work sites, the demands of the task situation remain constant regardless of the degree of mastery. Think of the assembly line, where repetition reaches a point of diminishing returns. In some others, where the student-worker takes on new tasks as she masters previous ones, they lead to a more productive learning trajectory. Either way, the question remains: whether practice promotes transfer of learning either in the classroom or in the field. Some work skills are too specialized to transfer. For the student who set up the anesthesia cart for surgical procedures, practice probably did not generalize to her school work or even to other medical sites. In limited ways, some work-practiced skills *could* be said to transfer to school-based activities. Linda, in the curriculum firm, honed her proofreading skills through practice, and those might have been helpful in her proofing her own papers for class. But the principle of practice often differs between school and field in ways that make it less fruitful as a source of learning transfer.

Academic and experiential settings can be compared on other conditions of transfer. College teachers certainly utilize explicit abstraction as a pedagogical strategy that helps students carry knowledge and skill from one course to another. A student might encounter the concept of social construction, for example, in a course on the sociology of race, and then deploy it again in a class on women's literature in Latin America. A professor of introductory economics might stress the law of supply and demand, and then a student might discover its relevance in a course on marketing. The use of abstractions underlies much of the pedagogy in discipline-based departments, which structure their majors around the assumption that those concepts, especially when they are explicitly pointed out, integrate their students' learning across courses.

On the other hand, observations suggest that interns and service-learning students are less likely to produce explicit abstractions of the experiences, or to create new forms of representations of concepts and processes (Bailey et al., 2004). Sometimes a supervisor does point out categories of some phenomenon as a way of organizing the worker's practice. Heather's boss, for example, once told her in a private meeting that there were several kinds of school classes: the well-prepared and focused, the bored and listless, the wild and disorganized. This typology may have served the function of triggering different teaching strategies. It might also have alerted Heather to similar differences in other kinds of audiences in other kinds of settings, so she could render similar judgments—though certainly her supervisor did not mention generalizability as a feature of the idea. In general, though, the use of explicit abstractions appears less frequently in field settings than in college classrooms.

Similarly, active self-monitoring and deep reflection seem not to be common among interns, especially as a function of their firsthand work experience. We do not often see them stepping back to examine and critique their performance, beyond wondering "How'm I doing?" Without being prompted, they do not typically ask themselves how group dynamics work, or why certain values are taken for granted, or who holds onto the bulk of power in the organization. These issues are left unexamined in actual workplaces, unless human relations consultants have been brought in to fix problematic work groups. Instead, people tend to do the work, and not to reflect extensively on their process (except perhaps to gripe about bosses and colleagues). Moreover, students doing internships tend not to be terribly self-reflective about the work and their engagement with situated knowledge, but rather take much of it for granted, as unproblematic. Instead, they spend their psychic energy trying to figure out how to get along, get by, and get over, how to avoid looking stupid to their supervisors and colleagues.

Self-monitoring, however, seems to be a rarity in college classrooms, too. Although many scholars of teaching recommend it as a teaching-learning practice (Bain, 2004; Brookfield, 2005; McKeachie, 2002), it does not appear that many professors support it, much less insist on it. Focused more on the content of their disciplines—theory, method, logic, history—academics tend to be unaware of these processes themselves. As a result, students rarely acquire the habit of reflecting on their own learning. On this dimension of transfer, field and classroom appear to be similarly deficient. Similarly, mindfulness is not a condition that either setting seems to acknowledge or practice. As we will see in the next chapter, teachers can promote it—and thus enhance transfer of learning—but most often they do not. Certainly social dynamics in the workplace are not particularly conducive to mindfulness, either.

Finally, the condition of cultural compatibility poses some complex challenges for both field and classroom. For one thing, there are actually three perspectives from which this dimension of transfer can be understood. First, the learner herself "comes from" a culture, a family and community setting with particular worldviews, customs, and norms. Then, from an organizational perspective, the workplace and the school manifest their own traditions, relations, and expectations, their own distinct cultures. The compatibility criterion, then, is tough to meet. Even holding aside particularities of ethnicity, class, and gender, cultural styles vary across communities and organizations. For at least a generation, scholars have investigated the points of difference between students' home cultures and their academic cultures, tracing what happens when a student from a working-class or minority background attends a traditional school (cf. Brice Heath, 1991; Erickson, 2004). This process varies substantially with different details of cultural style, and it affects both academic and situated pedagogy. College teachers know more about cultural difference than they did 25 years ago. So do workplace supervisors. How and to what extent they utilize that knowledge to accommodate (utilize, celebrate, and manage) cultural diversity is another question—and the answers are as numerous as the situations. We have seen few teachers or bosses explicitly exercise cultural sensitivity as a pedagogical practice.

In any case, the pedagogical conditions that promote transfer of learning appear erratically at best in both college classrooms and field settings. If, as researchers suggest, transfer happens most effectively if and when learners use new knowledge in repeated and diverse ways, when they are encouraged to construct meaningful abstractions about and from that knowledge, when they engage in active self-monitoring, and when the cultural features of Situation A and Situation B not only are compatible, but somehow align with their own experiences, then neither context seems ideal. Practice as repeated performance happens in both, but in different ways: Some workers tend to do the same thing over and over (the assembly-line effect), while others move on fairly quickly; college teachers assign problem sets and other exercises designed to give students enough practice to master a skill or bit of knowledge before moving on to the next level. Abstractions are common in college classrooms, but they tend to be produced by the professor more than by the learner; they also exist in workplaces and community settings, but are generally formed in the service of productive activity. Self-monitoring is rare in both settings, and cultural compatibility is always a challenge. The conditions for transfer, as we will see in the next chapter, demand explicit attention and intention from both classroom and experiential educators: They happen when someone decides to set them in motion, not as a function of customary practice.

Conclusions

In general, then, the pedagogical features of experience-based learning, as analyzed through the framework proposed earlier in this book, differ from classroom-based pedagogies in some important ways, though they are similar in some ways as well. On the dimension of access, college students have an advantage: They are given easy access to the full range of knowledge used in a course. By registering, they become eligible to attend classes, participate in discussions, get the assigned readings, do all the required work, and meet with the professor or a teaching assistant; if they choose, they can even go beyond the expected work, and read beyond the syllabus. In work-based internships or co-op placements, on the other hand, access is limited by the intersection between the student's role and the production process, as well as by the distribution of power in the organization. That is, the student-worker's participation in the situated community of practice is partial, fragmented, whereas the classroom-based student's participation is as comprehensive as that of any other student in the course—at least if she chooses to take advantage of the available resources and activities. As we will see in the next chapter, this difference creates a challenge for the internship instructor or civic-engagement professor: to coordinate a partial engagement with a comprehensive learning plan.

Similarly, workplaces structure newcomers' exposure to knowledge-use in ways very different from classroom instructors. In school, the syllabus organizes students' engagement with information, theory, and modes of inquiry around a rational analysis of the sequence, based on principles like chronological order, thematic relations, and degrees of difficulty. At work, knowledge is more often encountered on an instrumental, need-to-know basis. The pedagogical logic of the syllabus privileges the learning process, whereas that of the workplace serves the production process. Here is another challenge for the experiential educator: to lay out information and ideas in class in ways that align with or anticipate the order in which the intern encounters related knowledge in the field.

Role structures in the two settings are different, as well. In school, there are basically two roles—teacher and student—and everyone knows how they are enacted, who has the power, where the knowledge comes from. In some courses, students collaborate on team projects or in study groups, but most commonly college students are solo actors, and are judged on the basis of their individual performance. At work, the variety of role structures is far greater: boss and worker, to be sure, but also worker-worker, worker-customer/client, project teams, communities of practice. The distribution and exercise of power take more complex forms at work, and the intern may or may not have opportunities to exercise initiative and control. The role differences are not in themselves a pedagogical challenge for the college-based experiential educator—every reasonably intelligent adult can handle variations in social structures across contexts—but they create complicated social relations between the school and the work site: Who determines what the learner will do, when, how; who supports learning processes, and who drives task performance?

The nature of motivation varies within both school and out-of-school settings, and certainly between them. The claim that learners are more strongly motivated in nonclassroom contexts because their work is more authentic seems to me to be true only to a limited extent. Certainly the field experience is more "real" in the sense of having practical (economic, political, even moral) consequences that "academic" work typically does not. (Notice the intriguing linguistic fact that, in one language game, "academic" is the opposite of "real.") When Heather did the artifacts cart in the museum, it mattered whether she did it well: Elementary school kids learned something, the museum's reputation was secured. If she did the same talk as a presentation in a history class at school, the quality of her performance would not make much of a difference—except to her individual grade. That sort of authenticity does motivate learning, but more because the task is meaningful than simply because it is real. Plenty of student-interns perform real tasks that they find boring, repetitive, and meaningless: Witness my students who managed samples closets in fashion-related businesses. The authenticity of out-of-school work presents both a challenge and an opportunity for the experiential educator, which we will explore more fully in the next chapter.

Nor is the dimension of control as straightforward as some advocates of experiential learning claim (Sweitzer & King, 2004). If, as Ryan and Deci (2006) argue, people learn more easily in conditions of autonomy, the question becomes whether field-based experience tends toward autonomy or heteronomy—and, once again, the evidence is mixed. On the whole, classroom learning is heteronomous: The teacher controls the definition about what is to be learned, and the social processes by which it will be learned. But the situation is often not significantly different in the work arena, where the social organization of knowledge use is typically not in the hands of the individual intern. Some work groups do exhibit weak framing (Bernstein, 1975), giving the student opportunities for controlling her own access to and use of knowledge. But more often, the range of discretion is limited. The challenge—and opportunity—for the experiential educator may be to find ways to enable students to exercise some degree of control in their work and learning even when their external roles are shaped by the production organization, the service activity, or the community players.

The structuring of reflection as part of the learning experience in school depends on one or more of several processes. The instructor might describe, recommend, or require certain kinds of deep, transformational investigations of information, ideas, theories, and methods of inquiry; the college might build an iterative reflection process into the students' curricula, as Alverno College has done; or the individual student might, for whatever reason, take on that task. Typically, however, deep reflection—going beyond the normal abstractions and theorizing done in a college course—seems not to occur very much. Similarly, although field-based work processes often include various forms of processing (as described in the previous chapter), what happens most often entails feedback and assessment, and less often reconstrual of the problem space, reconsideration of the knowledge domain, or reconstruction of the self. That is, the normal pedagogical practices of neither college teaching nor situated work or service involve deep reflection. It happens on occasion, but not often.

Finally, the social conditions that promote transfer of learning appear only sporadically in either school or field. Frequent and repetitive practice does occur in both, but usually in different ways. College professors often ask their students to rehearse certain skills, procedures, and knowledge bases through devices like problem sets and reading responses. Those exercises change systematically in content as the class moves through the syllabus. Done at the right pace, this strategy does encourage transfer. In the field, practice is sometimes like assembly-line work: The intern repeats the task—setting up the materials for veterinary procedures, for example—over and over, and the learning curve flattens out. And sometimes the practicing shifts in content as the student gains competence. Active self-monitoring, like reflection, is relatively rare in both contexts, as is mindfulness. And cultural compatibility is a challenge on both fronts.

In general, then, the pedagogical features of college classrooms are rather different from those of work and service settings—but not in a way that would be likely to confuse or distract the student. The variations occur as much within environment types as between them. The challenges and opportunities for experiential educators center on devising moments for students to make sense of and interrogate their experience in ways that highlight the possible synergies between the two knowledge domains that they are operating in. We will explore some of the methods those teachers use, and the issues those methods raise, in the next chapter.

CHAPTER 7

Experiential Pedagogies in School

Interns come back to college from their field experiences—sometimes frequently, sometimes sporadically, sometimes only when they have completed the work—and their teachers have to decide what to do with them in order to guide, enhance, and monitor their learning. This chapter investigates and critiques the pedagogical practices that flow from those decisions. It represents not an empirical test of the outcomes of the teaching methods—I am not claiming to "prove" that experiential learning "works"—but a conceptual analysis of existing practices, a consideration of the issues they face, and a framework for thinking about alternatives. The basic questions addressed here are: What are experiential educators doing to try to squeeze more learning out of students' situated work and service activities, and what are the challenges and opportunities they encounter in that effort?

Drawing on previous chapters, this one will first outline the general issues that arise in experiential programs in colleges. Then it will examine some of the pedagogical devices used by experiential educators in the academy: the learning contract, the journal, the concurrent seminar, and the final paper. Using descriptions from our research projects and from contemporary websites, the critique will poke inside the practices in order to see where and how they grapple with the core issues. It turns out, as it often does, that in understanding the impact of these methods the devil is in the details; rhetorical claims about those matters reveal less than the particularities of experience. Finally, I will propose a scheme for considering the choices available to instructors, advisors, and administrators when they design such programs.

The reader will notice that this chapter again focuses more on work-based experiential learning programs (internships, cooperative education, etc.) than on service-learning, civic engagement, or adventure/outdoor programs, though these will receive some attention. The latter formats are hybrids, with one foot in the academy and one foot in the field. School-based educators have a greater range of control over the outside experience than internship coordinators do, for example: They often have ongoing partnerships with the field sites; they themselves often participate in the field activities; they often design those activities themselves, in collaboration with community-based actors. But they have less control over students' actual experience than classroom teachers do in their realm. Another reason I concentrate less on these civic-engagement formats is that the research and professional literatures on them are vastly more substantial than those on work-related internships (cf. Butin, 2010; Eyler & Giles, 1999; Jacoby, 2009; Sheffield, 2011), so more remains to be said about the latter. Still, many of the same issues arise in both categories of experiential programs, although the civic-engagement forms tend to handle them more effectively—or at least those practitioners think about the issues more rigorously. On occasion, then, this chapter will refer to service-learning projects as well as internships, but the work-related pedagogies will be our primary focus.

Pedagogical Issues

The issues raised by the problematic relationship between experiential learning and academic learning appeared in earlier sections of this discussion, but I want to reiterate them briefly before diving into the description of experiential pedagogies in the university. The first category of challenges stems from the *content* differences between the knowledge-use in the field and in the classroom. Even when the relevant concepts look similar, their meanings typically diverge. Take gentrification as an example. In college classes and in the disciplinary literature in, say, sociology, that term refers to an abstract, historical, generalized, collective social process. It might be defined in terms of certain kinds of demographic changes in a neighborhood over time, and might be tracked through statistics on (for example) median household income, average rents, and ethnic distributions. By contrast, in the community, the word might denote a concrete, political, personal experience understood, for example, through a boy's losing his best friend because the family had to move, or the disappearance of a local hardware store. Moreover, community activists treat gentrification as a problem about which they want to do something, not just a phenomenon that they want to understand. They think about the problem differently from the academics: define it differently, apply different logics to it, and act on it with different strategies and methods. And the concept of gentrification probably straddles the experiential and the academic more than most ideas.

The challenge to the experiential educator is thus to find and productively explore the empirical, conceptual, and theoretical relationships across those discursive domains.

Similarly, we have seen that the *modes of thought* employed in field settings are different from those in the classroom. The latter entail a propositional style—abstract, universal, decontextualized—whereas the former use the actional mode: concrete, particular, context-bound (Bruner, 1996b). Facility in one of those cognitive styles does not necessarily imply facility with the other (Lave, 1988; Olson & Torrance, 1996; Sternberg & Wagner, 1986). So the challenge for the school-based experiential educator is twofold: to become familiar with and to acknowledge the legitimacy of a mode of thought usually considered strange and inferior by mainstream academics, and to help her students translate between the two discourses.

A third category of issues centers on *curriculum structure*: not only the conceptual maps of the field and the classroom, but also the ordering of knowledge encounters in the two arenas. Where the conventional course syllabus in college lays out the material and the activities in a sequence according to a rational analysis of the knowledge domain and of learning processes, the natural curriculum of the workplace takes its shape more from the requirements of the production process. As a result, constructing a plan for a college course with an experiential component poses a significant challenge. Even the most carefully chosen field placement will rarely align neatly with the syllabus. Many internship courses, for example, build in a unit on ethical issues—but what happens when a student runs into a moral dilemma three weeks before that unit is scheduled? In a course on poverty, suppose the instructor has dedicated the first month of classroom discussion to the economic conditions of the poor, but a student comes back from a homeless shelter the second week asking, "Why don't they just get a job?" What then? The unpredictable and uncontrollable sequence of student experiences demands greater flexibility and agility than college professors typically need to muster.

Moreover, the curriculum structure of field experience, as we have seen, often exposes interns to only a partial range of knowledge-use: The student in the veterinary clinic learns about the anatomy of a cat's tail, but not much about the rest of feline physiology; the fashion magazine intern learns about generating story ideas, but not about marketing or circulation. The School-to-Work Opportunities Act of 1994 set a goal of helping students learn "all about an industry"—but internship experiences almost never meet that standard (Bailey et al., 2004). In any case, the fragmentary quality of the situated curriculum poses a challenge to the college teacher: to fill in the gaps in a way that is compatible with the course or the major.

Fourth, school-based educators have to accommodate the different *pedagogical* features of students' field experiences: their relationships with supervisors and colleagues, their organizational cultures, their engagement with power dynamics. When a student accustomed to taking orders from his supervisor in the workplace is asked back at school to invent a research question related to that setting, he may have to shake off the more docile mentality and recover agency. Conversely, a student working in a relatively wide-open placement may have trouble adjusting to a carefully and minutely planned syllabus. The fact that the social organization of knowledge-use is different in the two domains clearly poses a challenge for the college-based instructor.

Another pedagogical issue for experiential educators is *reflection*: Does reflecting deeply on an experience inevitably deepen the learning that one extracts from it? What sorts of reflection produce the broadest learning? Conversely, can the school-based professor ever simply take a laissez-faire attitude and allow the experience to speak for itself? Earlier we met an intern at a community newspaper who reported and wrote a piece on department-store Santas; we saw that she got excellent coaching from her editor. Should the classroom instructor elaborate on that process, or leave it alone? Clearly there are other situated experiences that cry out for reflection—we met a student at an airport hotel who found himself caught up in prickly labor-management relations, and had no one to talk with about his quandary—but what are the terms in which that reflection could proceed? Suppose the student is in a concurrent seminar. How much time should be spent talking about this particular situation, and how might the other members of the class be engaged? These are nagging pedagogical challenges.

Transfer of learning poses yet another issue for the educator. Given the conditions that researchers have discovered foster the translation of knowledge from one setting to another (Mestre, 2005; Perkins & Salomon, 1992), how can classroom teachers deploy those processes so that the situated learning will not be completely parochial, useless outside the context of its appearance? Especially in a classroom setting where students are interning in a variety of organizations, the translation problem is a major one for teachers. Without solving it, the school-based practice of experiential education becomes an exercise in futility.

On the level of the individual student, *motivation* represents another fundamental challenge. If, as scholars have long argued (Bransford et al., 2000; Illeris, 2006; Thorndike & Woodworth, 1901), learning does not occur unless the person is somehow motivated—whether intrinsically or extrinsically—to put in the necessary effort and time, how does an educator arouse that energy when the student comes back to school? In my own experience, students doing internships related to their career interests often resist and resent attempts to engage them in rigorous analysis of their activities and settings. They regard the work site as one domain, and school as another, and do not quickly see the personal value of straddling the two. So a question that must be put to experiential pedagogy is how motivation is generated and used to mobilize learning.

Finally, there is what might be called the *politics* question in experiential education. Any pedagogy, whether experiential or otherwise, and whether the teacher selects it consciously or not, inevitably embodies a set of values, beliefs, and political positions, and implies a set of practices that both reflect and shape power relations among members of society (cf. Giroux, 1984, 2011; Kincheloe, 2008). At least in part, this political stance relates to the goals the educator has for her students, for her school, and for society at large; it speaks to the question of who should know what, and how they should learn it (Apple, 2004). I have argued elsewhere (Moore, 2010) that the range of choices made by experiential educators can be usefully (if simplistically) described as falling into three general categories, from conservative to liberal to radical. These categories correspond roughly to several different organizational forms of experiential learning programs, from cooperative education to internships to service-learning and civic engagement. More recently, Sheffield (2011) made a similar argument about models of service-learning, portraying them as located on a spectrum from weak to strong, depending on how explicitly they engage students in critique. As we review the techniques that experiential educators actually and potentially use with students, we will explore the question of the political implications of their strategies.

Current Pedagogical Practices

This section investigates the properties of some of the major pedagogical devices commonly used by college-based experiential educators and analyzes them in terms of the issues just raised. These practices range from the preparation for the placement (the match and the contract) through the things teachers do during the term (journals, concurrent seminars) to the end-products (final papers). Many variations on and alternatives to these models exist in specific colleges. These descriptions are meant only to suggest broad possibilities, to demonstrate the complexities of trying to help students learn from firsthand experience in the world of work or service. Things are never quite so simple as either advocates or opponents of these programs suggest.

The Placement and the Learning Contract

The procedures for connecting a student with a specific site vary widely across programs in terms of faculty involvement, the intentionality of finding a match (indeed, in conceptions of what constitutes a match), and the application process. Many schools, especially but not only those that do not offer credit for the internship, rely entirely on the student's choice: She can apply wherever she wants, for whatever reasons. At Delaware Valley College in Pennsylvania, for example, students are required to complete 500 hours of work in an organization in their major field—animal husbandry, criminal justice, English—but anything that seems to fall within those broad terms is acceptable (Delaware Valley College, 2012). Departments in some colleges maintain a limited list of sites with whom they have developed an ongoing relationship—what is often called a partnership (Kelshaw et al., 2009; Maurrasse, 2001)—and ask students to choose among them. Instructors who require field-based work as a component of a course, especially a civic-engagement offering, may also maintain a short list of appropriate settings somehow compatible with the goals of the syllabus. In other programs, like my own at NYU, an internship director maintains a database of internship sites, organized roughly around broad terms like media, government, business, and the arts, and encourages students to search for suitable placements and then to contact a site themselves. The choice of sites, that is, varies from prescribed through loosely directed to completely open to the student.

The rhetoric of the match—the goodness of fit between the student and the site—sometimes appears in the literature on experiential learning (Kendall et al., 1986; Sweitzer & King, 2004), but there is no clear consensus on the dimensions on which the match can and should be achieved. Many practitioners buy into the claim that the most successful internships happen when the student's interests and learning styles align closely with the work content and organizational style of the placement site. Of course, that makes sense—provided that one prefers that the student stay inside her comfort zone. A student accustomed to contacts with strangers may be comfortable making cold calls to potential clients; a student who has done lots of public speaking may be fine with doing presentations in department meetings. The issue of content is more or less complex, depending on how narrowly one defines the student's interests and the organization's work. A student majoring in criminology may be intrigued by participating in restorative justice mediations, but not in filing records in the back office of a public defenders agency. In any event, the match has many dimensions, not all of which can be realized in any given case, not all of which are clear or consensual, and not all of which necessarily guarantee better learning. Here is a challenging thought experiment: If one wanted to create a computer-based matching system for prospective interns based on the methods used by internet dating services, what questions would one ask of the two parties? What would be the variables on which one would base a recommendation for a placement? In any case, some experiential educators do not appear to spend a great deal of energy on ensuring the depth and breadth of the matches their students make.

On the other hand, educators do often spend time encouraging students to think carefully and extensively before the fact about the nature of the experience they are about to have: about their goals, their prospective activities, their relationships with supervisors and colleagues, and so on. Frequently, these deliberations are recorded in a *learning contract*, a document that specifies what the student-intern will be doing in the site, what she hopes to learn, and the connections between them. The detailed terms of these contracts vary substantially across schools, across departments, even across courses within departments, but they tend to display certain general features. Typically, the student negotiates the contract with both her field supervisor and her academic instructor or adviser, and all three parties sign off on the document. The contract process occurs either before the internship begins or during the first week or two of the semester, on the premise that thinking through her goals and expectations up front will create a baseline against which she can reflect on and analyze the experience as it unfolds and when it concludes. The degree to which the student is held to the agreement varies widely across programs: Sometimes she is expected to demonstrate that she has in fact done the things she claimed she would do and learned the things she claimed she would learn; sometimes she is not, and the contract functions not so much as an accountability device as a reflection (and, if I may, a *pre*flection) tool.

A specific example will demonstrate the nature of the learning contract, and provide a foundation for discussing some of the pedagogical issues attached to this phase of the process. The Economics, Accounting, and Business Administration department of a small private college in the Midwest (which, like others in this section, will remain unnamed) has student-interns fill out a three-part form and get it signed by the site supervisor and the internship coordinator. The cover sheet is a legal-looking document with formal statements from each of the three parties; for instance, the site supervisor attests that

I have discussed this internship with the student and the Internship Coordinator. I agree to provide the Intern with an orientation to relevant organizational arrangements, procedures and functions. I agree to assign work to the Intern that supports the spirit and purpose of this Learning Contract. I agree to meet with the Intern regularly and make myself available for counsel and advice.

The student and the internship coordinator likewise agree to the terms of the contract, accepting the obligations to do certain things. The remainder of the document is divided into two parts: Part 1, "Job/Position Data & Description," asks for the work schedule, the job title, the salary, and, in an open-ended section, a "description of expected job duties and assignments"; Part 2, called the "Learning Agenda," is a page-size chart with three columns headed as follows:

- Learning Objectives (What do I intend to learn?)
- Strategies (What will I do/how will I learn it?)
- Evaluation Methods (How will I know if I've achieved it?)

These three elements appear in one configuration or another in most colleges' internship contracts, and in fact represent best practices in the field (cf. Qualters, 2010; Sweitzer & King, 2004); moreover, they align nicely with the establish-accomplish-process framework developed earlier. Interestingly, the departmental document from this particular school includes an extra page that provides some examples of learning-objective statements in an effort to clarify the level at which those declarations should be made:

Internship goals or objectives usually describe what you (the Intern) intends to learn during the course of the Internship. Be specific...and bold. Do you want to improve or develop skills, expand knowledge of a specific field or topic, apply or test a particular body of knowledge? Are you interested in validating a career interest and your own suitability for that career? Set specific goals focused on knowledge, skills and abilities; personal/professional development; and career exploration. Add other categories you feel are relevant. Include objectives that will "stretch" your thinking, such as: *Learn more about how (Operations Management) fits into/supports the organization's overall strategic operations. *Become more familiar with the role of Public Accountants and what it's like to be part of a Public Accounting firm. *Identify, apply, and evaluate specific leadership and management tools/techniques in interpersonal experiences.

The guidelines related to Strategies suggest that the student "describe specific actions, processes, and work assignments that will allow you to achieve each objective," including training sessions, performing specific tasks or projects, reading particular texts, and analyzing the organization. And the Evaluation section asks for "deliverables"—final reports, briefings, PowerPoint presentations—and the supervisor's expectations for each.

Now, this form strikes me as perfectly reasonable and productive as a tool for promoting learning in the internship process. But notice that it relies on several important—and contestable—assumptions. First, there is an implicit claim that the learning contract functions in the same way as a course syllabus: It specifies the learning goals and the activities through which students will achieve those goals. To be sure, one might question whether the syllabus in fact identifies the things students will learn in a course, but let us assume for the sake of argument that it does; at the least, it describes in broad terms the activities students will engage in: listening to lectures, doing readings, taking tests. But does the learning contract function in the same way? To the extent that the supervisor and the student can articulate the constituents of the intern's role in the organization—the things she will actually do—the contract does fulfill the basic purpose of the syllabus.

But from experience, we know that students often do things not anticipated in the contract, and do *not* do some activities specified in advance. That is, the details of the actual experience are far more variable and unpredictable—and, conversely, sometimes more repetitive and mundane—than they are in the classroom, where the instructor at least has (some) control over the general activities. Sometimes, as a consequence of an intern's particular interests and initiative, the learning activities go far beyond the expected, agreed-upon forms. In the city councilmember's office where Conrad created a bill-tracking system, his learning contract stipulated that his duties would be confined to answering the phone and handling constituent complaints; the expansion of his role in the office was a surprise to him, to his supervisor, and to the internship coordinator back at school. The work can also fall short of the agreement. In the curriculum development firm, Linda's learning contract had specified that she would perform some editing and writing functions—but for reasons too complex to outline here, she did not. Those developments do not obviate the value of the learning contract, of course—both students might have learned things by speculating in advance about what they might be doing, even if their predictions were inaccurate—but these stories do reveal one of the pedagogical challenges of experiential learning: operating in a realm that is far less controllable, far less predictable, and far less attentive to the learning needs of the student than the classroom is.

Another assumption embedded in the learning contract as a pedagogical device is that what I have called preflection is an educationally valuable process in its own right, that thinking in advance about what one is getting into enriches one's understanding and deepens one's learning. Now, again, that assumption may be correct—in fact, I believe it enough to use it with my own interns. But clearly, it does not always do what we hope it will. First, the terms in which students—and even site supervisors—articulate their learning goals and activities tend to be somewhat vague (the cautions against that style notwithstanding), or at least general. Take one listed above in the Economics program: "Learn more about how (Operations Management) fits into/supports the organization's overall strategic operations." That goal presumes and leaves unstated a number of conceptual tools that would help one learn how Operations Management fits into general corporate practices—indeed, it assumes that the student can easily distinguish Operations Management as a constituent of the organization, and strategic operations from other operations. Of course, the student may in fact have been taught those concepts in business administration classes. And perhaps the concepts as she learned them in school actually describe what happens in the specific organization where she works. But perhaps not.

Indeed, one of the putative values of experiential education resides in the difference between school-based knowledge and knowledge engaged in practice situations. When we move beyond the rhetoric of application— the claim that theories and skills acquired in the classroom map neatly and effectively onto real-world activities—we quickly discover that different organizations do things in different ways even when they use similar terminology for them. In any case, thinking about these issues in advance may help, or it may not. If the terms are vague and represent only the student's first untutored and unexamined impressions of what goes on in the internship site, if she tosses the words into the contract more or less arbitrarily, whimsically, or carelessly in order to satisfy the requirement, then the learning impact will be minimal—or even, in the cases where the terms close the intern off to experiencing and understanding the realities in more responsive and nuanced terms, negative.

Having read quite a few learning contract forms on college websites, I can say that the prompts they provide—like the ones above—point students in certain directions where they might not otherwise go. Thinking about these matters in advance, even in relatively simple terms, might serve to activate certain thinking processes, to alert the student to certain possibilities, to start the construction of a conceptual framework that can be amended and enlarged over time as the experience unfolds. Educationally, that process is likely to be positive. On the other hand, many of these prompts, to my eye, lack substance and rigor, and make assumptions of uniformity and predictability that turn out to be fallacious.

Another issue in the construction of learning contracts lies in the terminology typically used to describe goals. As we have seen, terms like "knowledge" and "skill," while used widely in the field, are contested in the literature in ways that challenge their use in this context. At the Second Annual Research Institute on the Future of Community Engagement in Higher Education (held at Boston University in June 2011), a panel of educators discussed the question of "core elements and core knowledge for the community engagement field." They began by asking, what does it mean to be a graduate of a service-learning or civic-engagement program? What common learning can we expect? The model they used for answering those questions was based on surveys of employers who were asked what "knowledge and skills" they expected of recent graduates applying for jobs. The answers (elaborated in a committee report at the 2012 version of the conference) were things like oral and written communications skills, critical thinking and problem-solving, the ability to apply knowledge (presumably gained in school) to real-world problems, teamwork, innovative spirit, and so on. Now, again, these terms constitute a perfectly reasonable form of discourse about the possible outcomes of an experiential learning program—but they also tend to treat knowledge and skills as discrete units of individual capacity, as things carried around in heads and bodies, rather than as modes of participation in situated activities. As such, the core competencies project may misrepresent the actual nature of experience-based learning, and project the responsibility for "outcomes" onto individuals.

Nonetheless, it does make sense, to my way of thinking, to articulate in advance, to the highest degree of specificity possible, and in tentative terms that will later be interrogated, the ways in which an intern will take part in certain kinds of activity with certain kinds of knowledge-use patterns. I believe that the Strategies section of the small-college learning contract described above works toward that goal. It asks, "Given these learning goals, what will I do that will enable me to achieve them?" Breaking down the goals into discrete skills and units strikes me as potentially misleading, in that it predicts what the student will carry from the experience in her head—and we can't really know that. But we *can* say how the intern will participate (e.g., as observer, as helper, as performer; as information retriever, as decision-maker, as order-taker) in certain kinds of knowledge-based activities. Thinking about that question in advance may well bear fruit.

Note another curious feature of this pedagogical strategy: It is virtually unknown in classroom-based learning enterprises. Many professors ask their students why they enrolled in a course ("Let's go around the circle; tell us your name, your major, and your reasons for being here"), and some even modify their syllabi a bit to accommodate trends. But it is rare—even in nontraditional colleges like my own—to give students the opportunity to decide for themselves what they want to learn from a class; that power resides primarily with the instructor. Imagine, by contrast, two students working at the history museum: They could conceivably settle on very different learning goals (understanding how little kids interact in groups, building public speaking skills, acquiring information about the history of the state), very different activities (leading tours, writing curriculum plans, consulting with curators on the design of exhibits), very different relationships with their supervisors and colleagues. To be sure, two students in the same college class can put different amounts of work into it, can focus on different elements of the syllabus, and can learn different things from it. But the range of variation in an internship is qualitatively greater, and that fact presents a pedagogical challenge: how to ensure that the student's learning benefits from the construction of the learning contract. It is not easy to do that when neither the student nor the faculty coordinator has deep knowledge of the internship site at the beginning of the semester; it is not easy to do that when the experience itself may unfold in ways unpredictable at the outset.

Still, as a teaching device the learning contract probably pays certain educational dividends. It finesses some questions about the content and structure of the curriculum, using concepts that ignore or understate the discursive differences between field and classroom. It assumes too much about the possibilities of learning transfer. And it tends to ignore politics and power. But it does make students think about their prospective experiences in ways they might otherwise avoid; it draws their attention to aspects of their work they might otherwise ignore, and thereby sets up at least some of the conditions for later transfer of learning.

The Journal

The second common teaching device used by experiential educators is the journal: The student writes regular descriptions of the internship experience, and reflects on them in some way and to some extent. As with the learning contract, the journal takes many different forms across schools and programs. In some, the exercise is wide open to the student's choice of style and content. It may end up being essentially a log, a record of what the student did during the field work: "On Tuesday, I straightened up the samples in the storage room, delivered samples to three clients, and helped prepare press kits for the show." This mode of journaling constitutes not so much reflection as documentation.

More typical is a form that starts with a more or less specific description of work activities, but then adds some reactions that might be about feelings, about careers, about general issues—but without systematic or rigorous analysis. Often the instructor gives vague and open-ended instructions: "Just tell me what you did and how you felt about it." Here is an example of a nondirected journal entry from a student (unidentified here) at a midwestern state college who was finishing an internship as a sports trainer assistant with a professional athletic team:

> When I left for [the team's hometown], I really had no idea what I was getting myself into. I had an idea of how lucky I was to be getting this opportunity, but that was all I had, an idea. I knew what I wanted to get out of the internship, but I did not know how to get that from the [team] . . . What the [team] needed from me was someone to do all the things the staff athletic trainers did not want nor have time to do, such as inventory, carrying Gatorade, setting up before practice, breaking down the trainers' area after practice, simple rehabilitation with the athletes, and comedic relief. I did all of those things the best and fastest way I knew how and I've come away with a great reference and an even greater appreciation for naps. What I wanted from the [team] was simple: a good reference. What I got was much more. I learned that although [the work is] prestigious, I do not want to work in the [league], ever. The players were nice enough and being on the sidelines for the games was surreal, but overall I don't think I would enjoy the job. The hours the staff trainers, and interns, put in are crazy, but that is only a small part of my disdain for the job. I can't swallow my pride enough to be successful. The trainers do not have the option of being respectful towards the players; they have to be. The players are only respectful if it suits them . . . Overall, I'm glad I went because I now know what I don't want to do once I grow up and leave college, which is almost as important as knowing what I do want to do.

Now, quoting this journal entry at length is in some respects unfair: Critiquing it is like shooting fish in a barrel. All four of the entries from this student's summer internship displayed the same tone and basic content: superficial reports of activities, emotional reactions, little analysis, but considerable humor. In fact, this journal represents a major genre of the form: the undirected reaction paper. Without guiding questions or probes, without substantive requirements for ways of presenting observations and reflections, the journal begins to look like a postcard home: "Having a great time, wish you were here!"

Ironically, and instructively for our purposes, this student actually touches on some intriguing issues that might have rewarded closer scrutiny.

The status distinction between professional athletes and their staff trainers, for instance, raises questions about organizational dynamics, power, and interactional styles. One could use Goffman's (1959) famous dramaturgical metaphor to examine the various ways the respective actors in the football locker room presented coherent and productive selves, and adjusted their performances to those of others in different statuses. But, as in many undirected journals, the moment slipped away.

Other programs and courses provide more extensive guidance for students as they work on their journals: They raise questions, call attention to certain issues, and ask for certain kinds of observations and interviews. I want to quote at length from the journal instructions provided by a program at a large southwestern university, because they suggest many of the features of this model. The document begins with an overview of the functions of the journal:

> A daily journal is a useful way of keeping track of what a student is learning during the internship. A daily journal provides an intern the opportunity to think about experiences and to record what he or she experiences and feels. To be most effective, the journal should not be merely a log of events. It should be a means to analyze or reflect on the activities the intern performs and the new information and ideas the intern acquires. In addition, it helps the intern to recognize important events and to relate his/her stated objectives to what he/she perceives he/she is learning and doing.

The document goes on to give more explicit and extensive instructions, organized around several substantive categories. I will quote only a few of them:

> Record something in your journal each day you work. Be sure to date each entry. Write at least several sentences each day. Use the following questions to help you decide what information to include in your journal entries…
> 2. The Organizational Setting
>   • What is the organizational structure? Who are the leaders? Who makes things happen?
>   • Who are the clients/customers of the organization?
>   • What is the work atmosphere at your site? How are decisions made? Is it a cooperative or competitive atmosphere? Is there a lot of group work, or do people work by themselves?
> 3. Journal entries
>   • What did you do/observe at your internship site?

- What new skills or knowledge have you learned since beginning the internship? How might these new skills or knowledge help you in future job searches?
- How would you describe a typical day at your site? . . .
- How have your duties changed since you first started? . . .
- Are there new terms that you encountered during your internship? (Write new terms and their definitions.)

These directions are not exactly rigorous or based on subtle, complex theories of organizational behavior and experience, but they do draw the student's attention to particular aspects of the internship process. They rely on some commonsense concepts, such as skills and knowledge, that I earlier suggested are problematic in some ways—but at least they raise useful questions.

Some instructors and coordinators go even further in structuring the journal-writing process. Sweitzer and King (2004, p. 12) review some of those methods:

- *Key Phrase* journals are those in which you are asked to identify certain key terms or phrases as you see them in your daily experience.
- *Double Entry* journals are divided into two columns. In one column you record what is happening and your reactions to it. In the other you record any ideas and concepts from classes or readings that pertain to what you have seen and experienced.
- In *Critical Incident* journals, you identify one incident that stands out over the course of a day, or a week, and write about it in some depth.

They also point to several processing techniques that enable students to examine their experiences more rigorously:

- The *Three-Column Processing* model developed by Weinstein (1981) asks the student to describe and analyze specific events in three parts: first, a bare-facts description of what happened; second, a statement of what the student was thinking when the event occurred; finally, a discussion of what she was feeling at the time.
- The *Integrative Processing* model designed by Kiser (2000) includes six steps: gathering objective data from concrete experience; reflecting on those data; identifying relevant theory and knowledge; examining dissonance; articulating learning; developing a plan. Kiser's scheme, although Sweitzer and King do not point this out, draws on Kolb's (1984) experiential learning cycle. Especially in the elements of

identifying theory and examining the dissonance between it and the experience, the device seems quite productive.

- *Process Recording*, a narrative-analytical technique widely used in social work, can be adapted to all sorts of settings. It can include such components as names and locations of participants; date, location, and length of session; purposes and goals; descriptions of actions; techniques, skills, and roles used; plans for future, etc. (Sweitzer & King 2004, pp. 12–15)

Some internship instructors, especially those with training in anthropology, ask their students to regard the journal as a form of ethnographic field notes. Drawing on approaches to that practice designed by such scholars as Schatzman and Strauss (1972) or Stake (2010), these instructors maintain that studying human experience—even one's own experience—yields greater insight when it acknowledges and analyzes the cultural context within which people operate, even in settings as limited as a single workplace. So, for instance, Schatzman and Strauss describe a three-part method of taking notes on situated activity:

- *Observational Notes* (ON) record the concrete activities in as much detail as possible: "He said...She said...They bent over the computer and adjusted the details of the organization chart."; I describe these observations as "verbal videotape."
- *Theoretical Notes* (TN) offer first-cut interpretations of the observations, raising issues and tentative explanations as the notes emerge: "The two of them seemed to be struggling over power, over the ability to control the other."
- *Methodological Notes* (MN) remind the writer-intern to do something or collect some particular information: "Interview X about that conversation, and find out what she thought was going on...Get a copy of the Annual Report." (Schatzman and Strauss 1972)

As the notes accumulate, and themes emerge in the TNs, the student-ethnographer can write *Analytic Memos* (AMs) developing her thoughts on an issue (e.g., gender politics in the workplace) more fully and rigorously, relating them to theories and readings. Ideally, these memos contribute to a final paper that goes far beyond description and emotional reaction, and proposes interpretations of the experience based on theory and systematic inquiry (cf. George, 2012).

To be sure, this journal-as-self-ethnography method takes more time, effort, and background understanding on the part of the students, and is therefore limited in its feasibility. But if they accept the challenge, their journals can generate considerable learning beyond the experience itself, and can connect that learning to ideas and concepts addressed in college courses and majors.

The journal is thus a pedagogical device that takes varied forms and yields varied results across programs and courses. It also faces some of the same issues mentioned in relation to the learning contract—but in spades. First, it assumes the educational value of reflection; it treats the experience itself and the learning it produces as somehow inadequate, incomplete. One might argue that that assumption is incorrect, that in fact the "mere" experience—leading the tours at the history museum, helping a veterinarian spay a cat, interviewing a department-store Santa Claus for a community newspaper—contains enough inherent learning to be justified as an element of a school-based program. But I will counterargue that (a) such experience tends to be partial, unsystematic, and particular, and (b) reflection on it can generate new insight and knowledge that will inform further experience— precisely the goal Dewey (1938) aimed at. Moreover, guided reflection can produce the preconditions for significant transfer of learning by calling the student's attention to certain generalizable ideas and issues.

A second challenge is that the journal, done right, imposes significant demands on both the student-intern and the instructor. It takes considerable time to write the notes if they are to be useful, to go beyond the cursory observations and reflections one often sees. Students often resist that effort, and believe that their energy is better spent on doing the work in the field site rather than processing it after the fact. They tend to adopt a silo-like separation of their field-based and school-based activities, regarding themselves as workers rather than as students when they engage in internship activities—and journal-writing often strikes them as an academic imposition with little obvious payoff on the job. What is more, the journal process demands significant time on the part of the instructor: reading them, at the very least, but preferably also commenting on them in writing.

That issue raises another: the faculty person's sense of (in)competence in responding to the journal. Frequently, my own colleagues, after reading journal notes from an advisee, complain that they simply don't know what to say in response. Trained in comparative literature or African history or environmental science, they argue that they have no business commenting on their students' descriptions of field-based experience: "What do I know about working for a fashion magazine?" The typical faculty member sees her competence in the domain of her disciplinary background, and assumes that she needs specialized knowledge to interpret and critique a student's experience in a different field. This challenge manifests strongly in the practice of the journal.

Finally, the modes of thought problem rears its ugly head here. Earlier, I cited Jerome Bruner's (1996b) persuasive argument that people think differently in different situations, using varieties of thought he called the actional, the narrative, the propositional. Bent Flyvbjerg (2001) notes Aristotle's three forms of intellectual virtue—*epistemé*, *techné*, and *phronesis*—and maintains that the university tends to privilege the first in liberal arts courses and the second in professional courses—generally omitting consideration of the ethical and social implications of activity. In *The Ends of Philosophy* (2002), Lawrence Cahoone distinguishes three different models of doing philosophy: as *inquiry* (the search for epistemic truth, based on intellectual and logical criteria); as *praxis* (the attempt to improve the world, based largely on social criteria); and as *poesis* (the creation of a mode of experience, with largely esthetic criteria). All three models lead to an important observation about the pedagogical practices of experiential education: We are trying to get students (and ourselves, for that matter) to think across styles, to generate forms of knowledge that answer to different standards. There is a question about whether these forms of thought are commensurable, about whether it is in fact possible to think and learn in ways that connect those modes, styles, or domains. If, as theorists we met in chapter 2 argue, all knowledge is situated, and if, as Perkins and Salomon (1992) assert, transfer of knowledge occurs only (or at least most reliably) under certain specifiable conditions, the question is whether the journaling process transcends that situatedness and meets those transfer conditions. Once again, my admittedly frustrating answer is: It depends. If the journal simply describes events and personal reactions to them, or deals in vague, unexamined assertions, then it is probably less than helpful. If, on the other hand, it pushes across diverse modes of thought, if it makes explicit connections between theory and practice, then it can contribute not only to the transfer of learning but to the construction of new knowledge.

The Concurrent Seminar

At the opposite end of the pedagogical spectrum from the sink-or-swim, laissez-faire model of experiential education stands the concurrent seminar, of which I will discuss two types: a classroom-based course that students take specifically to process an individual internship as it happens; and a service-learning course, like the PAR project on gentrification mentioned earlier, in which groups of students collaborate (under the instructor's guidance) on a community-based service activity. In a (very) few colleges, they also take a pre-field seminar, a course preparing them for the experiential learning process. Cornell's College of Human Ecology used to have a Field

Study Program in which students did full-semester internships either in the Ithaca region or in New York City; all of them were required to take the pre-field course where they read up on some of the issues they would be working on (housing, economic development, youth), practiced research methods such as ethnographic observations and interviewing, and examined their own styles of learning and interaction (e.g., by taking the Kolb Learning Styles Inventory and the Myers-Briggs Type Indicator) (Borzak, 1981). Northeastern University's cooperative education program also requires a pre-field preparation course, but focuses instruction on job-related skills, not academics: resume-writing, interviewing for a job, and professional etiquette in the workplace. The university also encourages returning co-op students to process their experiences in college classes, and to integrate the academics and direct work in a senior capstone course (Northeastern, 2012).

The model of the concurrent seminar, whether for interns or service-learning groups, affords students and instructors an opportunity to process the experience as it unfolds, to interrogate and critique it through a variety of theoretical and conceptual lenses. Civic-engagement courses have been described extensively in the literature (cf. Dallimore et al., 2010; Droge & Murphy, 1999; Harkavy & Donovan, 2000; Jacoby, 2009). A fairly typical example will illustrate the service-learning variety in which students do individual volunteering. At a large state university in a rural section of the Northeast, a course called *American Diversity: Identity and Culture* carries the following description:

> How would you characterize your social identity? In what ways are your beliefs about yourself linked to a community or culture you belong to? Among other materials, we'll read stories of immigrants and others who struggle to negotiate their identities. As one Indian-American said of her life in the U.S., it feels like standing with her left foot in one boat and her right foot in another—and the boats are traveling in different directions. *You'll volunteer in a community-based organization and continually make connections between the service and academic aspects of this course.* To prepare for your service placement, you'll learn about social identity, organizational culture, experiential learning, difference, privilege, power, and social justice. (Emphasis added)

The basic function of the course appears to sit at the intersection of theory and practice, to treat the phenomenon of diversity on experiential as well as theoretical planes—and to give the two nearly equal status. With three classroom hours per week, however, and reading and writing assignments as well, the field component constitutes only three to five hours a week—more would make unreasonable demands on the students' time by the standards of the credit system. (Some schools operate what they call a *three-plus-one* model, where a normal three-credit course will award an extra, fourth credit to students who complete a coordinated field placement.)

The other service-learning model of the concurrent seminar engages all the students together in a single community-based activity. Students in the PAR project mentioned earlier worked with community activists and residents to conduct a study of the social, economic, and political impact of gentrification in the neighborhood. The instructor had them read academic treatises on gentrification, and taught them methods of research: ethnographic interviewing, GIS, and so on. Earlier in the term, they discussed theories part of the time, and practiced methods part of the time. As the project evolved, they spent more and more time in the community talking with people, observing meetings, and collecting statistical data. As the data flowed in, they spent time analyzing it, discussing it with community leaders, and constructing a report. Ultimately, they presented the study at a neighborhood meeting where residents considered strategies for using the new information in their campaign to resist the gentrifiers. In this type of course, the instructor has greater (though far from complete) control over the sequence of events and their correlation to the readings and academic discussions.

These kinds of concurrent seminars operate most commonly in the domain of service-learning and civic engagement, and less often in the areas of work-based internships and cooperative education. There *are*, however, some efforts to build pedagogical practices around career-related internships. Northeastern University, one of the largest cooperative education schools in the country, has recently moved toward a system of courses through which students meet in classes *during* their placements rather than, as before, just after the fact. The standard pedagogy of co-op in the past has been (a) to provide courses related to the students' prospective professions (accounting, marketing, nursing) in school, (b) to alternate studies with total-immersion, full-time placements for a term at a time, and (c) to assume that the first provides a foundation for the second and the second deepens the first: that students learn concepts, theories, and skills in class that they then "apply" in their field placements, thus strengthening their grasp of the professional knowledge and preparing them for higher-level courses upon their return. The longevity of and widespread support for cooperative education suggests that those assumptions have been at least tenable. But some schools like Northeastern have begun exploring the possibility that the learning will be even broader and even deeper if students have an opportunity to explore and interrogate their field-derived knowledge while the internships are happening.

Some liberal arts-oriented internship programs—based in work experience, not service-learning—do engage students in concurrent seminars. I myself briefly taught an internship seminar in my school based on the premise that students needed to examine their experiences more fully than they would just by virtue of having a part-time job, and that the school needed to add some value to their experience, to enrich and problematize their learning. Because students received no extra credits for the seminar piece (their only incentive for taking the seminar, other than intellectual and professional curiosity, was that they received letter grades instead of pass/fail), I required no extra readings, and their writing assignments—the daily journal and a final paper—were the same as for the students doing the internships pass/fail. But I did expect them to write the journals more fully and more frequently than their regular advisors might have done; in fact, I taught them the Schatzman and Strauss model of field research described above (ONs, TNs, MNs, Analytic Memos), and encouraged them to regard their note-taking as a form of self-ethnography. Moreover, we met weekly to discuss the internship experiences, and I structured those conversations around concepts taken from the literatures on organizational behavior and workplace culture.

For example, I asked students to produce organizational charts for their respective settings, so we could discuss differences in ways of allocating resources, coordinating activities, and managing relationships across units. I asked them to draw process flow charts showing who did what, with what resources, with whom, in what sequence; we looked for points of friction, for bottlenecks, for communications issues. They had to identify core technologies, support functions, and maintenance functions in their organizations, as well as the kinds of tasks that were carried out by various participants and units (Hatch, 1997). They examined the relationship between their settings and the larger environments, asking about such factors as government regulations, market conditions, and technological change. And they teased out cultural features of their workplaces: dress codes, language-use, values and standards, customs, heroes and villains, and organizational climate. At the very least, this curriculum led students to explore their internships from perspectives broader than their own individual standpoint, more productive than the common motivating question for the college intern: How can I do this job without looking stupid?

Laurel George, a colleague of mine at NYU, provides another example of the work-related concurrent seminar. She teaches a seminar for students from a variety of departments in the College of Arts and Science that do not offer credit for the field experience; her interdepartmental course offers them that credit, but requires them to participate in the seminar as well so they can process their experiences in more rigorous ways. George, an anthropologist, draws on ethnographic methods to get her students to think about the experience from rich new perspectives. She has them read articles and write about such matters as workplace structures, dynamics, and cultures; and has them study broader social and political issues like globalization, labor rights, the casualization of labor, gender inequalities, and ethics. She argues,

> Learning to observe power dynamics, workplace culture, modes of speaking, and even uses of physical space can help students to understand not only their internship sites but also themselves as workers as part of larger social, cultural, and economic systems. For example, they may gain a language and frame for talking about the feelings of anonymity and disposability they often experience in their placements. (George, 2012)

Michael True, director of the internship program at Messiah College and a leading figure in the National Society for Experiential Education (NSEE), recently published a book called *InternQube: Professional Skills for the Workplace* (True, 2011) that encourages students to engage some of these questions even if they do not enroll in a concurrent seminar. Although some chapters raise questions about such academic concepts as organizational culture, ethics, and creativity, most of them focus on professional skills: email etiquette, oral communications, teamwork, dress codes. The book thus reflects the tendency of internship coordinators to regard job skills and employability as the principal educational goals of experiential learning. But it does provide a structure for reflection, for promoting greater learning transfer than would occur in, say, a part-time job or noncredit internship.

In other situations, the concurrent seminar is primarily about theory (or history, or academic concepts), and the field experience works as an add-on, a component mostly incidental to the more academic style of the course. In one New York City college, which we observed in the Teaching from Experience project, an urban studies professor taught a course on *Urban Politics, Law and Advocacy*; the syllabus revolved around theories and issues common in such classes (*The Federalist Papers*, Marx, Weber), but students were required to have an internship in a related organization—a city councilmember's office, a community legal clinic—for about three hours per week. I will describe one class session in this course at some length because it illustrates both the opportunities and the challenges in the pedagogical process of integrating student experience into discussions of academic concepts. I think that this instructor was making a valiant effort to achieve that integration, and that he was to some extent successful—but to some extent ran into serious problems.

On the day in question, the students had read an article by the German sociologist Max Weber on the profession of politics. The instructor tried to get the students to understand—and, more, to use—Weber's argument about the varied motivations for people engaged in politics: crudely put, money and personal gain on the one hand, ideals and the common good on the other. He started by initiating a discussion of an article in that day's newspaper about a controversy over the development of a basketball stadium in downtown Brooklyn. He gave some background on the issue, directed students to read the article, and then asked, "How does this situation relate to Weber's concepts?" They batted that question around a bit. So far, the conversation was a little more present-oriented than it would have been in some more strictly academic courses, but not a great deal. But then the professor asked the students to relate Weber's concepts to their personal experiences in the internship sites. One opined that the city councilwoman for whom he worked seemed to care about senior groups, Little Leagues, and other community-based organizations only to the extent that they might generate votes for her reelection. Another student working at a law-school clinic judged that his colleagues were driven more by ideals, by wanting to do good, than by anything like self-gain. The instructor summarized, "American society is a materialist culture, and this affects politics as well as other parts of life. What Weber's concepts give you is a way of analyzing this."

He returned to Weber's essay, and began working through a list of questions from the syllabus that students were supposed to have prepared to discuss. For example, "What is the definition of the state?" One student read from the essay—she had obviously thought about this question—and the professor wrote her answer on the board, then asked other students to explain what that concept meant. Another question was about Weber's famous distinction among types of leaders: traditional, charismatic, and legal/formal. At this point, the discussion would have seemed familiar to anyone who ever took a course in sociology: The instructor was looking for students to articulate the argument in a common reading. He occasionally summarized or clarified students' points, writing them on the board in Weber's terms. But then he did something uncommon in these scenes: After discussing the "ethics of ends" and the "ethics of responsibility" from the essay, he asked, "For your purposes, where do your people [that is, at the internship] fall on this spectrum? How do they think about it?" Interestingly, he posed that question only rhetorically—no students actually answered it—but said, "Again, this is a factor to look for when you're analyzing your situations at your internships."

He made a similar pedagogical move after inserting Marx and *The Communist Manifesto* into the conversation: He asked questions that led the students to identify the key elements of Marx's theory of class and his critique of capitalism (as much as one could do in twenty minutes!). Again, that teaching strategy would be totally familiar to denizens of the academy. Students cited specific passages of the text, offered interpretations, asked for clarifications. But then the instructor brought the conversation back to the students' experiences in their internships: "Does class according to Marx apply to your situations, your groups, especially the clients or constituents? Does it help you understand your situation better, or does another scheme— say, Weber—help you understand it better? Is it class, or are these groups grouped by something else, like ethnicity, or neighborhood, or religion? That's what you want to look for as far as applying this to your situation." Again, he posed the question but did not solicit responses.

With about five minutes left in the class, the professor asked, "How are your internships going?" Each student took a turn giving a brief update on the field experience, what projects they had been working on—but at that stage, nobody (including the teacher) related those reports to the concepts discussed earlier in the class.

In my judgment, this professor worked unusually hard at negotiating the complex relationship between the academic readings—Weber, Marx—and the students' internship experiences, especially considering that this was an academic course, not strictly an internship seminar. He repeatedly posed important questions and explored intriguing points about how the concepts (class, power, leadership) could shape one's understanding about the dynamics of behavior and relationships in the field sites. To be accurate, he more often asserted that one *could* make those theory-practice connections than he actually probed them; his point was as much methodological as substantive. And, not surprisingly, he did not treat the experiential elements of the course to the same extent in every class. In the very next session, for example, he spent far more time in a conventionally academic discussion of the notion of factions in *Federalist 10* than he did in searching for "applications" in the students' field experiences. Even in the first session described here, and especially in the second, he drew a pedagogical line between discussing texts and discussing the experiences: He ended the first one by asking how things were going in the field; he started the second the same way, asking, "Before we get down to Madison and Tocqueville, is anything going on in your internships"—first A, then B.

So the teaching methods were not perfectly consistent in treating the experiential as a full and respectable partner of the academic—but one would be hard-pressed to imagine what such a balance would look like, especially in a classroom conversation. The instructor did things that were totally familiar to anyone who has sat in a college-level politics class—and that, too, is fine, especially since he really worked to get students engaged in thinking through these concepts themselves, rather than spoon-feeding them through lecture or more directive questions.

Still, this episode illustrates both the benefits and the challenges of experience-based pedagogies. First, as I have argued before, the concepts and knowledge-forms used in the internship sites of the students in this class—in *any* class—do not map neatly onto the concepts and theories in the readings. Both Weber's essay and the instructor treated the mechanisms driving politicians' behavior as lying on a single-dimension spectrum, from personal gain to selfless ideals. Those terms might function as useful heuristics in the investigation of particular individuals engaged in political work, but they hardly cover all possible interpretations; there could be other motivations. Even if the ideals/gain spectrum *were* an adequate explanatory scheme for political behavior, it would not truly capture the details of that behavior from the perspective of the participants. That is, analyzing those motivations from an academic perspective differs significantly from what politicians—and even their interns—do when they are at work. In the field, they are engaged in action, not abstract analysis—or, if they do analyze a problematic situation (generating legislative support for a bill, for example), they do that analysis in ways different from what a political scientist would do. Their criteria for success revolve around consequences, around success in achieving practical ends, whereas the academics' criteria center on explanatory adequacy, on the elegance of the resulting theory.

Nonetheless, the exercise of analyzing their experiences through the lenses of Weber, Marx, Tocqueville, and others might have opened these students' eyes to new ways of understanding *and* functioning in these organizations. It might have raised questions—for instance, about ethics—that the practical politicians would not have entertained, and thus enlarged students' conception of the relevant range of issues in their practice. It might have given concrete referents to the students' abstract conceptions of class and power. Finally, the discussion might have given more nuance to their grasp of social theory.

Third, there are difficult and subtle matters of teaching technique here. Merely attaching an internship placement to a course clearly does not solve the challenge of making the course experiential. Rather, once again, the devil is in the details. When and how should the instructor raise questions about the practical experience in relation to the texts and theories in the syllabus? Should one do a "news of the week in review" at the beginning of each class session, asking students how things are going in the internship? How should one phrase queries that interrogate the practical work? Does it work to ask, "How would Weber interpret this situation"? A fascinating and significant research project could be designed around questions like that: What do experiential educators do to enhance and guide their students' learning, and what strategies and techniques appear to work most effectively—and what do we mean by effectively? This book cannot address that set of problems fully, but the point here is somewhat general: The intersection between the experiential and the academic is neither clear nor easy to navigate.

The Final Paper

Many interns, even those who do not participate in concurrent seminars, are required to write final papers somehow reflecting on their experiences, at least when they are earning credit for the work. Especially in colleges where the student is graded by a faculty member in the major department, the specific expectations for the paper vary tremendously. Some instructors ask for a library- or internet-based research paper somehow related to the work setting: a brief history of the fashion industry for an intern at a glamour magazine, a study of the recent financial crisis for a student working at an investment bank, a review of child development theory for a teacher's assistant in an elementary school. These papers are academic complements to the field work, in the sense that they are "about" the same domain. But as we have seen, the similarity in terms does not guarantee similarity in meaning. In this version of the final paper, the connections between the domains are typically left unexplored. The faculty person finds some relief in the fact that the student has at least done some legitimate academic work; the student finds some comfort in the familiarity of the term-paper genre.

Other teachers ask for a detailed description of the internship experience: what the organization was like, what the student did, thoughts on the learning. These are essays the student can produce without reference to texts or even, sometimes, to the journal: "Here's what I did, and here's what I thought about it." Moreover, their scope is often limited to the realm of the student's direct experience; the broader environment remains unexamined. Others, particularly instructors based in academic or preprofessional departments, demand the "application" of some form of theory to the experience. For example, a marketing intern in the public relations department of a famous fashion house used Michael Porter's (1998) notion of "five forces analysis" to understand the strategic opportunities and constraints in that industry: defining the industry and the market; identifying rivals, buyers, suppliers, and new entrants. She essentially used her company as a case study in the utility of that framework, but did not critique Porter's model from the perspective of her experience. In another school, a student who worked at a major television program conducted an ethnography of the company, describing the organizational structure, some of the local customs and language uses, and social relations among members. As it happened, she did not make much of the description in analytical terms, going into issues of power, gender, knowledge-use, and so on; this was not a Geertzian (1977) "thick description," but rather an ethnographic fly-by. Still, the essay did capture a more comprehensive picture of the setting than a mere travel brochure-style, "here's-what-I-did" paper.

Like the journal and the concurrent seminar, the final paper assignment has the potential to deepen an intern's analysis and understanding of her experience, and to connect that experience with theories more often found in college classes. Realizing that potential requires careful attention and feedback from the instructor, who needs to push the student to use methods and concepts not part of the natural thought practices in the work world. When that deeper reflection happens, however, it can promote the kinds of learning transfer and the new modes of thought that experiential learning is capable of.

Pedagogical Approaches: Some Choices

Finally, I want to describe a framework by which experiential educators might approach the pedagogical options facing them as they work with students engaged in learning outside the classroom. Possible strategies vary on several dimensions, which represent major questions teachers might ask themselves as they make plans:

- *Intervention*: To what extent do they need to structure, guide, and monitor students' out-of-classroom experience? This dimension might vary from laissez-faire to interventionist.
- *Knowledge domains*: To what extent should the teaching strategy focus on academic ideas and methods, and to what extent should it aim at practical learning? This dimension might run from totally academic to totally practical. Assuming neither extreme is desirable, what is the appropriate mix, and what are the epistemological terms on which it might be determined?
- *Politics*: To what extent should the teaching strategy call for a critique of local and/or societal issues related to political questions about the distribution and use of power, the principle of social justice, or the domination and exploitation of one group of people by another? This dimension might vary from scrupulously inattentive to power to completely committed to a critical position.

These dimensions do not lend themselves to a neat taxonomy of pedagogical strategies. The three elements do not fall into linear spectra, nor do they co-vary consistently in such a way that being at point 1 on dimension A means being at point 1 on dimension B. One can choose to be highly interventionist but resolutely apolitical; one can be attentive to power but analyze it in a largely theoretical way. Eric Sheffield (2011) distinguishes models of service-learning on my third dimension: He calls programs *strong* when they interrogate power relations and aim toward justice, and *weak* when they do not. I find that terminology useful for that particular aspect of engaged learning, but not for other elements of pedagogical strategy.

Instead, as a purely heuristic device, I could imagine a three-dimensional matrix, with each dimension on a spectrum from one pole (A) to another (Z): laissez-faire to highly interventionist; highly academic to highly practical; largely apolitical to highly critical. We could describe each dimension as divided into, say, three sections: very A, mixed, very Z. This 3 × 3 × 3 matrix would yield 27 "types" of teaching strategies for experiential educators. I am not making an empirical claim on that level of detail. Rather, I am suggesting that we can think about choices of teaching strategies as varying complexly on these dimensions.

Intervention

On the intervention dimension, pedagogies range from leaving the natural experience alone to attempting to control it in every respect. Noncredit internship programs based in career-services offices generally appear toward the laissez-faire end of that spectrum: They set the student up with a placement, and then leave her to her own devices, requiring no journals, no papers, no evaluations. In the low-middle range of this spectrum, teachers ask for general products: the basic learning contract ("I'll be at Company X, helping with marketing"), occasional journals reporting on activities and feelings ("I put together press kits; it was pretty boring"), and perhaps a summary paper at the end of the term ("here's what I did, here's how I liked it"). In the high-middle range, instructors might ask for more detail and more reflection, without exercising control over the field experience itself. They might draw on suggestions from workplace educators like Raelin (2008), Billett (2001), or Fenwick (2003), and ask students to construct organization charts or process flow charts, to examine the dynamics of production processes, to analyze industries and markets, and to identify the kinds of knowledge they are being asked to display. That is, the high-middle activism teachers insist on greater detail in students' reflection, and provide a set of questions and readings—but they may or may not intervene in the work or service site itself. That realm constitutes another element of the activism dimension: How much does the educator try to structure and manage the field experience?

The learning contract serves as one device for that external control, if the workplace supervisor and the student actually abide by its terms. Moreover, many internship instructors will intervene in the field site in case of a problem—the student has been assigned only to mundane tasks, or has been given no supervision, or has been mistreated in some way—but short of that extreme situation, they tend to let the student handle the experience as it comes.

On the other hand, service-learning instructors often move further toward the activist side in controlling the field experience. They may have frequent contacts with the project partners, making suggestions and giving feedback on the kinds of activities the students engage in. At the more interventionist pole, the instructors actually design the activities in collaboration with the partners, so they control just what the students are doing. In the PAR project, for example, some students were assigned to do interviews of neighborhood residents, while others collected and processed data for a GIS map correlating household income and location. In this arrangement, the instructor does not have perfect control over the field experience—the partners sometimes shape what goes on, and there is always some degree of unpredictability in that world—but they move toward that end of the spectrum.

Knowledge Domains

The distinction between academic knowledge and practical knowledge is, of course, nowhere near perfect, as we have seen; the terms function more as heuristic devices for naming orientations and conventions than as empirical categories. Postmodernists would criticize the words as binaries, and deconstruct them. That is precisely what I suggest about this spectrum as a tool for conceptualizing strategies for experiential learning: We can imagine a variety of configurations of curriculum content that give more privilege or less to the ideal type of academic thought or of practical knowledge. Even the reputedly purely academic inquiry in a school like, say, St. John's College (home of the "great books") aims at developing skills in its students; even a trade school expresses some of its lessons in theoretical, generalized terms.

In a cooperative education program, for example, classes might aim primarily at the mastery of practical skills—accounting procedures, techniques in art therapy or sports management—that could then be "applied" in professional settings. Its mixture puts it somewhere close to the practical end of the spectrum, but there are abstractions built in as well: for example, theories about the etiology of psychological conditions treated by an arts therapist. Toward the other end lie instructors like our political scientist, who care most about whether their students understand Tocqueville, Marx, and Weber, but who use the field experience for illustrative purposes. In any case, either describing or designing a pedagogical strategy for engaged learning requires one to decide on an appropriate mixture of the abstract/ universal and the concrete/particular.

Politics

Finally, the political dimension describes differences in the extent to which students and faculty attend to matters of power, justice, and morality. We might call one pole of that spectrum *apolitical*, but that term incorrectly implies that knowledge-use can sometimes be free of the exercise of power, and that pedagogy can be value-free (cf. Apple, 1995; Foucault, 1980; Kincheloe, 2008). We might call it *positivist*, in the sense of manifesting an epistemology that claims that there are persistent "things" in the world and that we can discover the "truth" about them (Moore, 1990, p. 274)—but not all opponents of addressing power and morality in academic discourse are strict positivists. For lack of a better term, let us use the term *noncritical*, and contrast it with the term *critical*. The latter refers to critical pedagogy, as mentioned in the previous chapter: teaching strategies aimed at the analysis of ideas and social phenomena in such a way as to reveal the underlying dynamics of power, to answer the question of who dominates and who is dominated, to comprehend the impact of such social forces as class, race, gender, and sexual orientation or identity—and, most of all, to *do* something about problems of hegemony and injustice.

Stances on this dimension might be described (provisionally, cautiously) as neoliberal, liberal, and radical. From the neoliberal position, market capitalism is the best form of political economy, and the function of higher education is to prepare young people to become competent participants in that system (cf. Giroux, 2011; Harvey, 2005). An example of an educational neoliberal would be E. D. Hirsch, whose controversial *Cultural Literacy* (1987) identified a long list of knowledge items that students should master. With some reservations, he regarded that knowledge as objective, unproblematic, and equally germane to all members of society, not as bound up in or manifesting relations of power. An experiential college program based on this assumption similarly regards knowledge as "out there," available to anyone who takes the trouble to acquire it. It does not investigate the sources or distribution of knowledge and power, but rather takes the student's experience at face value without attempting to determine how it got that way. Many, if not most, cooperative education programs, for example, do not raise questions about the social impact, political stance, or moral value of the industries and companies where they place their students. Rather, they take for granted the notion that there are jobs in the work world, that those jobs require certain kinds of knowledge and skill, and that their function is to prepare young people to acquire those things (Ryder & Wilson, 1987). Their basic criterion is utility, their basic goal is career preparation, and their basic stance is noncritical.

Moving along the politics spectrum, we find liberal workplace educators like Raelin (2008) and Billett (2001), who encourage learners to ask more and more rigorous and pointed questions about their organizations and their environments. Some versions of this approach do not interrogate the political economy within which the work goes on. Argyris and Schön (1974), for example, advance intriguing ideas about the use of theory in practice, but do not ask whether the corporations where these practices occur support democracy or justice. Others, like Fenwick (2003), do raise those issues. All of them, in any case, pose important queries about life in organizations, about the nature of knowledge-use, about structures and processes in the world of work.

Other analysts promote a form of inquiry that raises questions of morality and ethics. Sullivan and Rosin (2008), for example, propose a "new agenda for higher education," a model of teaching that operates at the intersection of liberal education and professional training, that functions in the service of the development of practical reason: the capacity to exercise judgment based on both deep understanding and immediate experience. Rather than either retreat to the life of the mind or acquiesce in the practical demands of the real world, this pedagogy brings one to bear on the other. In a similar vein, Flyvbjerg (2001) advocates an education that "makes social science matter" by building in students the capacity for what Aristotle called *phronesis*: an intellectual virtue that joins experience with ethics, that raises moral questions like "what is the good?" and political questions like "who benefits?" when engaging in situated practice. Many college-level civic-engagement programs, but relatively few internship programs, take this stance.

Finally, we move to the most overtly radical end of the political spectrum with the proponents of critical pedagogy, whose ideas and methods lead toward what Sheffield (2011) calls a strong form of experiential learning. One version of this approach to teaching, feminist pedagogy, draws on the ideas of people like Paulo Freire, whose *Pedagogy of the Oppressed* (1970) represented an opening salvo in the radical critique of mainstream education; bell hooks, whose *Teaching to Transgress* (1994) generated tremendous movement in the exploration of feminism as a mode of being in schools; and Berenice Fisher, whose *No Angel in the Classroom* (2001) described feminist pedagogy in great detail.

Writings like these flesh out a particularly rich conception of engaged learning by articulating several crucial principles underlying effective liberatory education (cf. Webb, 2005). First, the learner is regarded as an active participant in the generation and use of knowledge, not a passive recipient. The method recovers, acknowledges, and enlarges the voice of the learner (cf. Belenky et al., 1997)—and, by extension in the practice of civic engagement, the voice of oppressed and exploited community partners as well. This approach challenges the conventional power relations between teacher and student and between the university and society, aiming at the empowerment of all participants.

Feminist pedagogy also aims at the creation of community in the classroom and, in the context of engaged learning, in the larger world as well. It insists on respect for the diversity of participants' experiences and perspectives, and challenges traditional theories and practices. These principles, usually expressed in terms of life in the classroom, are completely compatible with a strong version of engaged learning outside the school as well. They speak not only to the kinds of knowledge generated by feminist inquiry—about power relations, about historical patterns of institutional behavior, about the dynamics of change—but also to modes of being in the world, to ways of relating to one another: democracy, care, respect, and reciprocity.

The other primary radical perspective on the theory and practice of experiential learning falls under the heading of critical pedagogy. This stance—which is far from monolithic in its expressions—draws on a variety of traditions: the critical theory of such Frankfurt School figures as Horkheimer, Adorno, Marcuse, and Habermas (cf. Jay, 1996); Gramsci (1971) on hegemony; feminism; Freire (1970), and various postmodernist, poststructuralist, and postcolonialist challenges to modernist, scientific, Western paradigms (cf. Kincheloe, 2008, p. 48). The central argument of the advocates of critical pedagogy is that educational institutions can contribute to a democratic society only by creating the conditions in which their members—students, faculty, and everyone else involved in the enterprise—can become citizens who are "critical, self-reflective, knowledgeable, and willing to make moral judgments and act in a socially responsible way" (Giroux, 2011, p. 3). The prominent advocate Ira Shor (1992) defines critical pedagogy as an educational practice that enables learners to

go beneath surface meaning, first impressions, dominant myths, official pronouncements, traditional cliches, received wisdom, and mere opinions, to understand the deep meaning, root causes, social context, ideology, and personal consequences of any action, event, object, process, organization, experience, text, subject matter, policy, mass media, or discourse. (p. 129)

Henry Giroux, another leading figure in the field, says that he wants his students to engage in "critique as a mode of analysis that interrogates texts, institutions, social relations, and ideologies as part of the script of official power" (Giroux, 2011, p. 4). Shor, Giroux, Kincheloe, and other proponents regard critical pedagogy as a tool for resisting and changing oppressive social relations, and insist that it must combine knowledge-construction with principled action in what Freire (1970) and others call *praxis*. Giroux argues, "Critical pedagogy is about more than a struggle over assigned meanings, official knowledge, and established modes of authority: it is also about encouraging students to take risks, act on their sense of social responsibility, and engage the world as an object of both critical analysis and hopeful transformation" (2011, p. 14).

As Dan Butin (2010) and Eric Sheffield (2011) show in their respective works, the issue of whether service-learning programs can or ought to practice some form of critical pedagogy arouses considerable controversy in higher education. Some people see it as totally consistent with the expressed values and purposes of civic-engagement programs, while others see it as risky and overreaching, even as inconsistent with their preferred postmodern approach, which avoids master narratives like Marxism. Since they and others (cf. Jacoby, 2009; Rhoads, 1997) have taken up that question at some length, I want to focus here on the implications of critical pedagogy for work-related experiential learning: internships, cooperative education, and so on.

For the intern working in a fashion house or an investment bank, what would critical pedagogy mean? It would *not* mean the professor's delivering lectures on Marxian critiques of late capitalism or Frankfurt School-like diatribes against mass culture. Rather, it would mean, for instance, that members of a concurrent seminar for interns would pose questions about their organizations: Whose interests are being served by this company? What values does the company promote by its products or services, and by the way it treats its workers and the larger community? How is power distributed and used in the organization, and to what end? Who has access to what kinds of knowledge, and who doesn't? That is, the stance means going beyond job preparation (though not ignoring it, either) to ask how jobs and organizations function, and in whose interest; it would place the experience in the larger context of the political economy.

Roger Simon, who once created a high school cooperative education program based on critical pedagogy, used to tell a fascinating story. A young woman in his class who worked at a local McDonald's raised a perplexing question: "Why is it," she asked, "that the girls have to work up front at the cash registers, dealing with nasty customers, while the boys get to be in the back flipping hamburgers, making French fries, and fooling around with each other?" Though the question grew out of her personal frustration at work, it sparked a lively conversation about gender roles in the workplace (cf. Simon et al., 1991). In a similar vein, I once supervised an advisee in a series of fashion-related internships: a clothing company, a magazine, a PR firm. At the same time, she took courses in cultural sociology and political theory, and read such authors as Adorno and Ewen on consumerism. As she neared graduation, she said to me, "I get up in the morning, look at myself in the mirror, and ask, What am I doing?!"

Now, the practice of critical pedagogy does not mean pushing students to reject all capitalist, consumer-oriented enterprise, or turning them into young revolutionaries. It *does*, however, mean encouraging them to ask deep questions, unsettling their taken-for-granted notions about business, challenging their easy assumptions about citizenship, justice, power, and democracy. After graduation, my advisee in fact decided to work in the fashion industry, despite her qualms. But I like to believe that she did it with a stronger sense of the social, political, and moral implications of what she was doing.

This chapter has reviewed some of the pedagogical issues confronting various forms of engaged learning, and has proposed ways of conceptualizing the choices educators face as they design and implement experiential programs. In the next and final chapter, we will consider a range of institutional issues stemming from the preceding analysis of the curriculum and pedagogy of field-based learning, and venture some conclusions about whether and how these programs fit into higher education.

CHAPTER 8

Institutional Mission(s) and Engaged Learning

U p to this point, we have been considering two large categories of challenges and possibilities faced by academics as they try to incorporate various forms of engaged learning into their programs: the *curricular*, having to do the with nature of knowledge used and valued in and out of college classrooms; and the *pedagogical*, having to do with the practices through which people encounter, engage, and produce knowledge—that is, through which they learn—in those different arenas. As we have seen, both in the literature on situated cognition and in the stories about actual interns, the intersection of knowledge-use inside and outside the academy presents enormous challenges and opportunities on both of those fronts. Even when people in the "academic" and "practical" worlds (the quotation marks reflect the highly problematic meanings of those commonsense concepts) are employing similar terms—say, gentrification—but especially when their discourses appear not to overlap, the substantial differences between the two knowledge domains highlight the question of whether they can be aligned and coordinated in productive ways. Similarly, the differences between the pedagogical dynamics of the two settings force us to consider whether and how faculty and students can devise methods to ensure that they both learn more than they would by virtue of mere out-of-school experience. In the curriculum and pedagogy sections, we explored some of the ways college people *could* exploit those differences educationally. But that analysis begs a further question: whether, given the mission(s) of higher education, educators *should* pursue that experiential strategy. In this final chapter, then, we will move our attention to the *institutional* context within which these explicitly educational concerns arise, and return to our central driving question: In what senses, to what extent, and under what conditions does out-of-school experience *fit* in higher education? When and how does it achieve and advance the mission of the university as an educational enterprise?

That last issue begs the question of what that mission *is*—and of course that problem has been sparking controversy since the institution arose nearly a thousand years ago. Part of this chapter, then, will identify and critique several versions of the positions on the mission problem, not as a comprehensive review of that debate but as a way of sketching out the relation of experiential learning to the respective solutions. People who lead and work in colleges and universities have a choice to make: whether to recognize, value, and engage forms of knowledge other than the scientistic, propositional, universalistic, abstract modes that have dominated higher education for hundreds of years, and specifically whether to utilize experience as a legitimate source of higher learning. Depending on one's stance on the mission question, different arguments on that issue will sound convincing. For some, experiential learning will seem to violate long-held standards of rigor, logic, and value. For others, it will provide a way to enhance and extend the ultimate ends of the university.

Finally, I will take a stance on the mission/experience question: I will identify the forms of experiential practice that I believe advance the integrity and impact of the institution of higher learning, and those that do not. My position may please neither the advocates nor the opponents of engaged learning, the advocates because I do not take for granted the premise that experience-based learning always improves the quality of education, and the opponents because I envision an institution far more engaged with the realm beyond its ivy-covered walls, far more open to diverse modes of knowing, learning, and acting in the world (cf. Moore, 1999, 2010).

Debates about the Mission

Conceptions of the proper mission of the academy have not evolved in a linear way since the founding of the University of Bologna in the eleventh century. There has been no steady march, for instance, from scholasticism to, say, a progressive or a technocratic model. Instead, especially in the Anglo-American realm, several roughly distinct versions of the purposes of higher education have vied for dominance. Sometimes one or another has prevailed, and sometimes the tensions among them have produced a diverse array of institutional forms and practices during a given period. My purpose here is not to trace the complex history of higher education in America (cf. Cohen, 1998; Rudolph, 1990; Veysey, 1965), but rather to lay out some of the key features of the several models and to explore their implications for the use of experience as a source of knowledge.

For heuristic purposes, I will divide these models into three categories: the conservative, the liberal, and the radical. This typology, which echoes the one proposed in the last chapter regarding experiential pedagogies, does not capture either the diverse realities of educational philosophy and practice or the basic underlying similarities in institutional forms (Altbach, 2001), and it elides subtle yet important debates within each category, but it does suggest the general dimensions of a useful scheme for thinking about differences among the visions: how they conceptualize knowledge and learning; how they imagine the roles of teacher, student, and researcher; and how they describe the relationship between the academic institution and the larger world.

The conservative model of the mission of the academy rests on a basic belief in the existence of a body of received knowledge, produced by authoritative thinkers and tested by time, that must be transmitted to rising generations. By this light, the purpose of the university is to preserve, protect, and disseminate what Matthew Arnold called "the best that has been thought and known in the world" (Arnold, 1960). This stance relies to some extent on an evolved reading of Plato's notion of knowledge and learning: that what is real is not the stuff of material existence and experience, but the Forms, transcendent ideas like Truth and Justice; that knowledge is the understanding of those Forms, and that learning is a matter of coming to that understanding through a process of dialectic (cf. Phillips & Soltis, 2004). While more modern conservatives do not subscribe to pure Plato, they share the assumption that knowledge concerns not the evanescent, changeable details of specific situations or phenomena, but the universal, the law-like, the epistemic, the authoritative.

The modern conservative conception of the roles of teacher and student differs from Plato's, as well. Where Plato (1984) saw learning as a process of recovering what the soul already knows, and teaching as facilitating that process (largely through asking Socratic questions, as in *The Meno*), more modern versions see the student as absorbing knowledge that the teacher has already mastered. In this view, learning is properly a matter not of either having or interrogating experience but of the study of canonical texts and ideas. The role of the researcher, which did not appear in Plato's theory of education (except in the remote sense of a person who actively reasons about the Forms), becomes for the modern conservative the rigorous, dispassionate, disinterested, and disengaged search for universal, decontextualized knowledge.

Finally, the conservative version of the mission of higher education places the university in a realm separate from the exigencies of the "real world." It is a domain protected from the sullying influence of politics, from the distorting demands of practical endeavor, from the confusing pull of competing perspectives. This description is, of course, a caricature—no serious theorist of higher education imagines that such a degree of purity is possible—but it captures an inclination, a longing toward an ivory tower where Truth reigns. This Platonic theory of the university "continues to dominate Western schooling systems to this day" (Benson et al., 2005, p. 195).

In the world of the Anglo-American university, this conservative stance has found a number of champions over the past two centuries. In 1828, the faculty of Yale College, in reaction to reforms creeping into such institutions as Harvard, issued a report insisting on a classical curriculum that furnished the minds of young men [*sic*] by means of exposing them to Greek, Latin, and such liberal arts as mathematics, astronomy, grammar, and rhetoric (Cohen, 1998, p. 76; Rudolph, 1990, p. 132). Thirty years later, John Henry Newman, founder of the Catholic University of Ireland (now University College Dublin) defended a version of the same classical curriculum (though with twists reconciling it with Catholic doctrine) against demands for a more practical, modern, and professionally oriented education. He advocated the quest for knowledge for its own sake. To the limited extent that Newman conceded a practical end for higher learning, it took the form of a claim that has been repeated by many liberal arts colleges since then: that the classical curriculum would produce more effective citizens. Like the Harvard mission statement cited in the introduction to this book, Newman saw classical education as serving society by producing "gentlemen" with refinement and intellect. For him, that was enough; for him, no explication was necessary of the specific way in which that curriculum prepared a student for productive citizenship.

More recent figures have also promoted versions of the Plato-Yale-Newman conception of the purpose of the university. In 1936, Robert Maynard Hutchins, the youthful president of the University of Chicago, rejected job preparation and vocationalism as missions, and advocated instead the study of the classics of Western civilization, and the liberal arts including grammar, rhetoric, logic, and arithmetic. In his plan, completing these fundamental college-level materials would qualify the student for higher-division university studies in metaphysics, the social sciences, and the natural sciences—none of them undertaken with a specific career in mind (Cohen, 1998, pp. 172–173; Hutchins, 1995).

Fifty years later, Allan Bloom, a philosopher then teaching at Chicago, took up Hutchins's cause in the controversial *The Closing of the American*

Mind (1987), in which he slammed the laxity and incoherence of modern college curricula, the demand for "relevance," and the politicization of the faculty, and argued for a return to the tradition of studying the classics. His was the surprising opening salvo in the higher education front in the "culture wars" of the next 20 years, heated debates over the proper mission and practice of the academy. Other conservative combatants in that battle have included Dinesh D'Souza (1991), William J. Bennett (2001), and Roger Kimball (1998), all of whom charge the modern faculty with corrupting higher education by injecting left politics into curriculum and teaching (cf. Hart, 2001; Kors & Silverglate, 1998). Interestingly for our purposes, none of these critics so much as mentions internships, service-learning, cooperative education, or any other form of experiential learning. They take for granted that issues of content and practice in the university arise in classrooms and laboratories, libraries and lectures, not in "the community." Like Plato, they regard experience as a distraction from study, as an unreliable source of knowledge, and as a matter for student services and the extracurriculum, not for serious discussions of higher learning.

One might infer from these expressions of the conservative mission of higher education a position on the fitness of experiential education as a feature of that institution: Don't do it, at least under the banner of the institution's learning program.

In contrast to the conservative camp, what I am calling the liberal position on the mission of the university defines knowledge and learning in terms now generally considered commonsensical: Knowledge is reliable, reasonably stable, descriptive, analytical, and explanatory information about the world, generated through rigorous inquiry—whether the scientific method or respectable thought in the humanities or social sciences—conducted by qualified scholars. It is progressive: It grows, adapts, becomes more trustworthy as it is tested and applied. And it is useful: It makes a difference in the way one functions in the world, whether through understanding, invention, or imagination. Learning, then, is a process of individuals' acquiring and mastering that knowledge, thereby becoming more and more competent participants in the arenas of family, community, economy, and society. This vision is liberal in the etymological sense of freeing the person from the constraints of ignorance (cf. Phillips & Soltis, 2004). It is *neo*liberal in the sense of taking for granted and not challenging the existing political economy, the hegemony of certain interests and institutions, or the power of particular ideologies (Harvey, 2005).

By this light, the role of the professor changes from the conservative notion of passing along the accumulated wisdom of the ages to the more generative one of engaging and enlarging knowledge about one or another domain of concern. The scholar, who is both researcher and teacher, actively works on solving problems, whether theoretical or practical. The student, in this scheme, participates in scholarship as a neophyte, learning from the professor the basic concepts, theories, and methods necessary for tackling those varied problems.

Where the conservative mission segregates the academy from the real world, the liberal mission imagines the university as being in service to society, as producing social amelioration through the creation and application of knowledge. This service function takes different forms in different versions of the liberal mission. To Andrew D. White, the first president of Cornell, it was to provide a supermarket of learning options: "I would found an institution where any person can find instruction in any study" (Rudolph, 1990, p. 266). To Daniel Coit Gilman, the founding president of The Johns Hopkins University, it was to create an arena for rigorous scholarship: "The university...renders services to the community which no demon of statistics can ever estimate...[namely] the acquisition, conservation, refinement, and distribution of knowledge" (Rudolph, 1990, p. 272). Pure scientific research, he maintained, would ultimately produce enormous benefits for the society, though its applications might not be immediately apparent.

During the Progressive Era, the Wisconsin Idea arose as a liberal statement about the function of the university in relation to the state and society. Faculty and staff spread out into the communities of the state to provide resources, training, and advice for farmers, businesspeople, homemakers, and other citizens. Research was aimed explicitly at meeting the political, economic, and social needs of the people and institutions of Wisconsin (Chambers, 2005). Half a century later, Clark Kerr, president of the University of California, described his vision of the "multiversity," a many-faceted, weakly coordinated institution that would provide services to many constituencies, from the elites to the working class, from the state to the corporate sector, from the local community to the larger world. It would provide technical expertise, resources, and incentives through a dizzying array of research institutes, business partnerships, university consortia, and public activities (Kerr, 2001). Both the Wisconsin Idea and Kerr's multiversity made claims to serve not only the practical needs of society but the cause of democracy, in the spirit both of the Jeffersonian ideal of promoting an educated public and of the liberal goal of affording access to people previously underrepresented in higher education.

In the realm of experiential education, the classic form of the liberal mission of higher education resides most clearly in the practice of cooperative education (cf. Ryder & Wilson, 1987). Co-op programs, which have been around since the University of Cincinnati created the model in 1906 (not coincidentally, during the Progressive Era in the United States), systematically prepare undergraduates for productive careers by having them alternate periods of advanced study (especially in such technical fields as engineering and accounting) with periods of full-time work in related enterprises. These programs recognize the work world for what it is, and provide students with a path into it. They are liberal in the sense that they enlarge and disseminate knowledge, provide a service to the larger society, and, especially, open doors to students who might otherwise be stuck on lower rungs of the occupational hierarchy. They are neoliberal in the sense that they accept (and, one might argue, reproduce) the structure of power in that larger world.

Regular internship programs—both the noncredit versions managed by career services offices and the for-credit versions in schools like my own—fall into the liberal category, as well, though on a more individual scale. Their function, as represented in Michael True's *InternQube* (2011) project, is to hook students up with employers, then get them to think about how to do their jobs most effectively, the ultimate goal being to secure gainful employment after graduation.

Some community service programs operate on a similarly liberal plane, but with a different motivation: to provide assistance to people in need. Whether students dish out food in a soup kitchen, tutor immigrant adults on English-language skills, or lead after-school programs in settlement houses, they are meeting some form of social need—and learning about both the problem and the people affected by it in the process (cf. Jacoby, 1996). In that sense, the programs fulfill the liberal mission of the academy. To the degree that they do not encourage students to inquire into the deeper causes and conditions of the problem, they are neoliberal. For example, students who participate in an alternative spring break with Habitat for Humanity, building houses for poor people in rural Alabama, may or may not ask a troubling question: Why do so many people in America lack decent housing? If democratic capitalism is the most productive, humane, and liberating form of political economy, how does the market leave so many people in substandard housing—or none at all? In a sense, the dividing line between the liberal and the radical models of experiential learning rests in that sort of question.

The liberal notion of the role of the academy in protecting and extending civil society, in teaching students the skills of democratic citizenship, and in operating for the public good permeates much of the more recent literature and activity of advocates of civic engagement in the university. It can be found in relatively early arguments for service-learning like Jane Kendall's *Combining Service and Learning* (1990), Robert Coles's *The Call of Service* (1993), and Barbara Jacoby's *Service-Learning in Higher*

Education: Concepts and Practices (1996), as well as in more recent collections like Dan Butin's *Service Learning in Higher Education* (2005) and Todd Kelshaw et al.'s *Partnerships for Service-Learning* (2009), all of which extol the impact of civic engagement on democracy as well as on student learning and community well-being. A number of national initiatives have been created to promote civic learning among college students: Campus Compact has grown since 1985 to include almost 1200 colleges, and promotes community and service-learning that develops students' citizenship skills and forges school-community partnerships (Campus Compact, 2011); *A Crucible Moment* (National Task Force, 2012) describes efforts by the Association of American Colleges and Universities (AAC&U) to promote the spirit and practices of engaged learning; the Center for Engaged Democracy at Merrimack College supports academic programs (certificates, majors, minors) based on civic engagement (Center for Engaged Democracy, 2012); the Kellogg Foundation sponsors the National Forum on Higher Education for the Public Good (cf. Kezar et al., 2005). These efforts—and scores of others—all seem compatible with a liberal conception of higher learning and its mission in a democratic society.

To be fair, however, some advocates of civic engagement articulate their principles and purposes in ways that move them into the third category of university missions—the radical—in the sense that they challenge the very foundations of the current neoliberal form of civil society, one dominated by entrenched economic interests and permeated by an individualist ideology. Author-activists like Harry Boyte (2005), Scott Peters (2010), and John Saltmarsh (2011) operate from a basic commitment to liberal democracy, but argue that the current distribution of power and privilege in society needs to be radically altered to restore voice, agency, and justice to all citizens. Leading figures in university-community engagement—Kenneth Reardon and the East St. Louis Action Research Project (ESLARP) (cf. Peters, 2010, Ch. 5); Ira Harkavy and the University of Pennsylvania's Netter Center for Community Partnerships (cf. Benson et al., 2000)—typically call for practices that transcend mere service and aim toward empowerment and change.

These proponents of civic engagement constitute the first of three more-or-less radical perspectives on the mission of the academy. All three go beyond the liberal goals of social amelioration, the promotion of democracy, and the achievement of justice through broader recognition of and access for underrepresented populations. None of these camps dominates higher education, or in fact constitutes a numerically prominent cohort in the field. Indeed, they operate basically at the margins of the academy. But they represent several different strategies for creating significant change in the way the university does its job.

The civic-engagement camp straddles the line between the liberal and the radical in its conception of knowledge as socially constructed, in the Deweyan sense (cf. Dewey, 1910, 1938), and as reasonably stable. Members are generally not postmodernists; they see knowledge as progressive, as situated and shaped by values and interests, and as subject to dispute, but not as ultimately vulnerable to deconstruction. The learner participates actively with the teacher in the construction of knowledge, both for herself and for her larger context; the teacher-researcher may have greater knowledge and skill, but nonetheless relates to students and community members as a colleague, not as a master. And the role of the university in society is not just to provide service or expertise, but to promote social change, to move society toward greater justice and equality.

A second caucus within the radical camp are the advocates of critical theory. Drawing on neo-Marxist and Frankfurt School scholarship, they begin with the premise that the social world displays huge imbalances of power and systemic exploitation of the many by the few. Their analysis of knowledge entails a critique of ideologies and social practices that blind regular people to the operation of systems of oppression. Knowledge in the form of ideology, that is, is said to disempower people, to reduce their agency (Brookfield, 2004). The university, these theorists argue, has historically been one of the key institutions through which ideological and political domination has been maintained (cf. Althusser, 1971). The function of a critical education, by this light, is to remove the blinders, to help people penetrate the systems of belief and action that sustain their oppression (cf. Willis, 1977), to enable people to move toward what Freire (1970) called *conscientization*, or critical consciousness not only of the hegemonic system but also of the possibilities for their own liberation (cf. Kincheloe, 2008). Real learning, that is, entails breaking through ideology and seeing the way the world actually works, whose interests are being served, and how things might be different.

To proponents of this model, the *actual* mission of the academy—whether couched in the conservative terms of Hutchins or in the neoliberal terms of Kerr—is to obfuscate the realities of exploitation and oppression, to convince students and communities that their interests are being served by preparing them to play their role in the political economy. The *preferred* mission for the radicals, of course, would be to equip people to see how that system operates and to work together to change it.

For the critical theorist-pedagogue, engaged learning—whether work-related internships, garden-variety service-learning, or more elaborate forms of civic engagement—becomes an occasion for students, faculty, and community members to critique and change existing relations of power. The question about the systemic need for low-income housing comes back on the table for the Habitat volunteer; the role of advertising in the rise of mindless consumerism becomes a matter for sustained inquiry and action to my fashion intern. Civic engagement challenges the traditional and neo-liberal relation between the university and the larger world, and becomes a primary device for accomplishing the work of critique and social change (cf. Mitchell, 2008, for a review of critical pedagogy in service-learning).

A third radical version of the proper function of the university can be teased out of certain strains of postmodern thought, including the ideas constituting the position known as antifoundationalism. Consistent with theories of situated cognition, this stance

> argues that there is no neutral, objective, or contentless "foundation" by which we can ever know the "truth" unmediated by our particular condition...Antifoundationalism makes us aware of the always contingent character of our presumptions and truths; there is, in Rorty's terminology, no "god's eye view" by which to adjudicate "the truth." Rather, truths are local, contingent, and intersubjective. (Butin, 2010, pp. 12–13)

This position aligns with varieties of postmodern thought that challenge the stability, unity, and trustworthiness of knowledge claims in general and metanarratives in particular, and see fragmentation, discontinuity, and uncertainty as hallmarks of contemporary life (cf. Lyotard, 1984). By these lights, the university emblematic of the Enlightenment and of modernity, which after Bacon and Comte sought an authoritative, totalizing explanation of the natural and social worlds, which regarded itself as the fount of all legitimate knowledge in society, has lost its meaning and its grip. Resting on such metanarratives as Christianity, Marxism, and scientific progress, the academy has struggled to maintain its central role in the constitution of social order—but in the face of postmodern forces becomes an institution on the cusp of either dissolution, irrelevance, or reinvention.

Where postmodernist critics like Lyotard (1984) expect that the end of the Enlightenment project and its epistemic correlates will push the academy in the direction of irrelevance, the sociologist Gerard Delanty offers a more hopeful, though still radical perspective in *Challenging Knowledge* (2001). He argues that society has been undergoing a major cognitive shift, a change in the source, structure, and institutional framework of knowledge. In the modern era, the university served as a site where much crucial knowledge was generated, legitimated, and disseminated; it was the place where "pure" science was done, where scholars took the responsibility of enlarging knowledge through respectable inquiry, and where professionals were trained. But as we move toward a postmodern society, Delanty observes, more and more people and institutions participate in the generation and use of knowledge, and there is less consensus, more dissensus. So the first element of his argument is that in a postmodern society, the customary modern function of the university as the authoritative source and arbiter of knowledge becomes increasingly contested.

His second basic observation is that the public sphere, the historical site of societal communication, has been colonized by money, power, and the media, stripping it of its capacity to enable citizens to participate in meaningful democratic dialogue or what Habermas called critical discourse (Delanty, 2001, p. 7; Habermas, 1989; Moore, 1990). In a neoliberal world in which knowledge comes to be regarded as a commercial tool, the public sphere becomes a market rather than a forum; knowledge becomes proprietary, focused on personal gain rather than public good; and learning becomes a savvy career move rather than an enriching human experience.

In this new historical situation, Delanty argues, with knowledge more diffuse, less certain, more contested, and less authoritative, the university has the potential to take on a new role and identity: to recover and occupy the space of the public sphere, by being

> the most important site of interconnectivity in what is now a knowledge society . . . It is the task of the university to open up sites of communication in society rather than, as it is currently in danger of doing, becoming a self-referential bureaucratic organization . . . [It should be] a community of dissensus. (Delanty, 2001, p. 7)

Delanty identifies some of the strategies by which the university could take on this new role, particularly three kinds of communicative interconnections: new links between the university and society, new links among the sciences, and changing relations between the university and the state. The first of those is most germane to our concerns here—but interestingly, he does not mention anything resembling civic-engagement programs or other enhanced forms of experiential education. I will argue, however, that these practices have the potential to be precisely the transformative strategy that Delanty imagines for the academy. The university can function as a social platform for citizens of many types to generate, try out, and contest various forms of knowledge and action. Community partnerships like the project in East St. Louis bring together citizens, students, and faculty to work on common problems, and give them occasion to learn from each other; they become, as Delanty urges, "an important site of public debate between expert and lay cultures" (p. 8). They challenge the monopoly of legitimate knowledge in the modern university, instead constituting a forum where all may participate.

There is, of course, a substantial obstacle in the path toward this version of the academy: As a raft of critics have asserted, the contemporary university has been commercialized and corporatized over the years, affecting the curriculum, research practices, administrative structures, and such institutional values as academic freedom and disinterested scholarship (cf. Aronowitz, 2001; Bok, 2004; Giroux, 2007; Kirp, 2003). Just as the open-source, libertarian early days of the Internet were quickly overtaken by the monetization of all manner of electronic media, the university has become a tool of moneyed interests, and itself has come to operate in many ways as a major corporate enterprise. If that be the case, the move toward reconstituting the academy as a site for public-sphere interconnectivity, for critical discourse in Habermas's (1979) sense, may provoke substantial resistance. But that movement is an exciting vision for the future of engaged learning.

There are strategic issues facing those who would mobilize the university around that vision. Put most simply, the issue is a choice between two primary options: to turn service-learning and civic engagement into a discipline, and locate them in a specialized department or program; or to spread the principles and practices of experiential learning across all kinds of schools, departments, and programs. The first strategy—departmentalization—is promoted by Dan Butin, one of the most insightful and enterprising theorist-practitioners in the field (cf. Butin, 2005, 2010). He has organized a series of national conferences attracting educators who are building majors, minors, and certificate programs around community engagement, and has created the Center for Engaged Democracy at Merrimack College (where he is the dean of the School of Education) to support these institutional efforts. Butin argues that efforts to make service-learning "a transformative pedagogical practice that would change the fundamental policies and practices of the academy" are misguided, that this model needs an academic home base: a discipline and a department (Butin, 2010, p. 69).

Surprisingly yet ingeniously, Butin draws on Stanley Fish, the postmodernist literary critic, who argues in *Save the World on Your Own Time* (2008) for a relatively narrow mission for the university. Academics should resist efforts to improve students' moral character, to combat injustice, or to promote social change. Rather, Fish asserts,

> College and university teachers can (legitimately) do two things: (1) introduce students to bodies of knowledge and traditions of inquiry that had not previously been part of their experience; and (2) equip those same students with the analytical skills—of argument, statistical modeling, laboratory procedure—that will enable them to move confidently within those traditions and to engage in independent research after a course is over. (Fish, 2008, pp. 12–13)

That is, the core business of the university is conducted by the several disciplines. Fish maintains that a narrow focus on discipline-based inquiry and teaching will protect the academy from criticism and incursions from the wider society. He is not a conservative pedagogue: He does want professors to unsettle students, to induce them to problematize their assumptions; he adopts an antifoundationalist position. But he specifically opposes the granting of academic credit for internships, service-learning, or community outreach—*unless* "a student who returns from an internship experience…writes an academic paper (as opposed to a day-by-day journal or a 'what-I-did-on-my-summer-vacation' essay) analyzing and generalizing on her experience" (p. 21). Butin takes up that exception to argue that civic engagement is precisely the pedagogy that can justify credit-for-experience, *if* proponents turn it into a serious discipline, including the institutional forms like departments, programs, and majors, and *if* they practice an antifoundationalist pedagogy. In essence, Butin cleverly joins the disciplinary focus of Fish with the engagement focus of the experientialists.

The alternative strategy—what might be called "experience across the curriculum"—receives support from such theorist-activists as Carol Geary Schneider, since 1998 the president of the Association of American Colleges and Universities (AAC&U). While extolling the value of civic learning and community engagement, Schneider observes that the movement has not caught on with the majority of faculty or students. The challenge, she says, is to "change the practices of undergraduate education so that *civic engagement and learning become central rather than elective*" (Schneider, 2005, p. 128; emphasis added). Interestingly, she criticizes some advocates of engaged learning for their implicit support of a modernist, universalist epistemology and its corollary ethics, a vision of such basic (Western) rights as justice, liberty, and self-determination (p. 130).

[These] universalizing tendencies in the twentieth-century approach to liberal education proved problematic rather than generative when it came to the task of fostering active civic engagement in college students' own communities. Both as premise and as practice, the twentieth-century conception of liberal education did not provide a rich sense of the public sphere, or of public work to change society. (p. 131)

Her general point, then, supports Delanty's notion of the new function of the postmodern university—and her strategy is to push for a change in the current epistemology and institutional form of the academy, partly by means of a reconceived version of civic engagement, one more responsive to and nurturant of the diverse modes of thought and action in a multiethnic and global world. By implication, Schneider rejects Butin's strategy of departmentalizing service-learning because it relies on an obsolescent bureaucratic form and a moribund epistemology.

In my opinion, Schneider mounts the stronger argument. Delanty's critique of the university—an institution shaped and dominated by the professions and the disciplines—makes a convincing case that the postmodern shift toward a knowledge society undermines both the epistemological and the organizational foundations of the modern academy. Hitching the wagon of civic engagement to an obsolescent structure seems a risky strategy. Certainly majors, minors, certificates, and departments devoted to community engagement can meet the needs of students and faculty already drawn to that sort of activity. The "academicizing" (Fish, 2008) of engaged learning can only enhance the rigor with which those people analyze their experience and the social issues it addresses.

Despite the growth of these programs, however, despite the many conferences and publications touting civic engagement, Butin (2012) himself noted recently that the field has reached an "engagement ceiling": The proportion of college faculty and students who engage in service-learning or other experiential programs has topped out at under 10 percent, and there is little growth in participation rates; meanwhile, as *The Crucible Moment* (National Task Force, 2012) and a national survey by Johnson and Levy (2012) indicate, students subscribe less and less to principles of democratic citizenship, more and more to neoliberal notions of personal success. Under those social and historical conditions, setting up a disciplinary home for those who want to perform and study civic engagement promises diminishing returns, and certainly does not lead to the transformation of the academy—and, ultimately, of society—that advocates yearn for.

Conclusions

These observations bring us back to our central questions: In what senses, to what extent, and under what conditions does out-of-school experience *fit* in higher education? When and how does it achieve and advance the mission of the university as an educational enterprise? As we have seen, where one comes out on these issues depends first on what one believes that mission is, and then on what should be done to accomplish it. For conservatives from Newman to Hutchins to Bloom, mere experience has no place in the curriculum of the university—that pronouncement settles the question. For the liberal who imagines the academy as an engine of social progress—as a device for enlarging the knowledge and expertise with which we can solve common (or even particular) problems, and as a way to expand access to the paths to individual success and social improvement—internships, cooperative education, and service-learning in the form of standard community service will seem appropriate and promising. Evidence that those programs succeed by those standards is mixed, but under certain conditions they do some good (cf. Bailey et al., 2004; Linn et al., 2004).

As I suggested in the sections on the epistemological and pedagogical aspects of experiential education, squeezing college-level learning out of firsthand experience poses a tremendous challenge for the serious academic. The kinds of knowledge encountered and used in workplaces and service activities do not align neatly with those found in the college classroom. Transfer of learning, the cognitive spanning of academic and external contexts, requires certain kinds of conditions and processes, and those do not manifest consistently either in workplace and community settings or in college classrooms. Simply asserting that a student reading sociological studies of poverty in school enriches her learning by also tutoring a poor child in a settlement house does not make that transfer happen. The student reading Max Weber on bureaucracy and concurrently interning at the New York City Department of Education did not connect those two forms of knowledge on her own. The two-way street is filled with bumps and potholes, and demands a lot of work.

On the other hand, when well-conceived and well-executed pedagogical strategies are employed both in the field and in the classroom, the potential does exist for making a great deal of the complex relationship between theory and practice, between ideas and actions. Indeed, many educators are already working on that two-way street. At NYU, for example, my colleague Laurel George (2012) uses ethnography as a tool to help students both to see the details of workplace culture and organizational dynamics and to step back from those details to place them in relation to larger social issues like globalization, the postindustrial labor market, and gender relations. Whether based in models of reflection proposed by workplace educators (Billett, 2001; Boud et al., 1993; Raelin, 2008), in critical theory (Kincheloe, 2008; Sheffield, 2011), in feminism (Fisher 2001; hooks, 1994), or in postmodernism (Delanty, 2001), methods do exist for tapping the learning possibilities inherent in the dialectical relation between experience and academic inquiry.

At the risk of sounding wishy-washy, I will declare that I am actually not dogmatic about the choice of pedagogical approach, though I favor some models and do not promote others. I used to think that critical discourse was the most effective model (Moore, 1990), and still believe it is useful, but I have come to believe that any method is effective that manages to induce the learner to look carefully at her experience, to question her own assumptions, to place the experience in relation to larger institutional and societal processes and discourses, to hear others' voices, to grapple with the question of why things happen the way they do, to imagine how things might be different, to read her experience in terms given by major social theories and to critique those theories from the perspective of her experience—to engage, in other words, in *serious* critical thinking. These methods have been particularly well developed in the realm of service-learning and community engagement (cf. Droge & Murphy, 1999; Harkavy & Donovan, 2000; Jacoby, 2009; Stewart & Webster, 2011), but can be adapted for cooperative education, internships, and other forms of experiential learning.

These pedagogies are radical in the sense that they get at the root of things, at the underlying social, political, and cultural dynamics within which experience occurs and knowledge is produced and used. Some of them, like critical theory, are explicitly radical in a political sense as well— and that fact raises important questions about the nature of engaged learning in the academy, about whether and to what extent teaching-learning activities should rest on preconceived value commitments and political positions.

While I generally subscribe to the premises and goals of critical pedagogy, two elements of that practice raise concerns: First, it risks attracting opposition not only from conservatives like David Horowitz (2006) determined to smoke out left-wing bias among university professors, but also from moderates and even progressives who, like Stanley Fish (2008), prefer to keep politics out of scholarly work, especially teaching. Identifying engaged learning with overtly radical beliefs may place it in some jeopardy, diverting its proponents' energies into fruitless debates and defenses. This reservation smacks of timidity, I know, but warrants attention. Second, and more importantly to me, it tends to subscribe to a master narrative, a set of premises taken as given—namely, that society is in fact unjust, that ideologies blind regular folks to the operations of hegemony, and so on—that ought to be taken as questions rather than as answers, that should be treated as matters for critical inquiry rather than as axioms. Having thought a great deal about these premises, I am ready to defend them as a participant in critical discourse, but I am not ready to insist that my students accept them as True. I would rather they reach their own conclusions—even if they differ from my own—through a process of engaged learning.

In the absence of these intensive strategies of reflection and critique, on the other hand, I am willing to say that conventional, neoliberal models of experiential education—whether co-op, work-related internships, or traditional community service—devolve into mere training or mere service, and may not be appropriate for higher education as envisioned in the radical mission. If Sunil, the intern who collects profit-and-earnings data on technology start-ups for an investment bank, does not have occasion back at school to ask questions about the economics, politics, and ethics of venture capital, he learns only to play an uncritical role in an unexamined game. Lisa, the fashion-magazine intern, needs to learn more than how to Google celebrities and how to generate a story; she ought to be encouraged to think about the nature of fashion as a cultural force, its impact on consumption, identity, and community. Even Heather, our history-museum guide, needs to think about more than the name of the last Dutch governor of New York and the opening of the Erie Canal, about more than effective public speaking. She needs to interrogate the nature of historical narratives—who produces them, in whose interest—as well as such matters as why so few families of color visit her facility.

If these extended inquiries do not happen—if the investment-bank intern learns only to collect data and enter it in a spreadsheet, if Lisa learns only the technology and jargon of fashion journalism—then one must ask whether their internships fit in the university, especially in the liberal arts. To be sure, many preprofessional programs offer courses that teach students to perform tasks that will be useful to them when they enter the work world—and there is nothing essentially wrong with a school's performing that function. But many, if not most, chores that I have watched or heard about college interns performing were not so technically advanced that the students could not have learned them on the job once they graduated. The push toward internships as a crucial part of the college experience stems more from changes in the labor market than from the technical difficulty of preparing for careers. If the road into a job at *The Daily Show* begins with an internship, it is not because full-time work there demands knowledge that an intern picks up in a part-time placement; it is because the entertainment industry uses college interns as a source of free labor and a mechanism for screening job applicants. As Ross Perlin argues in *Intern Nation* (2010), this is exploitation, not education. Even when an intern does acquire knowledge and skill that prepare her for a career, I am willing to argue that that is not sufficient—not wrong, not educationally irrelevant or misguided, indeed generally a good thing, but not sufficient, either.

As educators, we need to consider more than career training and job preparation, important as that function may be. Rather, we need to create conditions under which students learn to think rigorously about the nature of the professional and/or civic work they do, the settings in which it happens, and the dynamics of the larger society. They need to learn to critique social relations, to analyze power arrangements, to make sense of historical forces. They need to gain experience in acting in the world in concert (as well as in competition) with others, to exercise their rights and responsibilities as citizens of a democracy, to work effectively with diverse others in a globalizing era.

The laissez-faire approach to experiential learning—the model in which students are satisfied with getting a foot in the career door, in which faculty tolerate internships because the programs attract enrollments, and in which employers tap a source of cheap labor—does not accomplish that mission. It certainly does not achieve the conservative mission of the university: It distracts students from serious academic learning, claiming time and energy better spent in the classroom, library, and laboratory. In fact, that model fails to achieve even the liberal mission of the university: The learning is fragmentary and misaligned with the college curriculum, an inefficient way of passing on applied skills; the employment benefits accrue primarily to students who can afford unpaid work and are probably one step up on the career ladder already, thus perpetuating a system of unequal access; and the school becomes nothing more than a training ground for the dominant social and economic institutions. That is not what higher education should be about.

Serious, effective engaged learning takes careful planning and substantial resources. It takes professors who understand the complexities of this approach and have developed facility in the necessary teaching practices. It takes time and effort on the part of the students, who may initially prefer only to do the job so they can get the job, and may resist the deeper reflection required. And it demands an administration willing to reconstitute the institution's relation to the larger community, to convince faculty of the legitimacy of experiential knowledge, and to accommodate the organizational reconfiguration that the practice may entail. Making this antifoundationalist, expansive, collaborative, but pedagogically challenging model dominant in higher education—indeed, in any one university—will certainly be difficult, but I believe that is where the institution should try to head. As the academy struggles to serve a new function in a postmodern, knowledge-driven, communications-based, diverse, and democratic society, engaged learning—not just civic engagement but internships and cooperative education—can play a major role in that transformation.

References

Abbott, A. (2001). *Chaos of disciplines*. Chicago, IL: University of Chicago Press.

Altbach, P. G. (2001). Patterns in higher education development. In P. G. Altbach, R. O. Berdahl, & P. J. Gumport (Eds.), *American higher education in the twenty-first century: Social, political, and economic challenges* (pp. 15–37). Baltimore, MD: The Johns Hopkins University Press.

Althusser, L. (1971). *Lenin and philosophy and other essays*. New York: Monthly Review Press.

Ambrose, S. A., Bridges, M. W., DiPietro, M., Lovett, M. C., & Norman, M. K. (2010). *How learning works: Seven research-based principles for smart teaching*. San Francisco, CA: Jossey-Bass.

Amherst College (2011a). *About Amherst: Mission*. Retrieved February 9, 2011, from https://www.amherst.edu/aboutamherst/mission.

——— (2011b). *About the Center for Community Engagement*. Retrieved February 9, 2011, from https://www.amherst.edu/academiclife/cce/about.

——— (2011c). *Community-based learning courses*. Retrieved February 9, 2011, from https://www.amherst.edu/academiclife/cce/students/academic/current_cbl_courses.

Appelbaum, E., & Batt, R. (1994). *The new American workplace: Transforming work systems in the United States*. Ithaca, NY: ILR Press.

Apple, M. (1995). *Education and power*. New York: Routledge.

——— (2004). *Ideology and curriculum*. New York: Routledge.

Applebaum, H. (Ed.). (1984). *Work in market and industrial societies*. Albany, NY: SUNY Press.

Aramark. (2011). *College relations*. Retrieved February 2, 2011, from http://www.aramarkcollegerelations.com/parent-center/statistics.

Argyris, C. (1994). *Knowledge for action*. San Francisco, CA: Jossey-Bass.

Argyris, C., & Schön, D. A. (1974). *Theory in practice: Increasing professional effectiveness*. San Francisco, CA: Jossey-Bass.

——— (1978). *Organizational learning*. Reading, MA: Addison-Wesley.

——— (1996). *Organizational learning II*. Reading, MA: Addison-Wesley.

Aristotle (2009). *The Nichomachean ethics*. (D. Ross, Trans.). New York: Oxford University Press.

Arnold, M. (1960). *Culture and anarchy.* New York: Cambridge University Press.

Aronowitz, S. (2001). *The knowledge factory: Dismantling the corporate university and creating true higher learning.* New York: Beacon Press.

Arum, R., & Roksa, J. (2011). *Academically adrift: Limited learning on college campuses.* Chicago, IL: University of Chicago Press.

Astin, A. W. (1992). *What matters in college?: Four critical years revisited.* San Francisco, CA: Jossey-Bass.

Attewell, P. (1990). What is skill? *Work and Occupations, 17*(4), 422–448.

Bailey, T. (1989). Changes in the nature and structure of work: Implications for skill requirements and skill formation. New York: National Center on Education and Employment.

Bailey, T. R., Hughes, K. L., & Moore, D. T. (2004). *Working knowledge: Work-based learning and education reform.* New York: RoutledgeFalmer.

Bain, K. (2004). *What the best college teachers do.* Cambridge, MA: Harvard University Press.

Barry, P. (2002). *Beginning theory: An introduction to literary and cultural theory.* Manchester, UK: Manchester University Press.

Baum, H. S. (1990). *Organizational membership: Personal development in the workplace.* Albany, NY: SUNY Press.

Beauchamp, G. A. (1975). *Curriculum theory.* Wilmette, IL: Kagg.

Belenky, M. F., Clinchy, B. N., Rule, N., & Tarule, J. M. (1997). *Women's ways of knowing.* New York: Basic Books.

Bellack, A. A., Kliebard, H. M., Hyman, R. T., & Smith, F. L. (1966). *Language of the classroom.* New York: Teachers College Press.

Bennett, W. J. (2001). Introduction. In Intercollegiate Studies Institute, *Choosing the right college: The whole truth about America's top colleges.* Grand Rapids, MI: William B. Eerdmans Publishing Company.

Benson, L., Harkavy, I., & Puckett, J. (2000). An implementation revolution as a strategy for fulfilling the democratic promise of university-community partnerships: Penn-West Philadelphia as an experiment in progress. *Nonprofit and Voluntary Sector Quarterly, 29*(1), 24–45.

Benson, L., Harkavy, I., & Hartley, M. (2005). Integrating a commitment to the public good into the institutional fabric. In A. Kezar, T. Chambers, & J. C. Burckhardt (Eds.), *Higher education for the public good* (pp. 185–216). San Francisco, CA: Jossey-Bass.

Bereiter, C. (1997). Situated cognition and how to overcome it. In D. Kirschner & J. A. Whitson (Eds.), *Situated cognition: Social, semiotic, and psychological perspectives.* Mahwah, NJ: Lawrence Erlbaum Associates.

Bereiter, C. & Scardamalia, M. (1993). *Surpassing ourselves: An inquiry into the nature and implications of expertise.* Chicago, IL: Open Court.

Berger, P. & Luckmann, T. (1966). *The social construction of reality.* Englewood Cliffs, NJ: Prentice-Hall.

Bernstein, B. (1975). *Class, codes, and control: Volume 3: Towards a theory of educational transmission.* London: Routledge and Kegan Paul.

Billett, S. (2001). *Learning in the workplace.* Crow's Nest, New South Wales: Allen and Unwin.

———— (2011). Subjectivity, self, and personal agency in learning through and for work. In M. Malloch, L. Cairns, K. Evans, & B. O'Connor (Eds.), *The Sage handbook of workplace learning.* Los Angeles, CA: Sage Publications.

Bligh, D. A. (2000). *What's the use of lectures?* San Francisco, CA: Jossey-Bass.

Bloom, A. (1987). *The closing of the American mind.* New York: Simon and Schuster.

Bloom, B., Engelhart, M. D., Furst, E. J., Hill, W. H., & Krathwohl, D. R. (1956). *Taxonomy of educational objectives: The classification of educational goals—Handbook 1: The cognitive domain.* New York: Longman.

Blumer, H. (1969). *Symbolic interactionism.* Englewood Clioffs, NJ: Prentice-Hall.

Bok Center for Teaching and Learning (2011). *About the Bok Center.* Retrieved February 9, 2011, from http://bokcenter.harvard.edu/icb/icb.do?keyword=k1985&pageid=icb.page29716&pageContentId=icb.pagecontent79802&view=view.do&viewParam_name=prevCBLcourses.html.

———— (2012). *Activity-based learning.* Retrieved August 3, 2012, from http://bokcenter.harvard.edu/icb/icb.do?keyword=k1985&pageid=icb.page29716&pageContentId=icb.pagecontent79802&view=view.do&viewParam_name=prevCBLcourses.html.

Bok, D. (2004). *Universities in the marketplace: The commercialization of higher education.* Princeton, NJ: Princeton University Press.

Bonwell, C. C. & Eison, J. A. (1991). *Active learning: Creating excitement in the classroom.* San Francisco, CA: Jossey-Bass.

Borzak, L. (Ed.). (1981). *Field study.* Los Angeles, CA: Sage Publications.

Boud, D., Cohen, R., & Walker, D. (1993). *Using experience for learning.* Bristol, PA: Society for Research into Higher Education and the Open University Press.

Boud, D. & Garrick, J. (1999). *Understanding learning at work.* New York: Routledge.

Boud, D. & Miller, N. (1996). *Working with experience: Animating learning.* London: Routledge.

Bourdieu, P. (1977). *Outline of a theory of practice.* New York: Cambridge University Press.

Bourdieu, P. & Wacquant, J. D. (1992). *An invitation to reflexive sociology.* Chicago, IL: University of Chicago Press.

Boyte, H. C. (2005). *Everyday politics: Reconnecting citizens and public life.* Philadelphia, PA: University of Pennsylvania Press.

Bransford, J. D., Brown, A. L., & Cocking, R. R. (2000). *How people learn: Brain, mind, experience, and school.* Washington, DC: National Academy Press.

Braverman, H. (1974). *Labor and monopoly capital: The degradation of work in the twentieth century.* New York: Monthly Review Press.

Brennan, J. & Little, B. (1996). *a review of work-based learning in higher education.* London: Open University.

Brookfield, S. D. (2004). *The power of critical theory: Liberating adult learning and teaching.* San Francisco, CA: Jossey-Bass.

——— (2005). *Discussion as a way of teaching: Tools and techniques for democratic classrooms*. San Francisco, CA: Jossey-Bass.

——— (2006). *The skillful teacher: On technique, trust, and responsiveness in the classroom*. San Francisco, CA: Jossey-Bass.

Brown, J. S., Collins, A., & Duguid, P. (1989). Situated cognition and the culture of learning. *Educational Researcher*, *18* (January–February), 32–42.

Bruner, J. S. (1966). *Toward a theory of instruction*. Cambridge, MA: Harvard University Press.

——— (1973). *Beyond the information given*. New York: Basic Books.

——— (1996a). *The culture of education*. Cambridge, MA: Harvard University Press.

——— (1996b). Frames for thinking: Ways of making meaning. In D. R. Olson & N. Torrance (Eds.), *Modes of thought: Explorations in culture and cognition*. New York: Cambridge University Press.

——— (2003). *Making stories: Law, literature, life*. Cambridge, MA: Harvard University Press.

Burr, V. (2003). *Social constructionism*. Second edition. New York: Routledge.

Butin, D. W. (Ed.). (2005). *Service-learning in higher education: Critical issues and directions*. New York: Palgrave Macmillan.

——— (2005). Service-learning as postmodern pedagogy. In D. W. Butin (Ed.), *Service-learning in higher education: Critical issues and directions* (pp. 89–104). New York: Palgrave Macmillan.

——— (2008). Saving the university on his own time: Stanley Fish, service-learning, and knowledge limitation in the academy. *Michigan Journal of Community Service Learning*, *15*(1): 62–69.

——— (2010). *Service-learning in theory and practice*. New York: Palgrave Macmillan.

——— (2012, June). *When engagement is not enough: Academic programs as a key component in the institutionalization of community engagement*. Paper presentation at the Third Annual Summer Research Institute on the Future of Community Engagement in Higher Education, Merrimack College, North Andover, MA.

Buzzle. (2012). *Laboratory methods of teaching*. Retrieved July 31, 2012, from http://www.buzzle.com/articles/laboratory-methods-of-teaching.html.

Cahoone, L. E. (2002). *The ends of philosophy*. Oxford: Blackwell Publishers.

——— (2010). *The modern intellectual tradition: From Descartes to Derrida*. Chantilly, VA: The Great Courses.

Cairns, L. (2011). Learning in the workplace: Communities of practice and beyond. In M. Malloch, L. Cairns, K. Evans, & B. O'Connor (Eds.), *The Sage handbook of workplace learning* (pp. 73–85). Los Angeles: Sage.

Calderon, J. Z. (Ed.). (2007). *Race, poverty, and social justice: Multidisciplinary perspectives through service-learning*. Sterling, VA: Stylus.

Campus Compact. (2011). *About Campus Compact*. Retrieved February 10, 2011, from http://www.compact.org/about/.

Cantor, J. A. (1995). *Experiential learning in higher education: Linking classroom and community*. ASHE-ERIC Higher Education Reports, Volume 7. Washington, DC: George Washington University.

Carlson, A. (2001). *Authentic learning: What does it really mean?* Bellingham, WA: Center for Instructional Innovation and Assessment, Western Washington University. Retrieved June 25, 2012, from http://pandora.cii.wwu.edu/showcase 2001/authentic_learning.asp.

Carnegie Foundation for the Advancement of Teaching. (2012). *Community engagement.* Retrieved March 10, 2012, from http://classifications.carnegiefoundation .org/descriptions/community_engagement.php.

Casner-Lotto, J. & Benner, M. W. (2006). Are they really ready to work?: Employers' perspectives on the basic knowledge and applied skills of new entrants to the 21st-century U.S. workforce. New York: The Conference Board, The Partnership for 21st-Century Skills, Corporate Voices for Working Families, & The Society for Human Resource Management.

Center for Engaged Democracy. (2012). *About us.* Retrieved August 1, 2012, from http://center-for-engaged-democracy.wikispaces.com/.

Chaiklin, S., & Lave, J. (Eds.). (1993). *Understanding practice: Perspectives on activity and context.* New York: Cambridge University Press.

Chambers, T. C. (2005). The special role of higher education in society: As a public good for the public good. In A. J. Kezar, T. C. Chambers, & J. C. Burkhardt (Eds.), *Higher education for the public good.* San Francisco, CA: Jossey-Bass.

Chi, M. T. H., Glaser, R., & Farr, M. J. (Eds.). (1988). *The nature of expertise.* Hillsdale, NJ: Lawrence Erlbaum Associates.

Cohen, A. M. (1998). *The shaping of American higher education: Emergence and growth of the contemporary system.* San Francisco, CA: Jossey-Bass.

Cole, M., Hood, L., & McDermott, R. P. (1978). Ecological niche-picking: Ecological invalidity as an axiom of experimental cognitive psychology. Unpublished manuscript, The Rockefeller University, New York. Retrieved August 3, 2012, from http://132.239.241.8/assets/media/13189692664e9ddfb2 7b97c167519525.pdf.

Cole, M., & Means, B. (1986). *Comparative studies of how people think.* Cambridge, MA: Harvard University Press.

Coles, R. (1993). *The call of service: A witness to idealism.* Boston, MA: Houghton Mifflin.

Cooley, C. H. (1922). *Human nature and the social order.* New York: Scribner's.

Crawford, M. B. (2009). *Shop craft as soulcraft: An inquiry into the value of work.* New York: The Penguin Press.

Cree, V., & Macauley, C. (Eds.). (2001). *Transfer of learning in professional and vocational education.* New York: Routledge.

D'Souza, D. (1991). *Illiberal education: The politics of race and sex on campus.* New York: The Free Press.

Dallimore, E., Rochefort, D. A., & Simonelli, K. (2010). Community-based learning and research. In D. Qualters (Ed.), *Experiential education: Making the most of learning outside the classroom.* San Francisco, CA: Jossey-Bass.

Darrah, C. N. (1996). *Learning and work: An exploration in industrial ethnography.* New York: Garland Press.

Deal, T. E., & Kennedy, A. A. (2000). *Corporate cultures: The rites and rituals of corporate life*. New York: Basic Books.

Deal, T. E., & Peterson, K. D. (2009). *Shaping school culture: Pitfalls, paradoxes, and promises*. San Francisco, CA: Jossey-Bass.

Delanty, G. (1997). *Social science: Beyond constructivism and realism*. Minneapolis, MN: University of Minnesota Press.

——— (2001). *Challenging knowledge: The university in the knowledge society*. Philadelphia, PA: The Society for Research into Higher Education & Open University Press.

Delaware Valley College. (2012). *Center for Student Professional Development*. Retrieved August 1, 2012, from http://www.delval.edu/pages/career_life/C990/.

Descartes, R. (1960). Discourse on method. In M. C. Beardsley (Ed.), *The European philosophers from Descartes to Nietzsche*. New York: The Modern Library.

Dewey, J. (1910). *How we think*. Mineola, NY: Dover Publications.

——— (1916). *Democracy and education*. New York: Macmillan.

——— (1938). *Experience and education*. New York: Collier Books.

——— (1960). *The quest for certainty*. New York: G. P. Putnam's Sons.

——— (1964). Why reflective thinking must be an educational aim. In R. D. Archambault (Ed.), *John Dewey on education: Selected writings* (pp. 212–228). Chicago, IL: University of Chicago Press.

Digman, J. M. (1990). Personality structure: Emergence of the five-factor model. *Annual Review of Psychology, 41*, 417–440.

Dreyfus, H., & Dreyfus, S. (1988). *Mind over machine: The power of human intuition and expertise in the era of the computer*. New York: The Free Press.

——— (2005). Peripheral vision: Expertise in real-world contexts. *Organization Studies, 26*(5), 779–792.

Droge, D., & Murphy, B. O. (Eds.). (1999). *Voices of strong democracy: Concepts and models for service-learning in communication studies*. Washington, DC: American Association for Higher Education.

Dunne, J. (1993). *Back to the rough ground: Practical judgment and the lure of technique*. South Bend, IN: University of Notre Dame Press.

Durkheim, E. (1915). *The elementary forms of religious life*. New York: The Free Press.

Elkjaer, B. (2009). Pragmatism: A learning theory for the future. In K. Illeris (Ed.), *Contemporary theories of learning* (pp. 74–89). New York: Routledge.

Engestrom, Y. (2001). Expansive learning at work: Toward an activity-theoretical reconceptualization. *Journal of Education and Work, 14*(1), 133–156.

——— (2008). *From teams to knots: Activity-theoretical studies of collaboration and learning at work*. New York: Cambridge University Press.

Eraut, M. (2004). Informal learning in the workplace. *Studies in Continuing Education, 26*(2), 247–273.

Erickson, F. (2004). *Talk and social theory: Ecologies of speaking and listening in everyday life*. Malden, MA: Polity Press.

Erikson, E. (1963). *Childhood and society*. New York: W. W. Norton.

——— (1994). *Identity: Youth and crisis*. New York: W. W. Norton.

Eyler, J. (2009). The power of experiential learning. *Liberal Education*, *95*(4), 24–31.

Eyler, J. & Giles, D. E. (1999). *Where's the learning in service-learning?* San Francisco, CA: Jossey-Bass.

Eyler, J., Giles, D. E., & Schmiede, A. (1996). The practitioner's guide to reflection. Unpublished manuscript, Vanderbilt University, Nashville, TN.

Facione, P. A. (2011). *Critical thinking: What it is and why it counts*. Millbrae, CA: Measured Reasons.

Fedorko, J. (2006). *The intern files: How to get, keep, and make the most of your internship*. New York: Simon Spotlight.

Feldman, R. (2003). *Epistemology*. Upper Saddle River, NJ: Prentice-Hall.

Fenwick, T. (2003). *Learning through experience: Troubling orthodoxies and intersecting questions*. Malabar, FL: Krieger.

Fish, S. (2008). *Save the world on your own time*. New York: Oxford University Press.

Fisher, B. M. (2001). *No angel in the classroom: Teaching through feminist discourse*. Lanham, MD: Rowman & Littlefield.

Flanders, N. (1970). *Analyzing teacher behavior*. Reading, MA: Addison-Wesley.

Flavell, J. H. (1963). *The developmental psychology of Jean Piaget*. New York: Van Nostrand.

Flyvbjerg, B. (2001). *Making social science matter: Why social inquiry fails and how it can succeed again*. New York: Cambridge University Press.

Foucault, M. (1980). *Power/Knowledge: Selected interviews and other writings 1972–1977*. New York: Pantheon Books.

——— (1995). *Discipline and punish: The birth of the prison*. New York: Vintage Books/Random House.

——— (2010). *The archaeology of knowledge and the discourse on language*. New York: Vintage Books/Random House.

Freire, P. (1970). *Pedagogy of the oppressed*. New York: Herder and Herder.

Fuller, A. (2007). Critiquing theories of learning and communities of practice. In J. Hughes, N. Jewson, & L. Unwin (Eds.), *Communities of practice: Critical perspectives*. New York: Routledge.

Gardner, H. (1983). *Frames of mind: The theory of multiple intelligences*. New York: Basic Books.

——— (2006). *Multiple intelligences*. New York: Basic Books.

Gardner, S. (1999). *Kant and the* Critique of Pure Reason. New York: Routledge.

Garfinkel, H. (1967). *Studies in ethnomethodology*. Englewood Cliffs, NJ: Prentice-Hall.

Geertz, C. (1977). *The interpretation of cultures*. New York: Basic Books.

George, L. (2012, July 25). *Workplace ethnography 101: Interrogating the unpaid internship*. [Web log post]. Retrieved from http://savageminds.org/2012/07/25 /workplace-ethnography-101-interrogating-the-unpaid-internship/.

Gergen, K. J. (2009). *An invitation to social construction*. Second edition. Los Angeles: Sage.

Giddens, A. (1986). *The constitution of society: Outline of the theory of structuration*. Berkeley, CA: University of California Press.

Gilligan, C. (1982). *In a different voice.* Cambridge, MA: Harvard University Press.

Giroux, H. (1984). *Ideology, culture, and the process of schooling.* Philadelphia, PA: Temple University Press.

——— (2007). *The university in chains: Confronting the military-industrial-academic complex.* Boulder, CO: Paradigm Publishers.

——— (2011). *On critical pedagogy.* New York: Continuum Books.

Glaser, R., & Chi, M. T. H. (1988). Overview. In M. T. H. Chi, R. Glaser, & M. J. Farr (Eds.), *The nature of expertise* (pp. xv–xxviii). Hillsdale, NJ: Lawrence Erlbaum Associates.

Goffman, E. (1959). *The presentation of self in everyday life.* Garden City, NY: Doubleday.

——— (1974). *Frame analysis: An essay on the organization of experience.* New York: Harper and Row.

Goleman, D. (2006). *Emotional intelligence: Why it can matter more than IQ.* New York: Bantam.

——— (2007). *Social intelligence: The revolutionary new science of human relationships.* New York: Bantam.

Goodenough, W. (1957). Cultural anthropology and linguistics. In P. L. Gavin (Ed.), *Report on the 7th Annual Roundtable Meetings on Linguistics and Language Study.* Washington, DC: Georgetown University, Monograph Series on Language and Linguistics, No. 9, 167–173.

Goodman, R. B. (Ed.). (1995). *Pragmatism: a contemporary reader.* London: Routledge.

Gramsci, A. (1971). *Selections from the prison notebooks of Antonio Gramsci.* New York: International Publishers.

Grimmett, P. P., & Neufeld, J. (1994). *Teacher development and the struggle for authenticity: Professional growth and restructuring in the context of change.* New York: Teachers College Press.

Guilford, J. P. (1967). *The nature of human intelligence.* New York: McGraw-Hill.

Gumperz, J. J., & Hymes, D. (Eds.). *Directions in sociolinguistics: The ethnography of communication.* New York: Basil Blackwell.

Habermas, J. (1979). *Communication and the evolution of society.* Boston, MA: Beacon Press.

——— (1989). *The structural transformation of the public sphere.* Cambridge, MA: Polity Press.

Hager, P. (2011). Theories of workplace learning. In M. Malloch, L. Cairns, K. Evans, & B. O'Connor (Eds.), *The Sage handbook of workplace learning* (pp. 17–31). Los Angeles: Sage.

Hakel, M. D., & Halpern, D. F. (2005). How far can transfer go? Making transfer happen across physical, temporal, and conceptual space. In J. P. Mestre (Ed.), *Transfer of learning: From a modern multidisciplinary perspective.* Greenwich, CT: Information Age Publishing.

Hall, S. (Ed.). (1997). *Representation: Cultural representations and signifying practices.* London: Sage.

Hamada, T., & Sibley, W. E. (Eds.). (1994). *Anthropological perspectives on organizational culture*. Lanham, MD: University Press of America.

Hamilton, S. F. (1990). *Apprenticeship for adulthood: Preparing youth for the future*. New York: The Free Press.

Hanks, W. F. (1991). Foreword. In J. Lave, & E. Wenger, *Situated learning*. New York: Cambridge University Press.

Harkavy, I., & Donovan, B. M. (Eds.). (2000). *Connecting past and present: Concepts and models for service-learning in history*. Washington, DC: American Association for Higher Education.

Hart, J. (2001). *Smiling through the catastrophe: Toward the revival of higher education*. New Haven, CT: Yale University Press.

Harvard College. (2012a). *About the core program*. Retrieved July 29, 2012, from http://isites.harvard.edu/icb/icb.do?keyword=core&pageid=icb.page29341.

——— (2012b). *What is Harvard's mission statement?* Retrieved July 29, 2012, from http://www.harvard.edu/siteguide/faqs/faq110.php.

Harvey, D. (2005). *A brief history of neoliberalism*. New York: Oxford University Press.

Haskell, R. E. (2001). *Transfer of learning: Cognition, instruction, and reasoning*. New York: Academic Press.

Hatch, M. J. (1997). *Organization theory*. New York: Oxford University Press.

Hirsch, E. D. (1987). *Cultural literacy*. Boston, MA: Houghton Mifflin.

Hoffman, R. R. (Ed.). (1992). *The psychology of expertise: Cognitive research and empirical AI*. New York: Springer-Verlag.

hooks, b. (1994). *Teaching to transgress: Education as the practice of freedom*. New York: Routledge.

Horowitz, D. (2006). *The professors: The 101 most dangerous academics in America*. Washington, DC: Regnery Publishing.

Hughes, J. N., Jewson, N., & Unwin, L. (Eds.) (2007). *Communities of practice: Critical perspectives*. New York: Routledge.

Husserl, E. (1973). *Logical investigations*. London: Routledge.

Hutchins, E. (1993). Learning to navigate. In S. Chaiklin, & J. Lave (Eds.), *Understanding practice: Perspectives on activity and context*. New York: Cambridge University Press.

Hutchins, R. M. (1995). *The higher learning in America*. New York: Transaction.

Illeris, K. (2006). *How we learn: Learning and non-learning in school and beyond*. New York: Routledge.

——— (Ed.). (2009). *Contemporary theories of learning*. New York: Routledge.

Intern Bridge. (2012). *About Intern Bridge*. Retrieved March 12, 2012, from http://internbridge.com/.

Jacoby, B. (Ed.). (1996). *Service-learning in higher education: Concepts and practices*. San Francisco, CA: Jossey-Bass.

——— (Ed.). (2009). *Civic engagement in higher education: Concepts and practices*. San Francisco, CA: Jossey-Bass.

James, W. (1981). *Pragmatism: A new name for old ways of thinking*. Boston, MA: Hackett.

——— (1983). *Talks to teachers and students about psychology.* Cambridge, MA: Harvard University Press.

Jay, M. (1996). *The dialectical imagination: A history of the Frankfurt School and the Institute of Social Research, 1923–1950.* Berkeley, CA: University of California Press.

——— (2005). *Songs of experience: Modern American and European variations on a universal theme.* Berkeley, CA: University of California Press.

Johnson, M., & Levy, D. (2012). *The national assessment of service and community engagement: Results from 14,000 student surveys on 30 campuses.* Paper presentation at the Third Annual Summer Research Institute on the Future of Community Engagement in Higher Education, Merrimack College, North Andover, MA.

Kahn, C. (1979). *The art and thought of Heraclitus: Fragments with translation and commentary.* New York: Cambridge University Press.

Kant, I. (1998). *Critique of pure reason.* New York: Cambridge University Press.

Kanter, R. M., Stein, B. A., & Jick, T. D. (2003). *The challenge of organizational change: How companies experience it and how leaders guide it.* New York: The Free Press.

Keeton, M. (1976). *Experiential learning.* San Francisco, CA: Jossey-Bass.

Kelshaw, T., Lazarus, F., & Minier, J. (2009). *Partnerships for service-learning: Impacts on communities and students.* San Francisco, CA: Jossey-Bass.

Kendall, J. (Ed.). (1990). *Combining service and learning: A resource book for community and public service—Volume 1.* Raleigh, NC: National Society for Experiential Education.

Kendall, J., Duley, J. S., Little, T. C., Permaul, J., & Rubin, S. (1986). *Strengthening experiential education within your institution.* Raleigh, NC: National Society for Internships and Experiential Education.

Kerr, C. (2011). *The uses of the university.* Cambridge, MA: Harvard University Press.

Kezar, A. (2005a). Challenges for higher education in serving the public good. In A. Kezar, T. Chambers, & J. C. Burkhardt (Eds.) (2005). *Higher education for the public good: Emerging voices from a national movement* (pp. 23–42). San Francisco, CA: Jossey-Bass.

——— (2005b). Creating a metamovement: A vision toward regaining the public social charter. In A. Kezar, T. Chambers, & J. C. Burkhardt (Eds.) (2005). *Higher education for the public good: Emerging voices from a national movement* (pp. 43–54). San Francisco, CA: Jossey-Bass.

Kezar, A., Chambers, T., & Burkhardt, J. C. (Eds.). (2005). *Higher education for the public good: Emerging voices from a national movement.* San Francisco, CA: Jossey-Bass.

Kimball, R. (1998). *Tenured radicals: How politics has corrupted our higher education.* New York: Harper Collins.

Kincheloe, J. L. (2008). *Critical pedagogy: A primer.* New York: Peter Lang.

Kirp, D. L. (2003). *Shakespeare, Einstein, and the bottom line: The marketing of higher education.* Cambridge, MA: Harvard University Press.

Kiser, P. (2000). *Getting the most from your human services internship: Learning from experience.* Belmont, CA: Wadsworth.

Klein, J. T. (1990). *Interdisciplinarity: History, theory, and practice.* Detroit, MI: Wayne State University Press.

Knowles, M. S., Holton. E. F., & Swanson, R. A. (2011). *The adult learner.* 7th edition. Boston, MA: Butterworth/Heinemann/Elsevier.

Kohlberg, L. (1981). *The meaning and measurement of moral development.* Worcester, MA: Clark University Heinz Werner Institute.

Kolb, D. (1984). *Experiential learning.* Englewood Cliffs, NJ: Prentice-Hall.

——— (1985). *Learning styles inventory.* Boston, MA: McBer and Company.

Kors, A. C., & Silverglate, H. A. (1998). *The shadow university: The betrayal of liberty on America's campuses.* New York: The Free Press.

Kraft, R., & Kielsmeier, J. (1995). *Experiential learning in schools and higher education.* Boulder, CO: Association for Experiential Education.

Kraft, R., & Sakofs, M. (Eds.). (1982). *The theory of experiential education.* Boulder, CO: Association for Experiential Education.

Kronick, R. F., Cunningham, R. B., & Gourley, M. (2011). *Experiencing service-learning.* Knoxville, TN: University of Tennessee Press.

Kuhn, D. (1989). Children and adults as intuitive scientists. *Psychological Review, 96*(4), 674–689.

Kusterer, K. (1978). *Know-how on the job: The important working knowledge of unskilled workers.* Boulder, CO: Westview Press.

Lakoff, G., & Johnson, M. (2003). *Metaphors we live by.* Chicago, IL: University of Chicago Press.

Langer, E. J. (1989). *Mindfulness.* Cambridge, MA: Perseus Books.

——— (1997). *The power of mindful learning.* Cambridge, MA: Perseus Books.

Lave, J. (1988). *Cognition in practice.* New York: Cambridge University Press.

——— (2011). *Apprenticeship in critical ethnographic practice.* Chicago, IL: University of Chicago Press.

Lave, J., & Wenger, E. (1991). *Situated learning: Legitimate peripheral participation.* New York: Cambridge University Press.

Leamnson, R. (1999). *Thinking about teaching and learning: Developing habits of learning with first-year college and university students.* Sterling, VA: Stylus.

Leont'ev, A. N. (1979). The problem of activity in psychology. In J. Wertsch (Ed.), *The concept of activity in Soviet psychology.* Armonk, NY: M. E. Sharpe.

Levi-Strauss, C. (1968). *The savage mind.* Chicago, IL: University of Chicago Press.

Lewin, K. (1951). *Field theory in the social sciences.* New York: Harper and Row.

Lewis, A. J., & Miel, A. (1978). Key words relating to curriculum and instruction. In J. R. Gress, & D. Purpel, *Curriculum: An introduction to the field.* Berkeley, CA: McCutchan.

Liang, J. (2005). *Hello real world: a student's approach to great internships, co-ops, and entry-level positions.* Charleston, SC: BookSurge.

Linn, P. L., Howard, A., & Miller, E. (2004). *Handbook for research in cooperative education and internships.* Mahwah, NJ: Lawrence Erlbaum Associates.

Locke, J. (1996). *An essay concerning human understanding.* New York: Hackett.

Lombardi, M. M. (2007). *Authentic learning for the 21st century: An overview.* Boulder, CO: Educause.

Longo, N. V., & Shaffer, M. S. (2009). Leadership education and the revitalization of public life. In B. Jacoby (Ed.), *Civic engagement in higher education.* San Francisco, CA: Jossey-Bass.

Luria, A. R. (1976). *Cognitive development: Its cultural and social foundations.* Cambridge, MA: Harvard University Press.

Lyotard, J.-F. (1984). *The postmodern condition.* Minneapolis, MN: University of Minnesota Press.

Macaulay, C. (2001). Transfer of learning. In V. Cree, & C. Macaulay (Eds.), *Transfer of learning in professional and vocational education* (pp. 1–26). New York: Routledge.

Magee, B. (1998). *The story of philosophy.* New York: DK Publishing.

Malloch, M., Cairns, L., Evans, K., & O'Connor, B. (2011). *The Sage handbook of workplace learning.* Los Angeles, CA: Sage Publications.

Marsick, V. J., & Watkins, K. E. (1990). *Informal and incidental learning in the workplace.* New York: Routledge.

Martin, J. (1992). *Culture in organizations: Three perspectives.* New York: Oxford University Press.

Marzano, R. J., & Kendall, J. S. (2007). *The new taxonomy of educational objectives.* Thousand Oaks, CA: Corwin Press/Sage Publications.

Maurrasse, D. J. (2001). *Beyond the campus: How colleges and universities form partnerships with their communities.* New York: Routledge.

Mayer, J. D., Brackett, M. A., & Salovey, P. (2004). *Emotional intelligence: Key readings on the Mayer and Salovey model.* Port Chester, NY: Dude Publishing.

McEvoy, K. E. (2010). *Creating a learning environment: A case study of an innovative marketing internship program* (Unpublished doctoral dissertation). New York University, New York.

McIntyre, A. (2008). *Participatory action research.* Los Angeles, CA: Sage Publications.

McKeachie, W. J. (2002). *McKeachie's teaching tips: Strategies, research, and theory for college and university teachers.* 11th edition. Boston, MA: Houghton Mifflin.

Mead, G. H. (1934). *Mind, self, and society.* Chicago, IL: University of Chicago Press.

Mehan, H. (1979). *Learning lessons.* Cambridge, MA: Harvard University Press.

Mehan, H., & Wood, D. (1975). *The reality of ethnomethodology.* Cambridge, MA: Harvard University Press.

Merriam, S. B. (Ed.). (2001). *The new update on adult learning theory.* New directions for adult and continuing education, Number 89, Spring 2001. San Francisco, CA: Jossey-Bass.

Merton, R. K. (1949). *Social theory and social structure.* Glencoe, IL: Free Press.

Mestre, J. P. (Ed.). (2005). *Transfer of learning: From a modern multidisciplinary perspective.* Greenwich, CT: Information Age Publishing.

Meyers, C., & Jones, T. B. (1993). *Promoting active learning: Strategies for the college classroom.* San Francisco, CA: Jossey-Bass.

Mezirow, J. (1990). *Fostering critical reflection in adulthood: A guide to transformative and emancipatory learning.* San Francisco, CA: Jossey-Bass.

——— (2000). *Learning as transformation: Critical perspectives on a theory in progress.* San Francisco, CA: Jossey-Bass.

Mitchell, T. D. (2008). Traditional vs. critical service-learning: Engaging the literature to differentiate two models. *Michigan Journal of Community Service Learning,* *14*(2), 50–65.

Moon, J. A. (2004). *A handbook of experiential and reflective learning: Theory and practice.* New York: RoutledgeFalmer.

Moore, D. T. (1981a). Discovering the pedagogy of experience. *Harvard Educational Review, 51*(2), 286–300.

——— (1981b). *The social organization of educational encounters in non-school settings.* Washington, DC: National Institute of Education.

——— (1986). Knowledge at work: An approach to learning by interns. In K. Borsman, & J. Reisman (Eds.), *Becoming a worker.* Norwood, NJ: Ablex Publishing.

——— (1990). Experiential education as critical discourse. In J. Kendall (Ed.), *Combining service and learning.* Raleigh, NC: National Society for Experiential Education.

——— (1999). Behind the wizard's curtain: A challenge to the true believer. *NSEE Quarterly* (Fall), 1–4.

——— (2004). Curriculum at work: An educational perspective on the workplace as a learning environment. *Journal of Workplace Learning, 16*(6), 325–340.

——— (2007). Analyzing learning at work: An interdisciplinary framework. *Learning Inquiry, 1*(3), 175–188.

——— (2008). Workplace learning and the micropolitics of knowledge. In W. J. Nijhof, & L. F. M. Nieuwenhuis (Eds.), *The learning potential of the workplace* (pp. 117–128). Rotterdam, The Netherlands: Sense Publishers.

——— (2010). Forms and issues in experiential learning. In D. Qualters (Ed.), *Experiential education: Making the most of learning outside the classroom* (pp. 3–13). San Francisco, CA: Jossey-Bass.

Moran, J. (2010). *Interdisciplinarity: The new critical idiom.* New York: Routledge.

Murphy, G. L. (2002). *The big book of concepts.* Cambridge, MA: MIT Press.

NACE (National Association of Colleges and Employers). (2010). *Interns more likely.* Retrieved February 2, 2012, from http://www.naceweb.org/Publications/Spotlight_Online/2010/0526/Interns_More_Likely.

National Task Force on Civic Learning and Democratic Engagement. (2012). *A crucible moment: College learning and democracy's future.* Washington, DC: Association of American Colleges and Universities.

Neill, A. S. (1984). *Summerhill: A radical approach to childrearing.* New York: Pocket Books.

Newman, J. H. (1996). *The idea of a university.* New Haven, CT: Yale University Press.

Nijhof, W. J., & Nieuwenhuis, L. F. M. (Eds.). (2008). *The learning potential of the workplace.* Rotterdam, The Netherlands: Sense Publishers.

Northeastern University. (2012). *How co-op works.* Retrieved July 3, 2012, from http://www.northeastern.edu/experiential-learning/coop/howcoopworks/support.html.

NSEE (National Society for Experiential Education). (2011). *About us.* Retrieved February 10, 2011, from http://nsee.org/about-us.

NSSE (National Survey of Student Engagement). (2010). *Major differences: Examining student engagement by field of study–annual results 2010.* Bloomington: Indiana University Center for Postsecondary Research.

NYU (New York University). (2011a). *About civic engagement.* Retrieved February 10, 2011, from http://www.nyu.edu/civic.engagement/about/.

——— (2001b). *About jobs.* Retrieved February 10, 2011, from http://www.nyu.edu/careerdevelopment/students/jobs.php.

——— (2011c). *About student activities.* Retrieved February 10, 2011, from http://www.nyu.edu/about/leadership-university-administration/office-of-the-president/office-of-the-provost/university-life/office-of-studentaffairs/office-of-student-activities.html.

O'Brien, J. G., Millis, B. J., & Cohen, M. W. (2008). *The course syllabus: A learning-centered approach.* San Francisco, CA: Jossey-Bass.

O'Neil, J., & Marsick, V. J. (2007). *Understanding action learning.* New York: Amacom.

O'Neill, N. (2012). *Promising practices for personal and social responsibility: Findings from a national research collaborative.* Washington, DC: Association of American Colleges and Universities.

Olson, D. R., & Torrance, N. (Eds.). (1996). *Modes of thought.* New York: Cambridge University Press.

Ormrod, J. E. (2007). *Human learning.* Upper Saddle River, NJ: Prentice-Hall.

Parsons, T. (1964). *Essays in sociological theory.* New York: The Free Press.

Pascarella, E. T., & Terenzin, P. T. (2005). *How college affects students.* San Francisco, CA: Jossey-Bass.

Peirce, C. S. (1877). How to make our ideas clear. *Popular Science Monthly, 12,* 286–302.

Perkins, D. N. (1993). Person-plus: A distributed view of thinking and learning. In G. Salomon, *Distributed cognitions: Psychological and educational considerations* (pp. 88–110). New York: Cambridge University Press.

Perkins, D. N., & Salomon, G. (1989). Are cognitive skills context-bound? *Educational Researcher, 18*(1), 16–25.

——— (1992). Transfer of learning. *International encyclopedia of education.* Oxford: Pergamon Press.

Perlin, R. (2011). *Intern nation: How to earn nothing and learn little in the brave new economy.* New York: Verso.

Peters, S. J. (2010). *Democracy and higher education.* East Lansing, MI: Michigan State University Press.

Phillips, D. C., & Soltis, J. (2004). *Perspectives on learning.* New York: Teachers College Press.

Piaget, J. (1967). *Six psychological studies.* New York: Random House.

Pinar, W. F. (2004). *What is curriculum theory?* Mahwah, NJ: Lawrence Erlbaum Associates.

Plato (1984). *The great dialogues of Plato* (W. H. D. Rouse, Trans.). New York: New American Library.

Pohl, M. (2000). *Learning to think, thinking to learn.* Cheltenham, Victoria, Australia: Hawker Brownlow.

Polanyi, M. (1974). *Personal knowledge.* Chicago, IL: University of Chicago Press.

Poropat, A. E. (2009). A meta-analysis of the five-factor model of personality and academic performance. *Psychological Bulletin, 135*(2), 322–338.

Porter, M. (1998). *Competitive strategy.* New York: The Free Press.

Qualters, D. M. (Ed.). (2010). *Experiential education: Making the most of learning outside the classroom.* San Francisco, CA: Jossey-Bass.

Raelin, J. A. (2008). *Work-based learning: Bridging knowledge and action in the workplace.* New and revised edition. San Francisco, CA: Jossey-Bass.

Rainbird, H. A., Fuller, A., & Munro, A. (Eds.). (2004). *Workplace learning in context.* New York: Routledge.

Ramaley, J. A. (2005). Scholarship for the public good: Living in Pasteur's quadrant. In A. Kezar, T. Chambers, & J. C. Burkhardt (Eds.) (2005). *Higher education for the public good: Emerging voices from a national movement* (pp. 166–182). San Francisco, CA: Jossey-Bass.

Reed, E. S. (1996). *The necessity of experience.* New Haven, CT: Yale University Press.

Reich, R. B. (1991). *The work of nations: Preparing ourselves for the 21st century.* New York: Vintage Books.

——— (2011). *Aftershock: The next economy and America's future.* New York: Vintage Books.

Resnick, L. B. (1987). Learning in school and out. *Educational Researcher, 16*(9), 13–20.

Resnick, L. B., Levine, J. M., & Teasley, S. D. (1991). *Perspectives on socially shared cognition.* Washington, DC: American Psychological Association.

Rhoads, R. A. (1997). *Community service and higher learning.* Albany, NY: SUNY Press.

Roberts, J. W. (2012). *Beyond learning by doing: Theoretical currents in experiential education.* New York: Routledge.

Rogoff, B., & Lave, J. (1984). *Everyday cognition.* Cambridge, MA: Harvard University Press.

Rousseau, J.-J. (1993). *Emile.* London: Everyman/J.M. Dent

Rowden, R. W. (2007). *Workplace learning: Principles and practice.* Malabar, FL: Krieger.

Royer, J. M., Mestre, J. P., & Dufresne, R. J. (2005). Introduction: Framing the transfer problem. In J. P. Mestre (Ed.), *Transfer of learning: From a modern multidisciplinary perspective.* Greenwich, CT: Information Age Publishing.

Rudolph, F. (1990). *The American college and university: A history.* Athens, GA: University of Georgia Press.

Rush, F. (Ed.). (2004). *The Cambridge companion to critical theory.* New York: Cambridge University Press.

Ryan, R. M., & Deci, E. L. (2006). Self-regulation and the problem of human autonomy: Does psychology need choice, self-determination, and will? *Journal of Personality, 74,* 1557–1585.

Ryder, K. G., & Wilson, J. W. (Eds.). (1987). *Cooperative education in a new era: Understanding and strengthening the links between college and the workplace.* San Francisco, CA: Jossey-Bass.

Salomon, G. (1993a). Editor's introduction. In G. Salomon, *Distributed cognitions: Psychological and educational considerations* (pp. xi–xxi). New York: Cambridge University Press.

——— (Ed.). (1993b). *Distributed cognitions: Psychological and educational considerations.* New York: Cambridge University Press.

Saltmarsh, J. (2011). The civic promise of service-learning. In J. Saltmarsh, & M. Hartley (Eds.), *"To serve a larger purpose": Engagement for democracy and the transformation of higher education.* Philadelphia, PA: Temple University Press.

Saltmarsh, J., & Hartley, M. (Eds.). (2011). *"To serve a larger purpose": Engagement for democracy and the transformation of higher education.* Philadelphia, PA: Temple University Press.

Saltmarsh, J., & Zlotkowski, E. (Eds.). (2011). *Higher education and democracy: Essays on service-learning and civic engagement.* Philadelphia, PA: Temple University Press.

SCANS (Secretary's Commission on Necessary Skills). (1991). *What work requires of schools.* Washington, DC: US Department of Labor.

Schatzman, L., & Strauss, A. (1972). *Field research: Strategies for a natural sociology.* Englewood Cliffs, NJ: Prentice-Hall.

Schneider, C. G. (2005). Liberal education and the civic engagement gap. In A. Kezar, T. Chambers, & J. C. Burkhardt (Eds.) (2005). *Higher education for the public good: Emerging voices from a national movement* (pp. 127–145). San Francisco, CA: Jossey-Bass.

Schön, D. A. (1983). *The reflective practitioner: How professionals think in action.* New York: Basic Books.

——— (1990). *Educating the reflective practitioner: Toward a new design for teaching and learning in the professions.* San Francisco, CA: Jossey-Bass.

Schram, S. F., & Caterino, B. (Eds.). (2006). *Making political science matter: Debating knowledge, research, and method.* New York: NYU Press.

Schumpeter, J. (1994). *Capitalism, socialism, and democracy.* London: Routledge.

Schutz, A. (1970). *On phenomenology and social relations: Selected writings.* Chicago, IL: University of Chicago Press.

Scott, J. W. (1991). The evidence of experience. *Critical Inquiry, 17*(4), 773–797.

Scribner, S. (1986). Thinking in action: Some characteristics of practical thought. In R. J. Sternberg, & R. K. Wagner (Eds.), *Practical intelligence: Nature and origins of competence in the everyday world* (pp. 13–30). New York: Cambridge University Press.

Senge, P. (2006). *The fifth discipline.* New York: Broadway Business.

Sheffield, E. C. (2011). *Strong community service learning: Philosophical perspectives.* New York: Peter Lang.

Shor, I. (1992). *Empowering education: Critical teaching for social change.* Chicago, IL: University of Chicago Press.

Simon, R. I., Dippo, D., & Schenke, A. (1991). *Learning work: A critical pedagogy of work education.* New York: Bergin & Garvey.

Sinclair, J. M., & Coulthard, M. (1975). *Towards an analysis of discourse: The English used by teachers and pupils.* New York: Oxford University Press.

Skinner, B. F. (1965). *Science and human behavior.* New York: The Free Press.

——— (1972). *Beyond freedom and dignity.* New York: Bantam.

——— (1976). *Walden two.* New York: Macmillan.

Spenner, K. I. (1990). Skill: Meanings, methods, and measures. *Work and Occupations, 17*(4), 399–421.

Spradley, J. P. (1972). *Culture and cognition: Rules, maps, and plans.* San Francisco, CA: Chandler.

Stake, R. E. (2010). *Qualitative research: Studying how things work.* New York: The Guilford Press.

Sternberg, R. J. (1986). Introduction: The nature and scope of practical intelligence. In R. J. Sternberg, & R. K. Wagner, *Practical intelligence: Nature and origins of competence in the everyday world* (pp. 1–10). New York: Cambridge University Press.

Sternberg, R. J., & Wagner, R. K. (Eds.). (1986). *Practical intelligence: Nature and origins of competence in the everyday world.* New York: Cambridge University Press.

Stewart, T., & Webster, N. (Eds.). (2011). *Problematizing service-learning: Critical reflections for development and action.* Charlotte, NC: Information Age Publishing.

Sullivan, W. M. (2004). *Work and integrity: The crisis and promise of professionalism in America.* San Francisco, CA: Jossey-Bass.

Sullivan, W. M., & Rosin, M. S. (2008). *A new agenda for higher education: Shaping a life of the mind for practice.* San Francisco, CA: Jossey-Bass.

Svinicki, M., & McKeachie, W. J. (2010). *McKeachie's teaching tips: Strategies, research, and theory for college and university teachers.* Belmont, CA: Wadsworth Publishing.

Sweitzer, H. F., & King, M. A. (2004). *The successful internship: Transformation and empowerment in experiential learning.* Belmont, CA: Brooks/Cole.

Taba, H. (1999). *The dynamics of education.* New York: Oxford University Press.

Thorndike, E. L., & Woodworth, R. S. (1901). The influence of improvement in one mental function upon the efficiency of other functions. *Psychological Review, 8,* 247–261.

Tipper, M. O. (1982). *The creation of curriculum in internship settings* (Unpublished doctoral dissertation). Teachers College/Columbia University, New York.

True, M. (2011). *InternQube: Professional skills for the workplace.* Grantham, PA: Intrueition.

Turner, J. H. (1998). *The structure of sociological theory.* Sixth edition. Belmont, CA: Wadsworth Publishing.

UCLA (University of California at Los Angeles). (2011). *Community learning.* Retrieved February 9, 2011, from http://www.ugeducation.ucla.edu/community learning/.

Vallas, S. P. (1990). The concept of skill: A critical review. *Work and Occupations, 17*(4), 379–398.

Veysey, L. R. (1965). *The emergence of the American university.* Chicago, IL: University of Chicago Press.

Vygotsky, L. S. (1978). *Mind in society.* Cambridge, MA: Harvard University Press.

Warren, K., Mitten, D., & Loeffler, T. A. (Eds.). (2008). *Theory and practice of experiential education.* Boulder, CO: Association for Experiential Education.

Watson, J. B. (1998). *Behaviorism.* New York: Transaction Publications.

Webb, L. M. (2005). Feminist pedagogy: Identifying basic principles. *Academic Exchange Quarterly, 6*(1), 67–73.

Weinstein, G. (1981). Self science education. In J. Fried, *New directions for student services: Education for student development.* San Francisco, CA: Jossey-Bass.

Wenger, E. (1998). *Communities of practice: Learning, meaning, and identity.* New York: Cambridge University Press.

Wenger, E., McDermott, R., & Snyder, W. M. (2002). *Cultivating communities of practice: A guide to managing knowledge.* Boston, MA: Harvard Business School Press.

Wertsch, J. V. (1981). *The concept of activity in Soviet psychology.* Armonk, NY: M.E. Sharpe.

———— (1985). *Vygotsky and the social formation of mind.* Cambridge, MA: Harvard University Press.

Wertsch, J. V., Del Rio, P., & Alvarez, A. (1995). *Sociocultural studies of mind.* New York: Cambridge University Press.

Willis, P. (1977). *Learning to labour: How working class kids get working class jobs.* London: Routledge.

YouTube. (2012). *Harvard graduates explain seasons.* Retrieved July 31, 2012, from http://www.youtube.com/watch?v=p0wk4qG2mIg.

Zlotkowski, E. (2005). The disciplines and the public good. In A. Kezar, T. Chambers, & J. C. Burkhardt (Eds.) (2005). *Higher education for the public good: Emerging voices from a national movement* (pp. 146–165). San Francisco, CA: Jossey-Bass.

Index

Printed and bound in Great Britain by
CPI Antony Rowe, Chippenham and Eastbourne